Rio Grande Narrow Gauge Recollections

By John B. Norwood

Edited by Donald J. Heimburger
Layout by Marilyn M. Heimburger

Library of Congress Catalog Card Number: 86-81505
ISBN: 0-911581-07-3

First Edition
Printed in the United States of America

Heimburger House Publishing Company
310 Lathrop Ave.
River Forest, Illinois 60305

DEDICATION

The Mexicans who lived and worked along the Narrow Gauge believed implicitly in chisos and Patrones—spirits and guardian ghosts—who protected graveyards, lost mines and treasures from being despoiled or plundered.

This is a dedication and prayer to those chisos and Patrones, that they may always watch over the treasures of memories of the Narrow Gauge.

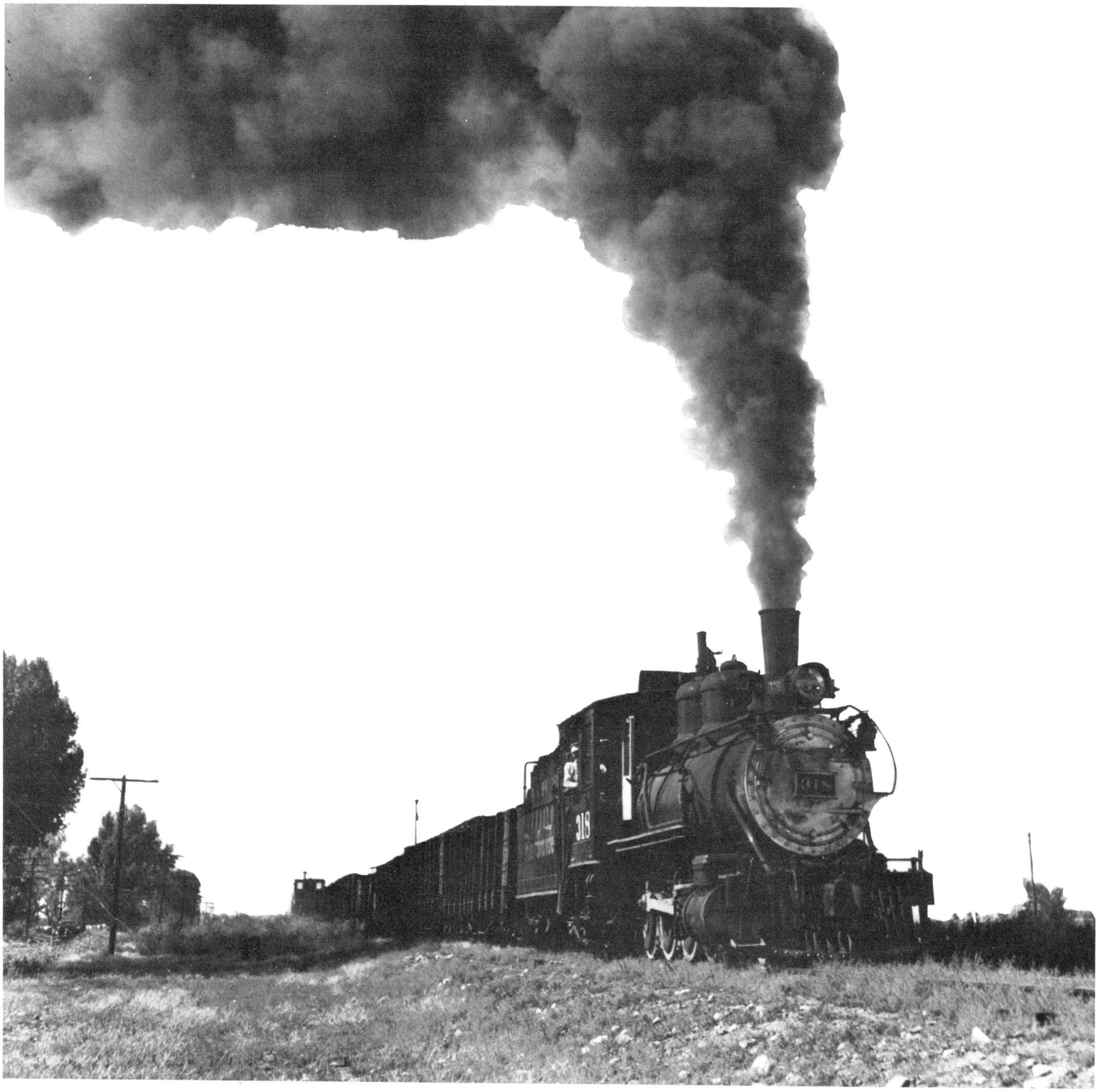

Ouray Branch, June, 1952, *John Krause/Dr. Richard Severance collection*

Contents

Foreword 6
Chapter 1—Monero, New Mexico 8
Chapter 2—Pagosa Junction 19
Chapter 3—Chama 27
Chapter 4—The Granddaddy of Snowstorms on Cumbres 37
Chapter 5—Slide Clearance on Silverton Branch 47
Chapter 6—1957 Snow Troubles 56
Chapter 7—Cumbres Pass Joint Railroad-Highway Survey 62
Chapter 8—No. 16 Is In The Gorge 66
Chapter 9—Silverton Branch High Water 73
Chapter 10—Narrow Gauge Trains 81
Chapter 11—Narrow Gauge Train Density 91
Chapter 12—Train Dispatcher 99
Chapter 13—Home Terminals and Working Districts 107
Chapter 14—Assignment with *Life* Magazine 112
Chapter 15—Herding Rail Buffs on the Silverton Branch 118
Chapter 16—Lonesome Operators at Hilltop Offices 123
Chapter 17—Narrow Gauge Languages 127
Four-Color Section 133
Chapter 18—One Hand For The Ship 147
Chapter 19—An' Some Of 'Em Was Brave An' Some Was Not 151
Chapter 20—Justifiable Mayhem 155
Chapter 21—Narrow Gauge Hemorrhoid Cure Without Surgery 160
Chapter 22—Gertrude 164
Chapter 23—Ayer, Hoy, Manana, Y Para Siempre 166
Chapter 24—Long Jim McIvor 169
Chapter 25—Telling My Beads—My Narrow Gauge Rosary 174
Chapter 26—Severe Storm Enroute From Artic Circle 200
Chapter 27—Bits And Pieces And Legends 215
Chapter 28—Mergers, Acquisitions And Abandonments 242
Appendix 254
Index 269

Foreword

When I retired from the Denver & Rio Grande Western in 1975, I swore a solemn oath that I would never until the day I died ever again have any connection with anything related to railroads. After nearly 40 years of close working relationships with the high iron, I was gut-sick with it—after all, there is absolutely nothing in the world that, if you have too much of it, will not produce a surfeit. And, after an early life as the son of a boomer telegrapher, I spent four decades as an employee of the Rio Grande more intimately involved in all phases of its operations and had more varied railroad experience than any one railroader could ever live through.

I stuck with my oath for a couple of years, then was seduced by a group of lawyers in Washington, D.C. into becoming their expert witness and fact-developer in cases they were handling as representatives of communities and organizations opposing abandonments, mergers and similar actions by railroads. The pay was unbelievable (compared to railroad standards), and there is no denying that you can become habituated to high living after having been on more or less unrestricted expense accounts for many years. So, I turned traitor, set up shop as an independent consultant, and using railroad experience in reverse, assisted in stopping several abandonments.

There was a decline in abandonment applications and the consulting work went into a slump—and, again I permitted myself to be sweet-talked into writing a book about the Rio Grande Narrow Gauge published by Heimburger House Publishing Company. I have yet to decide which of us worked hardest on the book—Don pushing me to write or I disciplining myself to sit at a typewriter when I preferred to be out hunting, fishing or just bumming around.

Finally, *Rio Grande Narrow Gauge* was published, and the first printing sold out in just a bit more than a year. The reviews were uniformly good and in many of them, and comments from readers, there have been only two criticisms. Most commonly given is the one that the book should have had more railroad stories and personal experiences. Next, that I failed to include similar material about the Marshall Pass route of the Narrow Gauge.

As to the last criticism: a book can be just so long, and cover only a given spectrum, or it becomes too costly to produce; the price escalates to where there is no margin of profit. Then, too, several other railroad authors have written excellent books about the Marshall Pass route. Frankly, I had a problem keeping my typewriter from jumping from Cumbres and the San Juan segment to Marshall Pass and the Gunnison route, but Don kept me on track over Cumbres Pass to Durango and Silverton.

DEMAND FOR STORIES

The demand for stories and experiences of the narrow gauge by rail fans has been great enough to induce Don and me to go for such a book prior to reprinting *Rio Grande Narrow Gauge*. This time the entire narrow gauge will be covered.

It is virtually impossible to convey the feeling, the essence, the aura of living and working on the narrow gauge portions of the Rio Grande during its last half century of its existence. It was almost as though you were isolated from the rest of the United States and living in an era and region not yet part of the nation. In fact, you instinctively resisted change and progress. It was only during the late fifties and the sixties that post WWII attitudes, thinking and developments encroached on the Narrow Gauge. As these burgeoned, the old easy-going life style died and, there being no resources left capable of supporting the rapidly increasing costs of living in the new era, the old ways were irretrievably lost.

The Marshall Pass route, especially the Gunnison River drainage Sargents to Montrose, depended upon cattle and sheep for an economic base. The Crested Butte and Baldwin branches were essentially coal mining districts with some livestock.

The Santa Fa branch, the first to go, in the final analysis then, was only a relic, the ending phase of Palmer's dream of a railroad to Mexico City. Except as a dream it never had any real reason to be built. It did not produce any worthwhile agricultural or livestock revenue, nor did it furnish any viable connection with other railroads. It was built into a Hispanic-Mission culture that did not begin to change appreciably until tourism started.

POPULATION MIX

Starting at Antonito westward on the San Juan route, the population mixture to Arboles consisted of some Anglos, a few south Europeans and Hispanics, the latter accounting for from 80 to 90 per cent of the inhabitants. West of Arboles the percentage dropped to about 50 per cent.

In the cattle-raising area around Gunnison, the ranch owners and cowboys retained the mannerisms and flavor of Texas-bred cowmen. In the Cimarron-Cerro Summit district, predominantly sheep country, the owners were either Mormons or Basques—and both were prototypes of their people. At the coal mining towns of the Crested Butte and Baldwin branches, it was with no difficulty you could imagine you were in villages of like kind in Italy or one of the Slavic countries. So isolated from influences of the outside U.S.A. were they that even the second and third generations had not become entirely Americanized.

On the Santa Fe branch and the San Juan route, the Anglo and Hispanic cultures lived and worked together, played the same, with neither assimilating the other to any degree. The Hispanics were, if anything, more religious, quieter, less contentious and with better morals than the Anglos. They knew how to enjoy galas, holidays and warm summer nights when romance was in the air better than the Anglos—and these aspects of narrow gauge life and living were soon adopted by the railroaders and others along the three-foot gauge.

All in all, it was an easy-going, carefree way of living with only a few individuals, Anglo, Hispanic or other, wanting to set the world on fire or garner riches. And the people in the narrow gauge sphere did not change until near the end of the railroad operation. The change came coincidentally with plentiful automobiles, improved roads, television and the emergence of giveaway government money, plus the availability of a plentiful liquor supply and the doctrine of free love.

Too bad it changed.

Locomotive #268, of the C-16 Class, is eastbound on the Marshall Pass (South Arkansas to Gunnison) line in May of 1955.
John Krause/Dr. Richard Severance collection

A doubleheader churns out black smoke eastbound at Monero towards the end of operation on the narrow gauge. A daylight extra eastbound was unusual at Monero. ***Colorado RR Museum/R.W. Richardson***

Chapter 1

Monero, New Mexico

Some of my fondest recollections in retrospect are of an unlikely place: Monero, New Mexico. My father bid in the Monero agency after a short time as second trick telegrapher at Chama.

Monero, at the time we moved there, was a relatively active town of about 300 people, 500 goats, 100 dogs and approximately the same number of scrawny, inbred pigs. The only streets were the coal hauling roads and the dirt road that ran from Chama to Dulce.

Among the permanent residents were five white families (including ours); one married black couple and two black

bachelors (one of these shortly married a young Mexican girl); two white bachelors, one of whom had an old one-eyed Mexican woman as his housekeeper. Temporary residents were a number of Jicarilla Apache Indians who came in from the Horse Lake section of their reservation to buy a few supplies and sell some of their tightly woven baskets or crude bows and arrows. Included in the supplies they bought was "sugar moon," a clear, potent alcoholic beverage brewed of sugar, yeast and water—it took a pint to make a white man drunk; a half-pint for an Apache.

I almost forgot to list the numerous burros that wandered around when not being used in the mines or as pack animals for sheepherders.

The second year we were there a school was opened for eight grades. The teacher (imported) had blue eyes, long blonde, naturally wavy hair. The school board voted $5.00 per month as salary for a janitor, and I took the job. It only required about two hours work daily, and then I was free to roam the hills with my .22 caliber rifle. Most of the game killed was rabbits, and I gave away a lot to people, including the school teacher. You can also believe that no school teacher had such a diligent and adoring janitor.

Adolescent adoration turned into fantasies when I took some dressed rabbits to the teacher's door one Saturday morning. She answered my knock on the door attired in only a new hat just received from a mail order house. She was the first nude woman I had ever seen, and I was so embarrassed all I could do was stammer, hand her the rabbits and beat a fast retreat. Fortunately, my photographic memory had developed at an early age—I carried away a vivid picture. I was 10 years younger than the teacher, so nothing came of the incident—except, occasionally when she came to school and I was there I mentally stripped the clothes off her.

While we were at Monero I trapped, learned telegraphy and station accounting, did a little mucking in the coal mines and worked as a helper on trucks and sleds hauling coal or lumber to the loading spurs of the Rio Grande. Every spare moment was spent with one of the white bachelors who was a retired machinist and mining engineer. I had to walk eight miles roundtrip to be with him, but it paid off later when I

You could ride'em, pack'em—or eat'em. Photo taken around 1900.
Courtesy Museum of New Mexico

The *San Juan* travels eastbound at Monero, New Mexico, past the water tank and approaches the trestle over Monero Creek. *Museum of New Mexico*

was able to take a Civil Service examination and qualify for a provisional appointment as a field geologist with the Bureau of Reclamation.

ADJUSTMENTS TO LIFE

The adjustment to life in a small town like Monero, after having lived in a metropolis such as Chama, a terminal town, was not too difficult to make. The agent's house was situated just across the "Hole Track" from the depot. It had been built of rough sawed pine boards nailed to a framework soon after the Rio Grande built through Monero. Over the possibly five decades it had housed agents' families, it had received, on the exterior, about a half-inch coating of the various colors of paint used by the railroad at any given year the paint gang repainted. Break off a chip and it was like reading tree rings. On the interior, the walls had first been built of the same rough sawed planks then covered with, variously, cheese cloth, muslin, old newspapers, wall paper, Kalsomine (water-based and tinted finely-ground calcium that, as it dried between coats, flaked off on everything), and at the time we moved in had been painted with the same dirty yellow paint used on the outside.

William Jackson Palmer

The floors were also of pine, not level, and the surface was knotty, literally, where hard pine knots had resisted wear better than the surrounding soft wood. Linoleum rugs had to be replaced twice a year. The interior was drab at best but fortunately there was so little light from the few small windows you could not see how bad it really was. And, to add to its unattractiveness, the surrounding yard like all of Monero was a deep layer of coal dust and adobe dirt. We wore out countless towsacks and door mats over the years trying to clean our shoes before entering the house, but my mother spent many hours scrubbing floors.

At the period we were at Monero, the regular meeting point between Nos. 116 and 115, the passenger trains, was at Monero, on the Hole Track. I finally became proficient enough in telegraphy to be able to copy the "middle order" addressed to the operator at the meeting point. And finally I could send well enough that my father would let me repeat the order to the dispatcher and ask for the clearance card. I still remember the wording of the order: "No 116 Eng 475 meet No 115 Eng 478 at Monero. No 115 pull by and back in on the Hole Track."

The depot was built on the curved track not quite at the top of the heavy grade of Amargo Canyon. It was the same construction as the living quarters and as old. To save time, when originally built, it had been raised to track level by a sub-structure of 8″ x 8″ pine timbers. Over the years the bases had rotted away unevenly, and the floor of pine was like the one in the house and displayed a sort of up and down surface where subsidence was uneven. There was a freight room; one small extra room (my bedroom), the office and the waiting room.

The passenger trains were the one big daily occurence. Every man, woman and child, along with various dogs, came to the depot to see the trains, if not otherwise occupied. One cold, wintry day, a riot broke out in the waiting room. It started from a hair-pulling fight between two women. My father broke it up with a stove poker, and questioning about the start, developed it was a remark from one woman to another. The remark: "Usted tiene pelo rojo en medio sus piernas"—You have red hair between your legs."

MAD BURRO

Another day, the trains had departed and the people were still standing around when a mad burro jack came running down from Caranta's store, braying and kicking out. Behind him was one of the Caranta boys with an automatic pistol, shooting into the body of the jack, trying to kill him. The shots of the small pistol were having no effect, and the jack was potentially dangerous. I ran to our house and got my 30-30 Winchester and dispatched the animal. The jack had been in a fight with another jack and got kicked in the testicles with had swollen to about the size of a football. The pain had driven him crazy.

Fresh meat (beef) was always in scarce supply during the summer months, for there was no refrigeration. One day a rancher named Bill Nolan came into town with the tonneau of his Dodge car piled high with cloth-wrapped meat. It was clean and mouth watering red and was quickly sold out. Our family acquired a loin cut that was cut into fine, thick steaks that we ate and enjoyed greatly—about the finest meat we ever ate.

Nolan did not come back to Monero for a couple of weeks, and when he did, my father questioned him about when he would have more meat available. Bill hummed and hawed a bit, then told my father the truth. During the past fall one of the passenger trains had killed one of his bulls and the Claim Department had refused to pay him for it. The day before he brought the meat in for sale he had been present when a freight train struck two of Caranta's burros that had strayed. Nolan butchered them and sold the meat to make up for the dead bull. Dad blew his top, but finally had to admit it had not hurt us and was the finest meat we had ever eaten.

My mother was a good cook and liked to feed people. There was not much opportunity to vary the diet at Monero, but she had a reputation for doing good things with what she had, and many people found ways to get an invite to our table. One that ate with us often was a Jicarilla Apache man named Norman TeQu. He was about 50 years of age with a high IQ and university education who, after some years in the white society in business, went back to the blanket. When he came to Monero he took pains to be clean and well dressed, anticipating an invite to eat with us. I don't know what he was like on the reservation, but in our home at the table his manners were exquisite, and after the meal he would sit and talk until nearly midnight about the world and our society. The Norwood family and anyone who dropped in listened spellbound.

Five crew members of the Rio Grande pose around locomotive #276, a Baldwin 2-8-0 of the C-16 Class. Note how sparse the boiler appears. Photo taken in Ouray, Colorado. ***Ruth Gregory collection***

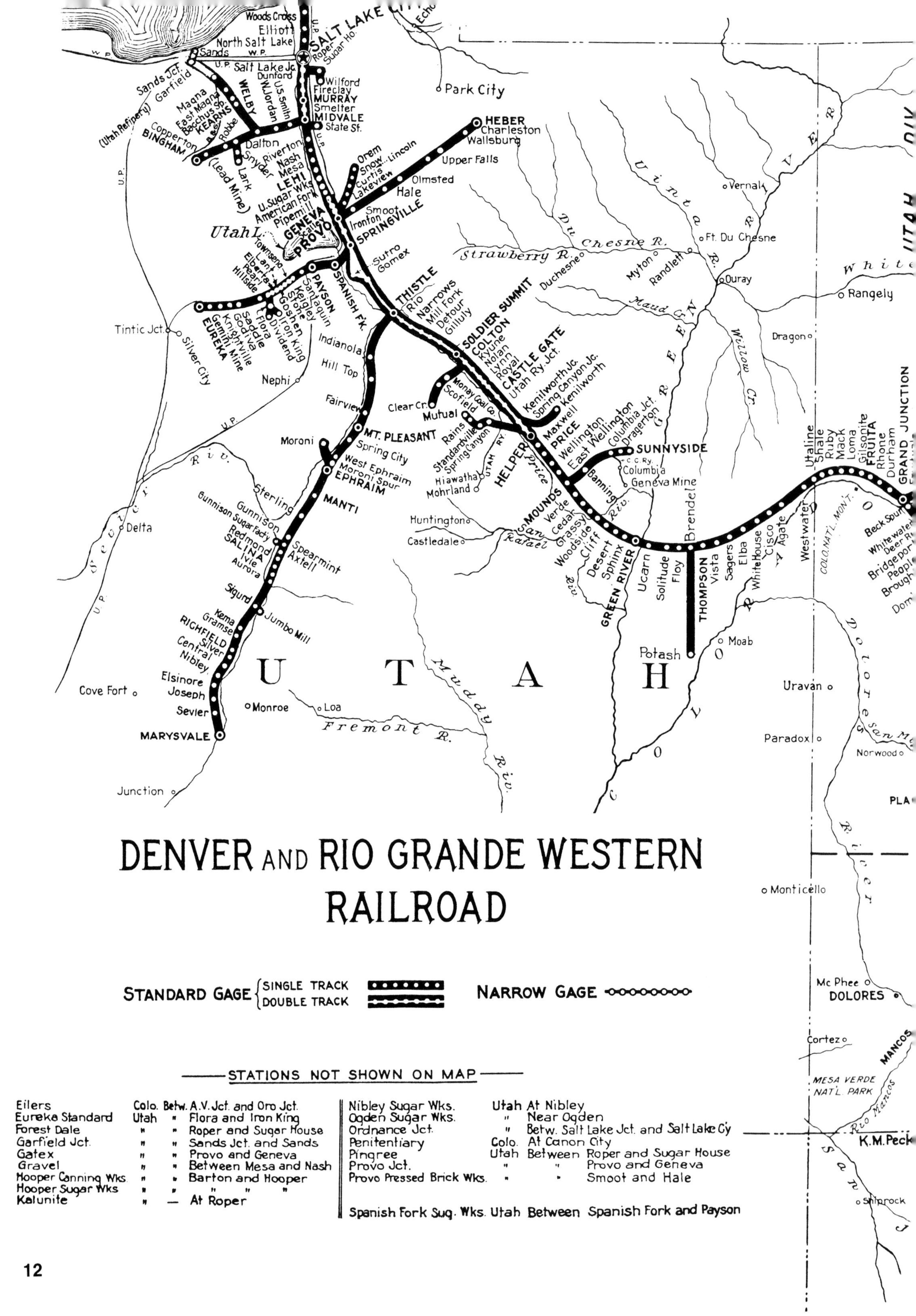

STATIONS NOT SHOWN ON MAP

Station	State	Location
Eilers	Colo.	Betw. A.V. Jct. and Oro Jct.
Eureka Standard	Utah	" Flora and Iron King
Forest Dale	"	" Roper and Sugar House
Garfield Jct.	"	" Sands Jct. and Sands
Gatex	"	" Provo and Geneva
Gravel	"	" Between Mesa and Nash
Hooper Canning Wks.	"	" Barton and Hooper
Hooper Sugar Wks.	"	" " " "
Kalunite	"	— At Roper
Nibley Sugar Wks.	Utah	At Nibley
Ogden Sugar Wks.	"	Near Ogden
Ordnance Jct.	"	Betw. Salt Lake Jct. and Salt Lake Cy
Penitentiary	Colo.	At Canon City
Pingree	Utah	Between Roper and Sugar House
Provo Jct.	"	" Provo and Geneva
Provo Pressed Brick Wks.	"	" Smoot and Hale
Spanish Fork Sug. Wks.	Utah	Between Spanish Fork and Payson

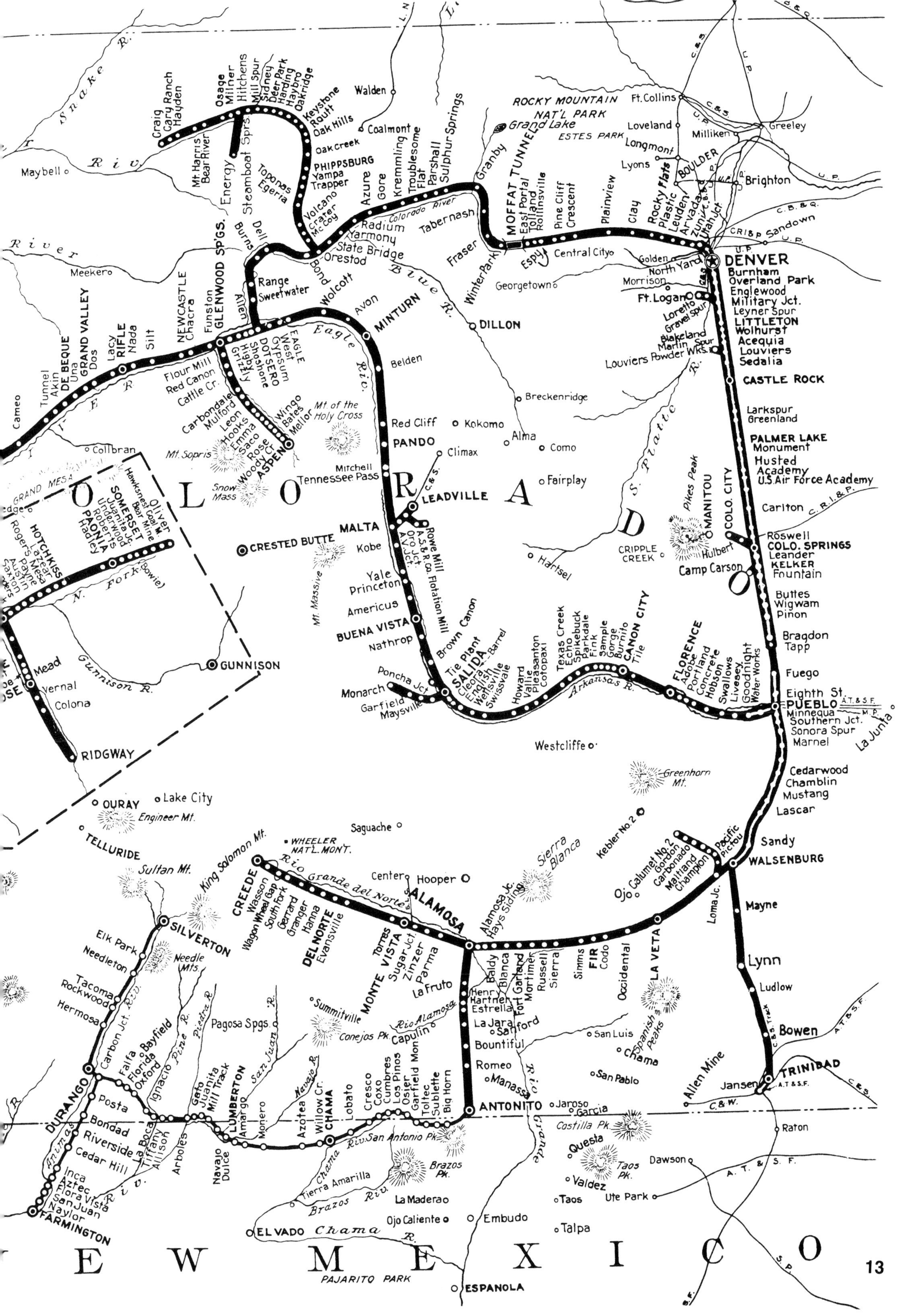

C O L O R A D O
N E W M E X I C O
DENVER
Burnham
Overland Park
Englewood
Military Jct.
Leyner Spur
LITTLETON
Wolhurst
Acequia
Louviers
Sedalia
CASTLE ROCK
Larkspur
Greenland
PALMER LAKE
Monument
Husted
Academy
U.S. Air Force Academy
Carlton
Roswell
COLO. SPRINGS
Leander
KELKER
Fountain
Buttes
Wigwam
Pinon
Bragdon
Tapp
Fuego
Eighth St.
PUEBLO
Minnequa
Southern Jct.
Sonora Spur
Marnel
La Junta
Cedarwood
Chamblin
Mustang
Lascar
Sandy
WALSENBURG
Mayne
Lynn
Ludlow
Bowen
TRINIDAD
Jansen
Raton
Dawson
Ute Park
Allen Mine
ROCKY MOUNTAIN NAT'L PARK
Grand Lake
ESTES PARK
MOFFAT TUNNEL
East Portal
Tolland
Rollinsville
Pine Cliff
Crescent
Plainview
Clay
Rocky Flats
Plastic
Leyden
Arvada
Zuni
Utah Jct.
Ft. Collins
Loveland
Longmont
Lyons
BOULDER
Milliken
Greeley
Brighton
Sandown
Golden
North Yard
Morrison
Ft. Logan
Loretto
Gravel Spur
Blakeland
Martin Spur
Louviers Powder Wks.
Central City
Georgetown
Espy
Winter Park
Fraser
Tabernash
Granby
Parshall
Sulphur Springs
Troublesome
Flat
Kremmling
Gore
Azure
Radium
Yarmony
State Bridge
Orestod
Bond
Volcano
Crater
McCoy
PHIPPSBURG
Yampa
Trapper
Oak Creek
Oak Hills
Keystone
Routt
Walden
Coalmont
Oakridge
Haybro
Harding
Deer Park
Sidney
Mill Spur
Hitchens
Milner
Osage
Hayden
Cary Ranch
Craig
Mt. Harris
Bear River
Energy
Steamboat Sprs.
Toponas
Egeria
Maybell
Burns
Dell
Range
Sweetwater
Wolcott
Avon
MINTURN
Belden
Red Cliff
PANDO
Mitchell
Tennessee Pass
LEADVILLE
MALTA
Kobe
Rowe Mill
A.S.&R.Co.
Oro Jct.
A.V. Jct.
Flotation Mill
Yale
Princeton
Americus
BUENA VISTA
Nathrop
Brown Canon
Tie Plant
SALIDA
Poncha Jct.
Monarch
Garfield
Maysville
Cleora
English
Wellsville
Swissvale
Barrel
Howard
Vallie
Pleasanton
Cotopaxi
Texas Creek
Echo
Spikebuck
Parkdale
Fink
Sample
Gorge
Burnito
CANON CITY
Tile
FLORENCE
Adobe
Portland
Concrete
Hobson
Swallows
Livesey
Goodnight
Water Works
Kokomo
Climax
Alma
Como
Fairplay
Breckenridge
DILLON
Hartsel
CRIPPLE CREEK
MANITOU
Pikes Peak
COLO. CITY
Hulbert
Camp Carson
Westcliffe
Greenhorn Mt.
CRESTED BUTTE
Mt. Massive
Mt. of the Holy Cross
EAGLE
West
Gypsum
DOTSERO
Shoshone
Hiegly
Grizzly
Wingo
Bates
Mellor
ASPEN
Woody Cr.
Rose
Saco
Emma
Hooks
Leon
Mulford
Carbondale
Cattle Cr.
Red Canon
Flour Mill
GLENWOOD SP'GS.
Funston
Allen
NEWCASTLE
Chacra
Silt
Nada
RIFLE
Lacy
GRAND VALLEY
Dos
DE BEQUE
Una
Akin
Tunnel
Cameo
Collbran
Mt. Sopris
Snow Mass
GRAND MESA
SOMERSET
Oliver
Coal M.
Bear Mine
Hawksnest
Juanita Jct.
Underwood
Roberts
PAONIA
Hadley
HOTCHKISS
Lazear
Mesa
Paxton
Austin
Bowie
Mead
Vernal
Colona
RIDGWAY
GUNNISON
OURAY
Lake City
Engineer Mt.
TELLURIDE
Sultan Mt.
SILVERTON
Elk Park
Needleton
Needle Mts.
Tacoma
Rockwood
Hermosa
Carbon Jct.
DURANGO
Posta
Bondad
Riverside
Cedar Hill
Inca
Aztec
Flora Vista
San Juan
Naylor
FARMINGTON
Falfa
Florida
Oxford
Bayfield
Ignacio
La Boca
Tiffany
Allison
Arboles
Gato
Juanita
Mill Track
LUMBERTON
Amargo
Monero
Navajo
Dulce
Azotea
Willow Cr.
CHAMA
Lobato
Cresco
Coxo
Cumbres
Los Pinos
Osier
Garfield Mon.
Sublette
Toltec
Big Horn
ANTONITO
Pagosa Spgs.
Summitville
Conejos Pk.
Capulin
San Antonio Pk.
Brazos Pk.
Tierra Amarilla
La Maderao
Ojo Caliente
EL VADO
Embudo
PAJARITO PARK
ESPANOLA
Jaroso
Garcia
Castilla Pk.
Questa
Taos Pk.
Valdez
Taos
Talpa
CREEDE
Wasson
Wagon Wheel Gap
South Fork
Gerrard
Granger
Hanna
DEL NORTE
Evansville
King Solomon Mt.
WHEELER NAT'L. MONT.
Saguache
Center
Hooper
ALAMOSA
MONTE VISTA
Torres
Sugar Jct.
Zinzer
Parma
La Fruto
Henry
Hartner
Estrella
La Jara
Sanford
Bountiful
Romeo
Manassa
Alamosa Jc.
Hays Siding
Baldy
Blanca
Fort Garland
Mortimer
Russell
Sierra
Simms
FIR
Codo
Occidental
LA VETA
Sierra Blanca
Ojo
Calumet No. 2
Gordon
Carbonado
Maitland
Champion
Pacific
Pictou
Loma Jc.
Kebler No. 2
San Luis
Spanish Peaks
Chama
San Pablo
Colorado River
Blue R.
Eagle Riv.
S. Platte R.
Arkansas R.
Gunnison R.
Rio Grande del Norte
Rio Alamosa
Rio Grande
Chama R.
Brazos Riv.
San Juan Riv.
Animas Riv.
Pine R.
Piedra R.
Navajo R.
N. Fork
Snake R.
C. & S.
U. P.
C. B. & Q.
C. R. I. & P.
A. T. & S. F.
M. P.
C. & W.
S. P.

THE DENVER AND RIO GRANDE WESTERN
RAILROAD COMPANY

1929 NOT GOOD ON TRAINS 7 AND 8 B1484

PASS C. D. Peirce,
City Freight Agent,
C.B.& Q. Railroad.

UNTIL DECEMBER 31, 1929, UNLESS OTHERWISE ORDERED OR SPECIFIED HEREON, AND SUBJECT TO CONDITIONS ON BACK.

VALID WHEN COUNTERSIGNED BY T. A. THOMPSON OR E. E. EMERSON.

COUNTERSIGNED E. E. Emerson

PRESIDENT

Collection of Doug Harley

Another almost regular invitee was the traveling priest who came to Monero monthly to hold Mass in the Catholic church. He always had his meals with us instead of his Catholic parishioners. We always put on our religious hats while he said grace, not usually the beginning of our meals. He was a short, rolly-polly Irishman, and I was always amazed at how much food he could hold. After the evening meal he and my father always talked a lot about many things but never about Masonry or Catholicism.

This priest made two extra trips per year to Monero—one just before Lent to strengthen his flock to resist temptation during the austere days ahead, and once after Lent to absolve those who had been weak, and to perform marriages which for some reason were more numerous at that time of year.

ANNUAL PHENOMENON

Another annual phenomenon was the many bailes held each year during the month before Lent began. They were held in the big room of the Peacock Coal Company's comisary and lasted from dusk to dawn. Both young and old really pulled out all the stops to get a surfeit of pleasure before the drouth. There was always one muchacha, sixteen or seventeen years old, who was reigning belle of the year. Almost invariably she was one of those married by the priest following Lent. Being an Anglo I was never eligible for any of the muchachas' favors, but I thoroughly enjoyed the gaiety and food.

One of the few (actually, the only one I know of) collissions involving the narrow gauge passenger trains happened just east of the Monero water tank on a curve where the track was laid on a shelf between Monero Creek and a sloping sandstone ledge.

About four miles east of Monero, No. 116 plowed into a freak drift of snow and was royally stuck. The 375 equipped with a wedge plow and a mudhen helper was dispatched from Durango. This outfit plowed up to the stalled train, then backed to Monero to set out the 375 so the mudhen could go up and pull out the passenger train. Conductor on the plow train was Stuttering Dick Bendure and No. 116's conductor was Henry Pollard. Due to an old feud they did not speak to each other and no explanation of operations was communicated.

While the plow was on its way back to Monero, the engine crew of No. 116, working with the steam hose, got loose enough to move and the train started backing to Monero—God knows why except maybe Pollard thought they could let the plow by to precede them to Chama.

The two trains met on the curve and the mudhen's pilot rammed deeply into the rear car of No. 116. This was a stroke of luck, for otherwise the coach would have rolled over into Monero Creek. Also, fortunately, there were no passengers in the parlor car. Both trainmen were on the car's platform

Engine No. 221 near Embudo Canyon, New Mexico sometime between 1908 and 1910 waiting to help an eastbound train up Barranca Hill. *Museum of New Mexico*

The engineer awaits the highball for a Rio Grande passenger train at the Santa Fe, New Mexico, depot circa 1939. The Santa Fe's railroad facilities are in the background. ***Museum of New Mexico***

with burning fusees; they saw the impending collision and joined the bird gang. Granny Duxstad jumped to the creek side and sustained some scratches and bruises. Alva (Alvy) Lyons left on the side of the sloping sandstone ledge. He lost the skin of his fingertips and some of his nails digging into the stone for handholds. If you looked carefully you could see eight deep furrows cut in the stone as he slowly slid down.

Monero seemed to attract out of normal occurrences. One fall night a trainload of sheep went through. Soon after daybreak an excited Mexican came to our door and informed my father there was a carload of sheep setting in the creek just west of the bridge. Sure enough there was—on its wheels and undamaged. The train's conductor when contacted at Chama said they had a break-in-two approaching Monero but all they had to do was back up and recouple. Apparently the couplers had opened at each end of the car and its momentum let it roll forward over the rails and down the creek's bank before the emergency air set up. (The same thing happened on the Chili Line and on the man-built shelf at Garfield Monument.)

Then there was the case of the stolen pigs. For several years there was a movement of feeder pigs from the Durango area that moved as Pig Specials to Santa Fe where they were transferred to the AT&SF for movement beyond. The shipments one fall began to arrive in Santa Fe with six to ten pigs missing.

MISCOUNTING

Special Agents started an investigation. The first and obvious answer was miscounting at loading time. Nothing out of line was found. Next checked out was the stop at Gato where the trains took water, sometimes coal, and the crews ate lunch. No pigs could have been taken there. The next regular stop was at Monero for water. All the time the way-stops were being checked, a Special Agent was riding the crummy of each pig train and discovering nothing.

Then Special Agent Hammond came undercover to Monero. He ate with us and slept in my bed during the day. At one meal my father remarked that he did not know why but the scrawny Mexican pigs for a couple of years had seemed to be getting larger and better fatted. Hammond allowed if they were, they must be getting an infusion of new blood, and just maybe the missing pigs were responsible.

The next Pig Special was instructed to slow down enough about a mile from the station so that Hammond could get aboard. This was done and Hammond started back over the top when the train stopped for water. Nearing the back of the Luchetti (Peacock Coal Co.) commissary building he heard a gabble of low voiced Mexican talk. He turned on his light and looked down—and the mystery was solved.

The old narrow gauge stock car doors were secured at one end by a hasp and pin and metal seal, but there was a lot of play. At the opposite side of the door the only security

ABOVE. A dozen cars, a caboose and two locomotives ply the rails in this earlier-day scene. NEXT PAGE. Placerville, Colorado stock pens were the shipping point for Norwood, Nucla, Paradox and Naturtia. ***Both photos Ruth Gregory collection***

was a chain attached to the door with a metal ring on the chain that fitted on a steel bar to act both as a slide and lock. Monero Mexicans had found they could spring this side of the door enough to let a small boy crawl inside the car where he could catch and push out small feeder pigs. The trains ran about on schedule; they stopped at Monero for water and there was the entrance of an old coal mine (the Crist) back of the commissary. The set up was perfect for a little pig rustling. Some were hid away, fattened and butchered. A few of the little boars were kept and put to the Mexican sows when they came in season.

I had one other snow experience at Monero several years before I became a full time Rio Grande employee. It was during one of the "Big Snow" winters on Cumbres, and all of the snow-fighting equipment was tied up on the opening. The storm that closed down through train operations also struck as far west as Monero. (Nearly all the remaining wild horses around Azotea died.) No trains had run between Durango and Chama for 10 days or two weeks, and there was concern about whether or not the first to be run could get through.

Consequently, a snow train with the 375 with wedge and a mudhen was made up and started east. Section men were picked up at Gato, Lumberton and Monero, plus some idle miners from Monero. I was hired as engine watchmen in case the crews went on breaks to extend their 16-hour service if it became necessary to stop while shoveling of snow was done.

ALL THE SCOOPS

At Monero a couple of cases of miners' candles and a good supply of scoop shovels were taken on. The candles were to be used to coat the scoops to prevent snow sticking to them. This was done by holding a scoop in the firebox to heat it, then the candle was rubbed on the top and bottom of the scoop. Before Chama was reached it would prove we needed all the scoops and all the candles.

The high wedge on the front of the 375 sliced through a number of six to ten foot drifts from Monero to just east of Biggs Spur where the going got tougher. By the time we were approaching the big cut at the Continental Divide east of Azotea section house, there was a whiteout from drifting

Monero, New Mexico in June, 1969; ten years later all was gone. ***Museum of New Mexico***

snow. The wedge struck a deep cut filled with snow at the summit and stuck. Some reconnoitering developed there was going to be several hours of shoveling ahead. The section men put on all the clothes they had and prepared for some cold work. The crews went on relief, and I went to work with nothing to do but throw in a few scoops of coal on the two engines occasionally and keep enough water showing in the glass.

About daylight the shovelers had a hole the wedge could get through, and we proceeded without incident to Willow Creek. The lead wheels of the flanger, trained behind the mudhen, split the west switch and derailed. The wheels were badly out of line, and the four rerailing frogs on the engines were not enough to make the necessary sets. There were two more on the crummy that could be brought forward. Walter Ashbrook, trainman and a giant of a man, volunteered for the job as he liked to show off his strength. He broke a trail back through the snow, got out the frogs and lined them up on the platform. He then stepped between and plowed back to the derailment. He was toting a lot of weight, for each frog weighed close to 100 pounds.

The aftermath of his stunt came later. Walter developed a bad case of hemorrhoids, and he drove everyone crazy telling about them and how they hurt. The tale of woe finally stopped when someone suggested he rub them with Sloan's Linament, a very powerful muscular linament. He did, and never thereafter mentioned his piles.

AGENCY CLOSED

Times got worse about the middle of the Big Depression and the Rio Grande petitioned to close the Monero agency. A vice-president, the superintendent and a couple of lawyers came for the hearing before the State Utilities Board, and my mother invited them to lunch. She served them a meal of trout I had caught the day before in the Chama River, with other fixings including a lettuce and watercress salad—the cress I had used to pack the trout in. The vice-president was generous with his praise and later sent her a one-pound box of chocolates to show his appreciation. However, her good cooking and Irish wiles did not keep him from closing the agency.

About 25 years later when I was Trainmaster at Alamosa, I had occasion to ride the *San Juan* frequently and pass through Monero. Only one white family was left, the Carantas, who were still operating one coal mine to furnish coal to the railroad. Each trip recalled memories, one of which I always wondered what it was all about, and what the final ending of the story was.

It involved the daughter of the Azotea Section Foreman. He had a Castillian wife (although he was one of the dark Mexicans), two sons and two daughters. One of the daughters and one of the sons were just run-of-the-mill specimens, but the other son and the second daughter, were magnificent examples of humanity. Especially the daughter. At 17 and 18 years of age she simply dazzled the eye with her form, proudly carried head, raven-wing hair, tawny skin and flirty eyes. She was some pumpkin and knew it, and although she had practiced cutting her eyes over her shoulders as she swayed away, she was inviolate—nothing but a teaser.

She had use of her father's pass and used it a lot to ride up and down the line visiting relatives and playing havoc with the libido of trainmen and all male passengers not accompanied by wives—maybe them, too.

Then one day, shortly before the agency was closed, the father brought her to Monero and bought her a one-way ticket to Denver. They sat in the waiting room talking quietly and without emotion.

No. 116 whistled for the station and they walked out to the platform. The girl carried some ordinary name, but the trainmen had named her *The Rose of Azotea.* And she was a rose, a full-blown one in a tightly-fitted red dress stretched above over high breasts and with Dietrich legs below.

As the train stopped, she threw her arms around the father, shed a few tears and said, "Adios, mi papa."

My mother was postmistress at Monero and no letters ever came for the father from the *Rose of Azotea*—and none of her family ever mentioned her from then on. But, years later as I rode the parlor car-dinette of the *San Juan* by Monero, I could still close my eyes and recall the picture of the *Rose of Azotea* as she climbed aboard and left a mystery behind.

Chapter 2

Pagosa Junction

I had my first experience with Pagosa Junction when I was about 14 years old and the Pagosa Springs branch was still being operated from Pagosa Springs to a junction with the main line at Pagosa Junction, later renamed Gato which was its original name before the branch was built.

At that time, it was still an active community of about 200 people. H.A. "Auz" Rogers and his wife, Helen, ran a small eatery with three guest rooms across the track from the depot. Two consecutive springs I rode the passenger train from Monero to Pagosa Junction and performed the spring cleanup and catch-up maintenance for the eatery and a home the Rogers had next door to it. These visits usually lasted a month or six weeks during which time I listened to a lot of Auz's railroad stories, and served as his listening post for hours as he argued to himself whether or not there was a God and a hereafter. He was neither an agnostic or atheist—he just was a thinker that could not accept the Bible's statements as other than the history and legends of ancient people passed down by word of mouth and later put into writing.

My second visit ended when crews on the Pagosa Springs branch and through crews sent word to my father to "bring that damned kid home. We are tired of eating rabbit fried, baked and stewed, and fish." Helen was a frugal woman and, although a fine cook, believed in utilizing the cheapest food. Rabbits and fish I provided looked to her like a means for saving.

My second experience came toward the end of 1937 and was my first regular agency on the narrow gauge, excluding a couple of relief jobs at Hooper and Romeo in the San Luis Valley, both on three-rail track. By the time I bid in the assignment, the dirt roads from Pagosa Springs and Arboles were both closed for the winter by mud and snow. After trading in our automobile at Chama for spring delivery of a new one, I loaded my wife and infant son on the passenger train, along with what few household items we had, and we rode the iron to Pagosa Junction. We were totally unprepared.

Photo of #482 balling the jack on a bridge at Salida in three-rail territory. *Author's collection*

SCRAPPED CARS

The agent's quarters, across the tracks from the depot, had been built of three scrapped refrigerator cars. Set in a U-form and painted with the current Rio Grande muddy yellow, they were not very promising. The only furnishings consisted of a flat-topped cast iron stove. There was a hole in the floor back of it, and the previous occupant had used it for a garbage receptable and flung the grease from his skillet against the wall. My wife was ready to cry, and I was not feeling very good about the setup.

We *did* have a crib for the baby son, bedding and pots and pans. Either Walter Zabriskie or Felix Gomez, operators of the two small general stores, loaned us a mattress so we set up housekeeping in the room with the stove and fired off an order for furniture to Montgomery Ward in Denver. It was a week or 10 days before it arrived and during the interim we got by. Goldie, my wife, scrubbed and scrubbed while I

The Railroad Red Book

THE DENVER & RIO GRANDE SYSTEM.

Round Trip Excursion Rates.

From May 15th to October 31st, 1905.

FROM	TO	Sunday only.	Saturday or Sunday to Monday.	Daily, good Ten Days.
Denver....	Canon City	......	......	$10 25
	Castle Rock........	$1 00	$1 30	† 1 85
	Colo. Springs	2 00	2 90	4 50
	Cripple Creek......	......	......	9 50
	Florence	......	......	9 65
	Larkspur	1 15	1 75	2 60
	Manitou............	2 00	3 00	4 65
	Monument.........	1 50	......	3 45
	Palmer Lake (Glen Park)	1 25	2 05	3 15
	Pueblo	......	......	7 00
	Sedalia............	75	1 00	†1 35
	Summit of Pike's Peak	6 00	7 25	9 40
Colo. Spgs.	Canon City.........	......	3 75	5 70
	Castle Rock........	1 15	1 60	......
	Cripple Creek......	......	......	* 7 50
	Denver.............	2 00	......	4 50
	Larkspur	85	1 20	1 90
	Palmer Lake (Glen Park)	75	85	1 35
	Parkdale...........	......	4 20	......
	Pueblo	1 25 Daily	......	2 50
	Summit of Pike's Peak	4 20	4 45	4 95

FROM	TO	Sunday only.	Saturday, or Sunday to Monday.	Daily, good Ten Days
Manitou...	Canon City	......	$3 85	$5 85
	Castle Rock........	$1 30	1 70	......
	Denver.............	2 00	......	4 65
	Littleton	1 90	......	......
	Monument.........	65	80	......
	Palmer Lake (Glen Park)	90	95	1 50
	Parkdale...........	......	4 30	......
	Pueblo	1 40	......	2 65
	Sedalia.............	1 60	2 00	......
Pueblo	Canon City.........	1 50	2 00	......
	Colo. Springs......	1 25	1 75	2 50
	Cripple Creek......	......	......	7 50
	Denver.............	3 25	......	7 00
	Florence	1 50	......	......
	La Veta	1 50	......	......
	Larkspur	1 85	2 95	4 60
	Manitou	1 40	1 85	2 65
	Palmer Lake (Glen Park)	1 75	2 60	4 05
	Parkdale...........	1 50	2 45	......
	Summit of Pike's Peak)	5 40	6 10	7 40
	La Veta Pass	......	4 65	......
	Trinidad	......	......	7 50
	Walsenburg	1 50	......	......

†Good five days. * Via Florence or Canon City. ‡ Daily.

ROUND TRIP LOCAL TOURIST RATES

Limit thirty days from date of sale.

	Denver.	Colo Spgs	Manitou	Pueblo.	Trinidad.
Alamosa	$17 70	$14 10	$14 30	$11 70	$10 15
Antonito	20 30	16 70	16 90	14 30	12 80
Aspen..............	18 00	18 00	18 00	18 00	25 50
Buena Vista.......	9 60	9 60	9 60	9 60	17 10
Canon City........	9 20	6 00	6 00	3 20	10 70
Cebolla............	16 00	16 00	16 00	16 00	23 00
Cimarron.	18 15	18 15	18 35	18 15	25 20
Creede	20 60	17 60	20 90	17 00	16 80
Del Norte	19 60	16 60	17 30	14 70	13 20
Delta..............	21 00	21 00	21 20	21 00	28 00
*Durango	28 00	28 00	28 00	28 00	28 80
*Glenwood Sp'gs.	16 00	16 00	16 00	16 00	23 50
Grand Junction ..	22 00	22 00	22 00	22 00	29 50
Gunnison	14 30	14 30	14 30	14 30	21 80
Iola	15 30	15 30	15 50	15 30	22 30
Lake City	20 25	20 25	20 45	20 25	27 30
Leadville..........	12 80	12 80	12 80	12 80	20 30
La Veta	13 50	8 90	9 10	6 10	4 55
Marshall Pass......	$12 10	$12 10	$12 30	$ 9 70	$16 75
Montrose...........	20 30	20 30	20 50	20 30	27 25
Monte Vista........	19 35	15 75	15 95	13 35	11 85
*Ogden	35 00	35 00	35 00	35 00	42 50
Ouray	23 70	23 70	23 90	23 70	30 75
Poncha.............	10 10	10 10	10 30	7 70	14 75
Pagosa Springs....	25 00	25 00	25 00	25 00	28 20
Parkdale	9 60	6 70	6 90	3 90	10 95
Salida	9 60	9 60	9 60	7 20	14 25
*Salt Lake City	35 00	35 00	35 00	35 00	42 00
Santa Fe	27 05	23 45	23 60	21 05	.....
Sapinero	16 70	16 70	16 90	16 70	23 75
Silverton...........	28 00	28 00	28 00	28 00	32 00
Trinidad	14 50	10 00	10 15	7 05	......
Twin Lakes........	11 50	11 50	11 50	11 50	19 00
Wagon Wheel Gap	19 60	16 60	16 80	16 00	16 00
Wolcott	16 00	16 00	16 00	16 00	23 05

*Limit sixty days.

Stop-over privileges will be granted in either direction within the above limits except on thirty day ticket to Canon City and Trinidad and from Trinidad to Denver, Colorado Springs and Pueblo.

Courtesy collection of Marvin Gregory

patched holes, built shelves and tried to make the place ready for the furniture. It was a good thing we were young, low on funds and jobs were scarce, yet at the end of the Big Depression.

The duties of the agent at Pagosa Junction were extremely light. Seldom did I take in more than $200 per month in freight revenue—and a great deal less from Western Union and Railway Express. To improve my ability as a Morse telegrapher (at the time it was only a shade better than lousy), I set myself an unbreakable schedule of sending one hour daily on a circuit I sat up on the pinboard and the same time copying messages, Western Union wires and train orders being transmitted between offices. A lot of reading and studying of correspondence courses consumed more of my time.

A night-call telegraph sounder and key were installed in the agent's quarters so when otherwise not needed at the depot, I was able to make a lot of home improvements. There was some good clear lumber in the freight room left over from a B&B project in the past. From it I built the furniture for our second bedroom, and we ordered a springs and mattress from Montgomery Ward. Nothing luxurious, but comfortable and my wife was a good cook. We soon had traveling rail super-

NEXT PAGE

No. 315 was originally Florence & Cripple Creek No. 3, the "Elkton." It came to the D&RG in 1917. In 1950 it was donated to the city of Durango for display. ***John Krause/Dr. Richard Severance collection***

315
315

visors finding excuses to stay overnight with us and a means for a little extra spending money. We kept it, together with the few dollars of Railway Express and Western Union commissions, for those items we did not think we could afford from the railroad salary.

AUDITOR STAYS

One of the travelers who stayed with us about four times per year was the Traveling Auditor, Hugh Edmisten. Back then, under the old Account Current bookkeeping system, each agency, no matter how small, was periodically thoroughly checked by a Traveling Auditor. For a station as small as Pagosa Junction, the procedure bordered on the ludicrous. Unannounced the auditor stepped off the passenger train with his briefcase and hurried to the office. There he placed a seal on the cash drawer, pulled down the roll-cover of the ticket case and spun the combination to close the safe—all this while the agent was occupied unloading mail and express.

Engine No. 268 pulls a train on the Sapinero Branch in the canyon along the Gunnison River. The time is September, 1953. ***John Krause/Dr. Richard Severance collection***

On one trip Edmisten found me 35¢ short in the cash and asked for an explanation. I recalled I had sent a telegram for Walter Zabriskie the day before and had not yet collected for it. I offered Hugh the amount from my pocket, but he refused and made me go forthwith and collect from Zabriskie. On my return with the money, I was subjected to a quarter-hour lecture on the fact the railroad company did not do business on a credit basis. Priority was given to auditing rail accounts, and when those were finished, the express and Western Union accounts were just as closely audited. Woe betide the culprit who had made an error in any of the accounts. Of course, after awhile you learned the lectures were given by rote and, barring an evident mishandling of money, every agent received a good report when sent in by the auditor.

Hugh's only family was an old maid sister. He was very precise and soft spoken—put you in mind of a Methodist preacher. He took to my wife, and the evenings he spent with us played with the young son. Up until he died, each Christmas he checked where we were and sent my wife either a box of chocolates or a nice Christmas greeting. He always wrote a letter with the greeting, and always referred to how much he had enjoyed and appreciated the evenings spent with us.

At the time we moved to Pagosa Junction the population had dwindled to only about 50 people in what could be called the town proper. Another 150 to 200 people lived within a 10 mile radius in addition. Public relief had yet to become a way of life, and these people lived from hand to mouth on small subsistence-type farms with the only cash coming from sheepherding jobs of the menfolks. There was a pumper who kept the water tanks at Pagosa Junction, Arboles and Navajo full, a section foreman and three laborers. These had regular checks monthly, but their rates of pay were low. Also, there was a schoolteacher who drew about $75 per month. The natives depended on the barter system as much as the cash one.

ALMOST 'RICH'

There were two almost rich families: Walter Zabriskie's and Felix Gomez's. Both owned small general stores, and I do mean 'general'. Food staples, some luxury foods, clothing, shoes, horseshoes and harness, shoes for people, standard non-prescription drugs, a few dusty ladies hats and decorations, common tools and building supplies, window glass, hay, corn, oats—you name it, they had it. Even by today's standards, both were well-to-do, but they had started at Pagosa Junction when the sawmills were active, made their money and knowing no other way of living, just stayed where they were. Neither family was misers—they just did not know what to do with their wealth. Truth to tell, many of the old Mexican couples were able to eat simply because Walter and Felix did not keep very close control of their credit accounts.

In the late seventies, we stopped in Pagosa Junction to visit Felix and his wife, Elena. The Zabriskie store had fallen to ruin, but the Gomez General Mercantile still stood, and the two old folks lived in the attached living quarters. Elena served us fried goat cheese, tortillas and hot Mexican cocoa. After the repast, Felix took us into the old store section that had been closed for a number of years. It still looked like I remembered it except for a heavy layer of dust. There were hundreds of items on the shelves and hanging from wires and hooks that belonged in museums. Felix said he did not want to be bothered by collectors.

Elena served our food on a solid oak round table covered with a fine Irish linen cloth bearing exquisite old china. During the meal I commented on the silverware, and when we finished, Elena opened a chest of silver sufficient to set up for at least 20 people. The handles of the knives and forks

A La Madera branch mixed train at Taos Junction in 1924. Three years later, the mixed service was offered only once a week. Abandonment was granted in mid-1930. ***Museum of New Mexico***

were of 19th Century designs and solid silver, not hollowware. I told her I was a silversmith and could make her something to cherish with some of the pieces. We finally agreed on a cross she could set on the mantle. I took four knives and later cut off the blades, formed a cross with the handles by silver soldering them together and mounted it on a polished walnut base. The thank-you note I received was written in Spencerian script using a fine pen, black ink and on embossed stationery, a relic of the past in itself—it was written in very correct Castillian, although Elena's English was better than mine.

We could not afford a radio (battery powered), so the first winter our evening was spent reading. On sunny days, and there were a lot of them, on Sundays (I worked six days per week), we took a coffee pot and lunch materials and hiked miles up and down the track to a good fishing hole and caught fresh meat—maybe killing a rabbit or squirrel enroute. Honestly, it was neither a boring nor unhappy way of living, and it was easy to understand why the Zabriskies and Gomez's stayed at Pagosa Junction as it became a ghost town.

EARLY SPRING

Spring comes early at Pagosa Junction. When it did, I seeded the area in front of the quarters to grass, using oats in the mixture to give quick greening and to shade the new bluegrass. By mid-June it was thriving. Between the house and the water tank I planted a garden. Watered from a pipe run from the water tank and planted in a six-inch layer of head end cinders mixed with decomposed manure from the stockyards, everything I planted grew exuberantly. The local subsistence farmers, used to scrawny corn, small squash and puny vegetables, could not believe what they were seeing. They came to the depot and to the garden and made me tell them over and over what to do.

We nearly lost our son, just starting to crawl, one day while I was working in the garden. His mother brought him out and put him on a quilt near where I was working. She cautioned me to keep an eye on him but, you know how it is, I maybe did not watch closely enough. Straightening up I happened to look toward the river bank and saw some dust in the air—and no son. Running to the bank, I saw him floating face down in the spring runoff. I do not remember how I got him out of the swift water, but I did, held him up by his heels to let the muddy water run out of his lungs, and then blew into his lungs until his chest starting to heaving and he began yelling for mama.

That river bank was too close to the house for comfort. I fenced it for safety, but had to admit it did serve one worthwhile purpose. Our outhouse (privy) was built on heavy bridge timbers well anchored and sat out over the flood—no need for the usual semi-annual ritual of moving the privy. The river did not freeze at this point, and we always had good disposal. Of course, this was before the days of EPA and even cities were still dumping live sewage into rivers.

During the period I held tenure as agent at Pagosa Junction, no earth shaking events occurred to break the even flow of time. The folks still left there were well beyond the hell-raising age and content to just watch the seasons roll by. There were enough children to justify Archuleta County in maintaining a one-room schoolhouse for grade school pupils. Those of marriagable age, male and female, had all left the community seeking employment so there were no bailes—and no structure large enough to hold one in any event. Just as at the other small communities along the narrow gauge west of Chama, the daily arrivals and departures of the two passenger trains were the highlight of each midday.

One day the westbound was held up several hours while a washout was cleared between Carracas and Arboles. Aboard was a coach load of female school teachers enroute to Durango for a teachers convention. They made the grand tour of the community, oohing and aahing at the simply incredible things, especially all the very interesting things to be found on the shelves of the two stores. They even bought a few dusty knickknacks from Felix Gomez. The small Mexican children were simply adorable; the old people were quaint and so native. (Most of the teachers had the same kind of children in their classes—and more than one of them came from the same background, but had worked hard to bury their roots.)

And it was absolutely marvelous, incredible, that information and conversations could be transmitted and received by that unbelievable language of clickety-clack (read it dots-and-dashes). The ringing of the telegraphone and the voice of the Arboles section foreman giving the all clear were welcome sounds—I had a surfeit of female schoolmarms on holiday.

WATER SUPPLY

The system for supplying water to the tank at Pagosa Junction dated back to the beginning, with the exception that the original steamboiler pump had been replaced by a gasoline engine pump. The water, taken direct from the San Juan river, was fed to a sump at the pumphouse. Almost every spring after the high water receded, it was necessary to clean the ditch that carried the water. The ditch could have been replaced by a pipeline that would not be fouled with silt and debris, and over the years saved its cost many times. Apparently nobody ever thought of doing so. Another feature of this anachronistic system was, with the silt-laden water coming directly from the river, the tank bottom had to be cleaned of the accumulation every so often.

This chore was performed by Water Service Man Ralph Springett. Ralph had put in a hitch in the Navy, and his vocabulary was salted with phrases and words not normall used in polite society. About every third word was an e› pletive, or worse. He was a small, hot tempered man—wor thick lensed glasses and smoked cigarettes constantly.

His outfit car was set out by an eastward freight behind the depot and Ralph prepared to go to work. I had nothing to do so I went along to observe the operation.

The draining of the tank involved removing a large water-soaked wooden plug from the bottom just above the permanent access ladder. Ralph approached the plug with a heavy sledge prepared to knock it out. I suppose he had done it before, but the maneuver looked risky to me and I told Ralph so. He informed me in highly colored language he did not need any advice from a (string of expletives) officer worker, lit a fresh cigarette and swung the maul at the plug.

The plug came—and with it a cascade of dirty, muddy silt. Ralph lost his maul; the plug struck his arm and tore loose his grip on the ladder. The bedrenched little man, blinded by water and mud, frantically regained handholds on the ladder and saved a fall, but his descent, of necessity, was slow and awkward while all the while he was being deluged with water and silt.

He reached the bottom of the ladder and stumbled away from the pouring water. His glasses were hanging from one ear, and half a cigarette had been swallowed (it soon upset his stomach). He was a woebegone figure as he automatically reached to his shirt pocket for another cigarette. What he found was only a soggy mass of paper and tobacco.

The torrent of cusswords and phrases that erupted from him was artistry. I knew the kind of temper Ralph had, and was not sure what his reactions would be if I laughed in his presence, so I beat a hasty retreat to the depot before giving in to my urge to chortle.

About an hour later, cleaned of mud and in dry clothing, he came to my office and sheepishly admitted maybe in the future he might listen to what office men had to say.

UNPLEASANT JOB

One of the nastiest, most unpleasant jobs I ever had to perform on the narrow gauge occurred at Pagosa Junction.

In the thirties the Rio Grande still used a "Conductor's Manifest" system for recording freight train data. That is, upon reporting for duty the conductor was furnished a switch list of the cars, from head to rear, in his train. Using this he walked his train and confirmed numbers and train order. Waybills for each car were given him, and enroute he lined them up in train order, and from them entered waybill data on manifest sheets. These were on a heavy paper set up to show by columns necessary information from each waybill. The manifests and waybills were carried in a folder about 5″x12″ made of heavy parchment backs covered with waterproof black oilcloth. When not in use, after entering data, the folder was secured with one or more heavy rubber bands. Conductors most often carried the folder in a rear pocket of their bib overalls which was standard attire in freight service.

Stame Edmiston, conductor on an eastward freight train, one morning while the engine was being watered and coaled at Pagosa Junction, had a call of nature and took the opportunity to use the station's outdoor toilet. When the proceed whistle sounded, Stame hurriedly adjusted his clothing and ran to the trackside to catch the crummy as it went by. Somewhere between Pagosa Junction and Dulce, the next

Northbound daily passenger train at Otowi, New Mexico. Note bridge and non-agency station. ***Museum of New Mexico***

open telegraph office, he discovered his manifest book was missing. Running over locations it could have been lost, he settled on the logical place as being the toilet at Pagosa Junction.

He stopped the train at Dulce and had the agent get hold of me to look for the lost records, and if found, to send them to Chama on the shortly-due eastward passenger train—and to let him know at Chama the result of my search.

I did not find the book on the floor of the toilet so made a search along the track for a distance east of the depot. Nothing was found and this left me one last place to look. I obtained a flashlight and returned to the toilet to look in the pit.

There floating on top the ordure was the lost book—the effluvium, it being summer, was heavy and noxious. However, when duty calls, unpleasant chores must be performed. I obtained a length of stiff wire and bent a hook in one end with which I was able to retrieve the stinking bundle of data. The waybills being protected somewhat by the oilcloth cover had not absorbed too much liquid, but the cover was a mess that required several washings to be cleaned. And, I am sure the waybills at their final destinations still had some aroma left.

Anyway, I was able to get them on No. 116 and wire Stame that the lost was found and enroute.

Later in the day I hand-lettered a large sign and posted it on the wall of the toilet: "If you have waybills in your pocket, remove and lay down on the seat before dropping your pants."

Engine No. 268 leads the parade of box cars on a train sometime in the 1950's. ***John Krause/Dr. Richard Severance collection***

This is Chama Main Street in the 1950's. ***Museum of New Mexico***

Chapter 3

Chama

Of all the towns and cities I lived and worked in on the narrow gauge (and standard gauge), Chama was my favorite. I can only explain it by saying it felt like homebase. But there had to be more, for Chama was never an attractive town. There was little or no system in the way it was laid out, and only in recent years has there been any pavement, water or electric systems. Maybe it was because Chama, as long as the railroad was there, retained an essence of the frontier. The single worse thing against Chama was that each residence provided its own water and outdoor sanitation facility. The water wells were dug down to the water table through a deposit of glacial moraine and river deposits. And, somewhere near, the privy was located, a pit-dug hole in the ground and a wooden structure over it. There were periods constantly when Montezuma took revenge on the populace with recurring bouts of dysentery.

My first acquaintance with Chama came when my father bid in the second trick telegraph job. I was then 14 years old. Chama had a so-called high school, about 30 students, and the principal taught all the classes. I got through two years of it. Then, up until the time I married, Chama was more or less my headquarters out of which I worked many kinds of jobs (the Depression was on)—trapping, oil fields, surveying (rodman and axeman), coal and hardrock mining, lumbermills and logging. I went anywhere there was work.

POUND BROTHERS

The Pound Brothers Lumber Company was the most active industry, not only at Chama, but for 50 miles around. They operated a large commissary (actually a general store), the Chama Mercantile. A niece of theirs worked in it as cashier. Up until I became acquainted with her due to bumming around so much and working so many jobs, I had little knowledge of the female specie. As the old saying goes, I fell like a ton of bricks, and we got married. Our two children were born at Chama, delivered by the Rio Grande company doctor, Dr. J.I. Dunham. More about him later, for he was a "character"—there were a lot of characters in Chama, no real bad ones but interesting in being products of the times and place.

We were living in Chama when a Bureau of Reclamation

project ran out of money (I was field geologist), and I had to look for other employment. The Rio Grande then became my next (and final) employer. I had learned the Morse Code and some station work when I was 12-14 years old and had retained enough knowledge so that I was hired as a telegrapher.

The first assignment was at Romeo, Colorado, followed by Hooper and Del Norte, all temporary jobs. My first regular agency was Gato (Pagosa Jct). A senior agent whose station had been closed bumped me, and in turn, I bumped in on the night operator job at Chama.

Chama proved an excellent training ground for developing habits that would stand me in good stead in the years ahead in the official ranks. I learned to do with little or no sleep because the trout fishing was fantastic, hunting also, and there were high meadows and lakes to hike to. All more important than sleeping. Also, I learned how to cool off irate conductors and enginemen along with other classes of employees.

M.E. (Milton) Trotter was the regular agent when I went to Chama as operator. Milton's hobby, almost an obsession, was hybridizing sweet corn. He had developed a bit of cinder laden ground near the roundhouse, fertilized and fenced it and on it grew some championship roasting ears. Milton was a good agent to work with. He was a very busy man during the day so we reached an agreement that I would keep the Railway Express and Western Union reports for him and share in the commissions. At that time they were considerable and the additional income made it possible for me to indulge more in the outdoor sports. Operators then only made about $125 per month. The agent had free living quarters, fuel, ice and kerosene. The operator had no fringe benefits.

WINTER AT OSIER

Milton told a story of a winter he spent at Osier on an OS-snow reporting job. There were two operators assigned that winter at Osier. The second one was Eddy Oliver who eventually worked up to a Trainmaster's assignment. The two batched in the telegraph office and once a week one of them would ride No. 115 to Chama to replenish the supplies.

On one of the trips Oliver made, he returned to Osier with less groceries than he should have, a jug, and three coyote traps. Eddy had been working the night trick and saw a lot of coyotes running over the crusted snow near the office. He had reached a conclusion they could make some additional money by trapping coyotes. Of course, neither one had any experience, but Milton was easily convinced that with so many coyotes due to the bad winter they would be hungry and easily trapped. So the day following Eddy's return, they bundled up and went out to set the traps.

The surmise about the coyotes being hungry proved true. The second morning after setting the traps they looked out a window and saw a coyote in one of the traps. Jubilant, they put on heavy clothes and, armed with a cutoff broom handle, went out to start gathering their extra income. Finally, after much falling and dodging in the snow, Oliver landed a blow on the coyote's head. It fell, supposedly dead. The trap was reset after the "dead" coyote was removed. Eddy picked up the animal and slung it, head down, over his shoulder and the two Nimrods started back through the snow to the office.

About halfway back the "dead" coyote came alive—and took a healthy bite in Eddy's buttock. Then took off across the crusted snow with his tail sticking straight out behind him.

Back at the office when Eddy lowered his pants the extent of the coyote's attack was found to be only four toothmarks a bit more than skin deep. They were washed and an antiseptic applied.

Trotter bundled up again and went out to pick up the traps. So ended their dreams of making a fortune in furs.

SILVER DOLLARS

Milton laid off during the summer for a vacation. I did not exercise my prerogative to relieve him (fishing was at a peak), so W.B. Stackhouse came in as relief agent. Soon after he arrived, the Rio Arriba State Bank ordered in a large shipment of silver dollars to be available for the lumber mill's payday. It came in by Railway Express and was unloaded to the baggage truck from No. 115. Stackhouse got occupied copying some train orders, so the mailman took the mailsacks; passengers took their baggage and nothing was left on the truck but three canvas bags. Stackhouse was still occupied in the office and someone moved the truck out of the way against the depot wall.

Next morning while Stackhouse was opening up, the callboy came over from the roundhouse office and questioned him: "Say, Stack, there are three sacks of express out there on the baggage truck—says on them that they contain $1,000

Silver each. Better put them inside, somebody may walk off with them."

Well, they had laid there in plain sight for the better part of a day and no one, railroader or other, had tried to steal them—nor taken the time or effort to tell Stack about them. There were a lot of honest people in Chama. All the time we lived there we never used, never had, any keys for our house.

Chama did have a bank robbery, however. Dean Amox, a fireman, got liquored up, and thought he was one of the James boys. He filled his Model T with gasoline and his old pistol with cartridges. Then he walked into the Rio Arriba State Bank and told W.O. Evans, owner and president, and Myrtle Ray, the cashier to "put 'em up and give me the money."

They did, and Amox backed out to his Ford and took off in a cloud of dust up Main Street toward Chromo Pass.

Evans says, "Myrtle, hand me that rifle from behind the counter." With it in his hand, he stepped out the door, jacked a round into the chamber and got ready to shoot himself a bank robber.

He fired toward the fleeing car until the rifle was empty. Later, the watertank at the east end of our yard sprouted three small leaks. The blue sky of New Mexico was punctured by the other three.

FINALLY CAUGHT

The Pagosa Springs sheriff was notified, as were the ranchers around Chromo. Two or three carloads of possemen set out from Chama in pursuit. The ranchers threw up a roadblock at Chromo. Amox, by now sober and scared about what was going to happen to him, stopped some distance from the ranchers. One of the pursuing cars caught up and a brave posseman walked toward Amox and told him to surrender. The posseman all the time pointing his gun in a threatening manner. It was later discovered his weapon was a brand new Daisy air rifle he had grabbed from the firearms shelf of the Chama Mercantile. Amox was sentenced to three years in the New Mexico penitentiary at Santa Fe.

Prior to the establishment of mega-dairies and creameries, a lot of cream moved by baggage car from small producers along the line to creameries at Pueblo and Denver. It moved

The old D&RG depot at Chama as of October 27, 1973. A lot of trains have left from here. ***Museum of New Mexico***

Locomotive #499 pulls a passenger train with three cabooses upfront somewhere between Chama and Durango. ***John Krause/Dr. Richard Severance collection***

in 5- or 10-gallon galvanized cans. Chama usually had 10 or 12 cans daily, but it was too active a station to permit the agent, or me, to be guilty of a bit of petty larceny considered almost legitimate at one-man agencies. That was, lifting the lid and taking a pint or two of cream from each can. All of us at the small agencies got our supply of cream that we churned for our butter and buttermilk that way.

Unfortunately, by the time I was working as an agent, there was another practice reserved to one-man agents I could not enjoy. In pre-Prohibition days whisky was shipped in oak barrels (After Prohibition it was bottled and moved in cartons). When it moved in barrels, agents kept a small auger and a mallet handy. The mallet was used to knock a barrel-band up a ways, then the auger was used to make a small hole in which a piece of rubber tubing was inserted. When a quart fruit jar of whisky had been siphoned off, the hole was plugged with a splinter and the band knocked back into place.

Speaking of whisky and Prohibition brings to mind one more memorable character. Pat Reddington, an engineer, was blacklisted and not put back to work after the 1923 strike. So, he bought a hardscrabble ranch up the Horse Lake drainage south of Monero. There was a large, rambling adobe house on it and some utility buildings also of adobe. The livestock consisted of three or four scrawny mixed-breed milk cows, maybe a dozen sheep and about 50 goats. A small stream ran most of the year through the center of the graze and there were dense thickets of scrub oak and manzanilla bush around the open portion and extending up a couple of concealed small canyons.

PREMIUM PRICE

Up one canyon was an everflowing spring of fine water. This was the main reason Pat bought the place, for he had plans for making a living putting to use his knowledge of making poteen taught him by his father. Prohibition was in full bloom, and Pat figured men would pay a premium price for good liquor. He did not want to be bothered with mundane chores, so he hired a one-eyed Mexican women (she looked like a Halloween witch) and her cretin son to keep house and care for the livestock. Then he set up his illicit still up the hidden canyon, bought the necessary supplies and went into a very excellent 100-proof whisky production.

Another thing Pat had inherited from his father in addition to the art of making fine whisky was the mind, memory, and golden tongue of an Irish shanachie (pronounced shawn-a-kee). Pat could charm the coyotes out of the hills and mesmerize an audience with his voice and stories.

The end of Prohibition did not put Pat out of business. He continued his distilling and sold his production at $2 per pint with no trouble even though Old Mister Boston and Old Quaker whiskies came on the market quickly after repeal and cost only $1 per pint. Besides the sales made to various convention chairmen, including annual sheriffs' conventions, Pat periodically boarded No. 116 at Monero, checked his trunk (a metal bound one about the size of a footlocker) and rode the varnish to Chama to dispose of the liquid contents of the trunk. Often he would be sold out between the time No. 116 arrived and dark.

Then, after selling all his goods, he would repair to the waiting room to spend an evening with cronies he had worked with. One such evening he was in an exceptionally good tongue and one story followed another. I leaned on the ticket counter with the window open to listen—nothing but a frantic string of Morse '9s' by a dispatcher could have torn me away. A loud-mouthed young fireman kept interrupting Pat's stories to tell about his experiences (he had been working a couple of years, at least). After awhile Pat knocked the dottle out of his pipe and reloaded it while Loud-mouth was talking. Then he asked the gang if he had ever told them of a head-on collision he once was in. The consensus was he had not. Loud-mouth was all ears and pop eyes.

'RUN WILD'

"I was firing for Old Dad Boyer, going east with a hot train of bulls with engine 166 on the point. At Cumbres we picked up orders to "run wild" to Antonito, which meant the railroad was ours. We made our inspection before we whistled off at Cumbres, then Old Dad just put that 166 down in the corner and wound her up tight. Hell, he was plain gutting that teapot, and I was throwing coal even on the downgrade.

Well, anyway we were going so fast I think Old Dad was missing his count on some of the joints, and not giving a damn, anyway. I know we was 'way over the 15 MPH speed limit most of the time.

We took water at Sublette without taking time to eat any of our 1000-miler lunch. The sun was just coming up as we headed into the big cut through the gravel and rocks a couple miles east of Sublette, and I was down heaving them black diamonds again.

The cowcatcher had just turned the corner in the cut when Old Dad rared back on the Johnson bar, hit the brakes and pulled down on the whistle cord hard.

Then he yelled at me, "Boy, you better join the bird gang, quick—they's an engine coming right at us, fast."

I didn't ask questions or hesitate, just went out that gangway with all feet and arms aflapping. Hadn't took time to look for a landing place but just took wing off that engine."

Pat stuck his pipe back in his mouth, scratched a match on his shoe sole and started breathing deep to get a good light. He belched out a few puffs of smoke and got up to leave. Loud-mouth could not stand it, "Then what happened, Pat?"

Pat took in a few more deliberate drags of the pipe and says, with a straight face, "I don't rightly know, Boyo. I hit the side of that cut hard, and was killed."

For many reasons Dr. J.I. Dunham, the Rio Grande company doctor, was my favorite Chama "character." Too often the fact is overlooked that during the healthy years of our railroads, before Medicare and Medicaid, the company doctor was an integral part of railroads and a recognized member of the railroad fraternity. Especially was this true in the more isolated, smaller communities. "Doc" Dunham was surely all of this at Chama, besides being a fine conversation piece for our bull sessions. His antics, peccadillos, and falls from grace by drinking, and no less, his miraculous cures of ailments and salvation of mangled limbs, were always good for comment.

Doc was born in the Tennessee hills and obtained one of those legendary educations some hillbillies aspired to. In Doc's case his included becoming a medical and surgical doctor. Many of his characteristics, actions, weaknesses, and strengths developed as a young man in the Tennessee hills stayed with him throughout his life. One weakness he brought to Chama with him when he had to move to a higher, drier climate when he contracted tuberculosis. That was a fondness, a periodical rage, for hard liquor. His sprees and consumption of the stuff put to shame Wyatt Earp's buddy, "Doc" Holliday.

MILITARY MOUSTACHE

He sported a well-trimmed military moustache and his attire was WWI military and was always the same. His shirts were expensive woolen garbardine and his pants were the type made popular by WWI officers and of cavalry twill. His

The main street of Aztec, New Mexico—it reaped benefits from the gas boom, too. *Museum of New Mexico*

MINING CAMPS

Along the line of the Denver & Rio Grande and Rio Grande Western

ASPEN—On Aspen branch, 408 miles from Denver and 41 miles southeast of Glenwood Springs, at which point branch leaves main line.

ALTMAN—On the C. S. & C. C. D. Ry. and F. & C. C. R. R. in the Cripple Creek District.

ANACONDA—On the C. S. & C. C. D. Ry. and F. & C. C. R. R. in the Cripple Creek District.

AMIZETT—Near the head of the Rio Hondo, 32 miles northeast of Tres Piedras on Espanola Branch, 314 miles from Denver.

ALHAMBRA—North of Parkdale, a point on standard gauge main line, 171 miles from Denver.

AMES—On the Rio Grande Southern Railroad, 41 miles from Ridgway and 120 miles from Durango.

ASHCROFT—Reached by stage from Aspen, 408 miles from Denver.

BADGER—Twenty miles northeast of Salida, 216 miles from Denver. Stages tri-weekly.

BLAND, N. M.—Forty-five miles from Santa Fe on the Santa Fe Branch, 406 miles from Denver. Stage line daily.

BONANZA—Sixteen miles from Villa Grove, on San Luis Valley Branch, 247 miles from Denver. Stages daily except Sunday.

BACHELOR—Three miles from Jimtown, on Creede Branch, 319 miles from Denver. Stages daily.

BELDEN—On main standard gauge line, four miles west of Red Cliff and 302 miles from Denver.

BINGHAM—On the Bingham branch, 14 miles from Bingham Junction, 25 miles from Salt Lake City.

BIRD'S EYE—On Dillon branch, five miles from Leadville and 283 miles from Denver.

BEAR CREEK—Eighteen miles southeast of Silverton, western terminus of Southern Colorado and New Mexico division, 495 miles from Denver.

BLUFF CITY, UTAH—Ninety miles from Dolores, a point on Rio Grande Southern railroad, 60 miles from Durango and 102 miles from Ridgway. Stages semi-weekly.

CARBONDALE—On Aspen branch, 28 miles southeast of Glenwood Springs and 379 miles from Denver.

CREEDE—At terminus of Creede branch, 70 miles from Alamosa and 320 miles from Denver.

CRESTED BUTTE—On Crested Butte branch, 28 miles from Gunnison and 316 miles from Denver.

CRIPPLE CREEK—46 miles from Colorado Springs on the C. S. & C. C. D. Ry. and 41 miles from Florence or Canon City, on the F. & C. C. R. R.

CAPITAL CITY—Near Lake City, terminus of Lake City branch, 37 miles from Sapinero and 352 miles from Denver.

CHIHUAHUA—Near Dillon, on Dillon branch, 36 miles northeast of Leadville and 318 miles from Denver.

COCHETOPA—Twenty miles from Parlin, on narrow gauge main line, 279 miles from Denver and 11 miles east of Gunnison.

CLARKSVILLE—North of Parkdale, a point on standard gauge main line, 171 miles from Denver.

CARSON—Reached by stage from Creede, terminus of Creede branch, 320 miles from Denver.

CHATTANOOGA—On Silverton railroad. 9 miles north of Silverton and 504 miles from Denver.

COCHITI—Reached by stage from Santa Fe, N. M., 404 miles from Denver.

DURANGO—On Southern Colorado and New Mexico division, 45 miles from Denver.

DAKIN—Twelve miles from Castle Rock, which is 33 miles south of Denver.

DUNCAN—Twenty-two miles from Hooper, on the San Luis Valley branch, 282 miles from Denver. Stages daily except Sunday.

DUBOIS—Eighteen miles from Iola, on main narrow gauge line 301 miles from Denver. Stages daily except Sunday.

DILLON—On Dillon branch, 36 miles northeast of Leadville and 313 miles from Denver.

DIFFICULT CREEK—Near Aspen, on Aspen branch, 408 miles from Denver and 41 miles southeast of Glenwood Springs.

EUREKA, COLO.—On Silverton Northern railroad, near Silverton. terminus of Southern Colorado and New Mexico division, 495 miles from Denver.

EUREKA, UTAH—On the Tintic branch, 40 miles from Springville and 90 miles from Salt Lake City.

ELKTON—On the C. S. & C. C. D. Ry and F. & C. C. R. R. in the Cripple Creek District.

FULFORD—Eighteen miles from Eagle on main standard gauge line, 335 miles from Denver. Stages daily except Sunday.

FRISCO—On Blue River branch, 35 miles from Leadville and 310 miles from Denver.

GILMAN—Three miles from Red Cliff, on main standard gauge line, 300 miles from Denver. Stages daily.

GOLDFIELD—On the C. S. & C. C. D. Ry. and F. & C. C. R. R. in the Cripple Creek District.

GRANITE—On main standard gauge line, 18 miles south from Leadville, and 259 miles from Denver.

GUNNISON—On main narrow gauge line, 290 miles from Denver.

GOTHIC—Near Crested Butte. on Crested Butte branch, 28 miles from Gunnison and 318 miles from Denver.

HARRINGTON—Fifteen miles north of Salida, on main standard gauge line, 216 miles from Denver. Stages tri-weekly.

HOLY CROSS—Eighteen miles from Red Cliff, 300 miles from Denver. Stages semi-weekly.

HOPEWELL—Eighteen miles west of Tres Piedras, on Espanola branch, 314 miles from Denver.

HOWARDSVILLE — On the Silverton Northern Railroad, near Silverton, terminus of Southern Colorado and New Mexico division, 495 miles from Denver.

IBEX—Seven miles from Leadville on the Chrysolite Extension, 283 miles from Denver.

INDEPENDENCE—On the C. S. & C. C. D. Ry. and F. & C. C. R. R. in the Cripple Creek district.

IRIS—South of Gunnison, on main narrow gauge line, 290 miles from Denver.

IRONTON—Nine miles from Ouray, on Ouray Branch, 380 miles from Denver. Stages daily except Sunday, or all rail route via Durango, 512 miles from Denver.

IRWIN—On Ruby Anthracite Branch. 3 miles from Crested Butte and 326 miles from Denver.

KOKOMO—On Dillon Branch, 20 miles northeast of Leadville and 296 miles from Denver.

LEADVILLE—On main standard gauge line, 277 miles from Denver.

LA PLATA—Nine miles from Hesperus, on Rio Grande Southern Railroad, 16 miles from Durango. Stages daily.

LAKE CITY—Terminus of Lake City Branch, 37 miles from Sapinero and 352 miles from Denver.

LA BELLE—Reached by stage from Antonito, on Southern Colorado and New Mexico division, 279 miles from Denver.

MARYSVALE—On the San Pete and Sevier Branch, 133 miles from Thistle Junction and 234 miles from Salt Lake City.

MAMMOTH—On the Tintic Branch, 42 miles from Springville and 92 miles from Salt Lake City.

MERCUR—On the Salt Lake and Mercur Railroad, 50 miles southwest of Salt Lake City.

MONARCH—On the Monarch Branch, 15 miles from Poncha Junction and 236 miles from Denver.

MARBLE CITY—Thirty miles from Carbondale, on Aspen Branch, 379 miles from Denver.

MIDWAY—On the C. S. & C. C. D. Ry. and F. & C. C. R. R. in the Cripple Creek District.

MONTEZUMA—Near Dillon, on Dillon Branch, 36 miles northeast of Leadville and 313 miles from Denver.

NEEDLETON—Thirty-one miles north of Durango, on Silverton Branch, and 481 miles from Denver.

NELSON—Nine miles northeast of Salida, on main standard gauge line, 216 miles from Denver. Stages tri-weekly.

OHIO CITY—Eight miles from Parlin, on main narrow gauge line, 11 miles east of Gunnison and 278 miles from Denver. Stages daily except Sunday.

OURAY—Terminus Ouray branch, 36 miles south of Montrose and 389 miles from Denver.

OPHIR—On Rio Grande Southern railroad, 45 miles from Ridgway and 424 miles from Denver.

PARK CITY—On the Park City branch, 35 miles from Salt Lake City.

PITKIN—Fifteen miles from Parlin, on main narrow gauge line, 11 miles east of Gunnison and 278 miles from Denver. Stages daily except Sunday.

POWDERHORN—Twenty miles from Iola, on main narrow gauge line, 301 miles from Denver. Stages daily except Sunday.

PLACER—On Veta Pass line, 38 miles from Alamosa and 213 miles from Denver.

RED CLIFF—On main standard gauge line, 23 miles west of Leadville and 300 miles from Denver.

RED RIVER CITY, N. M.—Sixty-five miles southeast of Antonito, on the Southern Colorado and New Mexico division, 279 miles from Denver. Stages tri-weekly.

RED MOUNTAIN—Twelve miles south of Ouray, on Ouray branch, 36 miles south of Montrose and 389 miles from Denver.

RICO—On Rio Grande Southern railroad, 66 miles south of Ridgway and 96 miles north of Durango.

RUBY—On Ruby Anthracite branch, 11 miles from Crested Butte and 329 miles from Denver.

ROBINSON—On Blue River branch, 20 miles from Leadville and 294 miles from Denver.

SALIDA—On main standard gauge line, 216 miles west of Denver; junctional point of four divisions D. & R. G. R. R.

SPENCER—Eleven miles from Iola, on main narrow gauge line, 301 miles from Denver. Stage daily except Sunday.

SILVERTON—Western terminus Southern Colorado and New Mexico division, 495 miles from Denver.

SILVER CLIFF—Two miles from West Cliff, on the West Cliff branch, 25 miles from Texas Creek, 211 miles from Denver.

SNEFFLES—Eight miles from Ouray, on Ouray branch, 389 miles from Denver. Stage daily except Sunday.

SAW PIT—On Rio Grande Southern railroad, 30 miles from Ridgway and 409 miles from Denver.

ST. KEVIN—About six miles from Leadville, on main standard gauge line, 277 miles from Denver. Stages daily.

SAGUACHE—Twenty miles from Villa Grove, on San Luis Valley branch, 247 miles from Denver. Stages daily.

SILVER CITY—On Tintic branch, 44 miles from Springville and 94 miles from Salt Lake City.

SPANISH PEAKS—Near La Veta, on Veta Pass line, 191 miles from Denver.

SUNNYSIDE—Three miles west of Creede, terminus of Creede branch, 320 miles from Denver.

SPAR CITY—Near Creede, terminus of Creede branch, 320 miles from Denver.

TOLIFARO—Twenty-two miles from Iola, on main narrow gauge line, 301 miles from Denver. Stages daily except Sunday.

TELLURIDE—On Telluride branch Rio Grande Southern railroad, 45 miles from Ridgway, 104 miles from Durango and 424 miles from Denver.

TRES PIEDRAS—On the Santa Fe branch, 315 miles from Denver.

TURRET—Fifteen miles north of Salida, on main standard gauge line, 216 miles from Denver. Stage daily except Sunday.

TWIN LAKES—Nine miles west of Granite, on main standard gauge line, 259 miles from Denver; stages daily except Sunday.

TIN CUP—Northeast of Crested Butte, on Crested Butte branch, 28 miles from Gunnison and 318 miles from Denver.

VULCAN—Twelve miles from Iola, on main narrow gauge line, 301 miles from Denver. Stages daily except Sunday.

VICTOR—Forty-five miles from Colorado Springs, on the C. S. & C. C. D. Ry., and 35 miles from Florence or Canon City, on the F. & C. C. R. R.

WEST CLIFF—On the West Cliff branch, 25 miles from Texas Creek, 209 miles from Denver.

WHITE PINE—Twelve miles west of Sargent, on main narrow gauge line, 250 miles from Denver. Stages daily except Sunday.

From Marvin Gregory collection

With #490 leading, a freight doubleheader shares the load near Antonito in 1954. ***John Krause/Dr. Richard Severance collection***

boots were cordovan in color and laced well over his calves. They were always with a split-polish sheen.

Doc delivered both of our children. The last one, our daughter, because the only assistant he could find late at night was a grand old Irish biddy named Nora Krenz, Doc drafted me to be on hand to apply the ether cone. I was amazed at his tenderness during the delivery and care of my wife, for Doc had worked on me several times, and he was anything but tender.

My first experience with Doc was when he laid me face down on his table, wiped my bare back with alcohol, then proceeded to dig a bunch of birdshot out that a careless hunting partner had blasted into me. The next was to sew back on my right thumb that was severed when caught between a loop of my lariat and the saddle horn. (Thanks to his abilities, I still have a usable thumb, although almost nailless.) On another occasion, as I was walking by his office with another man, he called us in to help hold a Mexican sawmill worker who had been slashed across the abdomen. The cut had not gone into the abdominal cavity and Doc said if the bastard was tough enough to be fighting with knives, he would be damned if he would waste ether on him. So we held the guy's arms and legs and Doc sewed him up.

My last experience with Doc, he came to the office after

Locomotive #490 brings up the rear of an eastbound freight train below Windy Point near Coxo in August of 1952. ***John Krause/Dr. Richard Severance collection***

being called by the agent, Milton Trotter, to attend me. It was about midnight, and I had a hole in my left thigh made by a .41 caliber hunk of lead going through it. It was sheep shipping season, and I had a Colt's Single Action pistol in a pigeonhole of my desk. When I was relieved (we had a third operator on during stock season), I stuck the pistol in the slash pocket of my jacket. I leaned over to show my relief something, and the gun fell out landing on the butt. It went off with the muzzle pointing up toward my thigh. (I always carried the gun with the firing pin on an empty chamber, but apparently while I was out of the office, someone had fooled with the weapon and spun the cylinder.)

Before going for Doc, Milton, who had been called from his living quarters, came in and brought a half pint of whisky with him for me. (Neither of us knew that whisky should never be drunk if you are bleeding.) Anyway, I made use of it, and when Doc arrived, his first question was to determine who had been drinking. I told him I had to keep down the shock.

Doc says, "Son, that was damned foolishness, but if you like alcohol, I'll give you a little more."

LITTLE PAIN

He cocked my leg up on a table top, pulled my pants down around my ankles, and swabbed out the bullet hole; there was a wound from just above my knee that exited under my hip. Fortunately, no bones, nerves, or large vessels had been hit and no cloth had been carried into the wound. And, there was very little pain until Doc elevated my leg a bit higher, squeezed the wound open and poured alcohol down through it as an antiseptic. I let out a howl and wet my pants a little.

Doc then applied bandages, and he and Milton took me home. My wife came to the door and asked what was wrong. Milton answered I was shot. She comes back with, "Oh, yeah? Looks to me more like he's half shot. Bring him on in."

I thought being shot I would not have to work for a few days. Doc says I was wrong and he would not okay a sick leave. So I went to work each afternoon and hobbled around enough to do the office work. Milton Trotter got out and sealed all the stock cars we loaded. (It was several years later before we quit sealing stock shipments.)

I was in the dining room of Ma Foster's restaurant one evening when Doc was there eating with some more of us rails. There was a man and woman there from the East just touring around, and we overheard them talking about the fact they had decided all the stories about a Wild West was melarkey. Doc winked at us (he was cold sober), got up and pulled out a pistol and started putting on a drunken act, declaring he was the deadliest shot in five states. On a wall about 30 feet away was a large John Deere calendar with a picture of a man on a tractor. Doc took careful aim at the farmer's head and squeezed off a couple of shots and blew the guy's head off. The couple sat in their chairs, petrified.

Doc was attached almost as much to his firearms as he was to the bottle. He had a large collection among which was a beautiful .22 caliber Winchester. Sometimes in the evening (until he married and his wife made a few changes) he would set on his back porch and ring the bell in the steeple of an old church across the street with that .22.

On another occasion he used his guns (or the threat of using them) to enforce a quarantine. Ensenada, a small Mexican settlement in the Tierra Amarilla district, had an outbreak of smallpox. The Rio Arriba County officers refused to quarantine the community. All the county officers were Mexicans and great number of the natives, at that time, firmly believed that if you had survived smallpox, and as a result

An eastbound freight with #490 as a helper has just cleared the Lobato Trestle. The time is September, 1954. ***John Krause/Dr. Richard Severance***

were heavily pockmarked, you would go through purgatory without receiving any punishment.

Doc loaded up a shotgun and a couple of pistols, along with his medical supplies, and went to Ensenada where he established and enforced his own quarantine.

BERSERK MAN

Returning from a call out of town one afternoon, Doc noticed a crowd of people on the sidewalk in front of the bank and general store watching a berserk man pounding an old tree stump near the post office with a heavy iron pipe. A Swede roundhouse laborer had gone off his rocker and chased everyone out of the roundhouse, then ran up the hill from the railroad tracks to Main Street. There he started venting his rage on the stump, and people just stood and watched him.

Doc parked his car, got out and took a pistol from his black bag. He checked the loads and started toward the mad Swede. Crossing the street he kicked a rounded fist-sized rock out of the surface and fitted it in his right hand: the gun in his left. He approached the berserk man with calming words, but when he was three or four steps from him, the madman started toward Doc. The Tenessean must have killed a lot of small game with rocks—his arm came up and back then blurred coming forward. The rock struck the Swede's forehead hard and he dropped unconscious. Doc went back to his black bag and filled a hypodermic needle with a sedative. The injection kept the out of control man quiet for several hours, and when he awakened, he had no recollection of what had happened.

There were a lot of people who joined Doc's wife and children mourning when Doc died in an automobile accident.

Today, Chama still nestles in the pocket of hills at the foot of Cumbres Pass, but it is just another tourist town that has some resemblance to a railroad town because the Cumbres and Toltec Scenic Railroad has its main headquarters and operations there. But there is a world of difference between one train a day departing then returning to Chama after a day's railfanning on Cumbres, and the many rail movements of the narrow gauge's heyday.

Chapter 4

The Granddaddy of Snowstorms on Cumbres 1952

December 28, 1951, was one of those winter days at Chama of turquoise skies and warm breezes. It was possible to work outdoors without gloves or coats. Old snow was melting to slush, then to water. The sharp crests of the San Juan mountains were clear against the cloudless blue. Nothing in any weather report indicated other than a continuation of the conditions.

A Chama-Cumbres Turn departed Chama at 8:50 p.m. to shuttle a string of coal loads and lumber to the top of the hill to be picked up by a following train. Engineer Joe Dalla and fireman Johnny Lira were on the helper engine and lined up to cut off at Cumbres to run light to Alamosa. In view of the existing conditions, they did not anticipate any untoward delays, so they carried no extra food or heavy clothing.

About an hour after the Cumbres Turn left Chama, a heaving black cloud raced in from the west wiping out the stars as it came. A misty rain started falling in Chama. Nobody paid any special attention, although the conductor of the Cumbres Turn, upon return from Cumbres, reported that the wind at the top of the pass was blowing hard and the clouds were low and heavy. It was snowing some and drifting, enough to make it necessary to call section men to clean switches before setting out. This was not out of the ordinary.

About three hours after midnight, the train dispatcher became concerned when Joe Dalla and engine 491 had not been reported by Antonito, and he began checking for its location.

Cumbres station answered the callbell and was asked for a weather report. The report was that it was plain hell and that there was a tomcat of a blizzard in progress.

A doubleheader wedge snowplow opens the set out track at Cumbres. Note the semaphore signal has replaced the Swift-type signal of 1918. ***Colorado RR Museum/R.W. Richardson***

NO ANSWERS

There were no answers from either the Osier or Sublette section headquarters. The dispatcher kept on ringing, while he and Cumbres discussed the situation. While they were doing so, a voice broke in and said, "It may be bad at Cumbres, but it is worse here at Big Horn."

The Sublette and Osier gangs had combined forces for a track job and when finished, started by motorcar back to Sublette where both gangs intended to spend the night. Some two miles west of the old Big Horn sectionhouse, then abandoned but with a phone still installed, they stalled in the snow. They got part way back to Big Horn when snow cut them off. After a wet, cold struggle, they reached the old building on foot and were able to tear up some flooring and get a fire going, but they had no food.

Neither had they seen or heard anything of Joe Dalla and engine 491. At 6:00 a.m., December 29, there was still no report. At 8:00 a.m. a snowplow train (without a rotary) left Alamosa to pick up the section men at Big Horn and continue west to try to find engine 491. This was potentially a dangerous move in case engine 491 was moving east, but later developments removed any doubt about the opposing engine still being enroute.

At 10:30 p.m. this plow train reported from Osier that it had got to a point about a mile west of Osier and had to return to Osier. Backing into Osier the caboose derailed and then the Jordan spreader, a small flanger and the tank wheels of engine 492 derailed.

The Narrow Gauge had a mess on its hand. At Chama a snow train was made up of a plow engine and helper and a car for section men, equipment and a food supply. A rotary train was started west from Alamosa.

The train from Chama slugged it out with the snow to MP 331, one mile from Cumbres, where it rammed into a heavy slide and became stuck. I was with this train and went to Cumbres through the snow, reported, and was filled in with details of the situation at that time. Obtaining snowshoes at Cumbres, I returned to the eastward snowplow to line up operations there.

RECEIVED A SLED

Returning to Cumbres, I obtained a sled and food supplies and started east through the blizzard to try to find Joe Dalla and Johnny Lira. I found them just before dark about three miles west of Osier, stuck in a deep drift and completely covered by more drifting snow. The men were hungry, but otherwise in good condition. The snow insulated them, and they had been able to keep a fire for heat alive in the firebox. A meal was cooked using the coal scoop, and a cleared out waste bucket, then we settled in for the night. Next morning the blizzard still raged, but I was able to reach Osier. Dalla and Lira stayed on the engine.

On the last day of 1951, I returned to engine 491 with more food and heavy clothing. New Year's eve the three of us celebrated on the buried engine drinking coffee. On New Year's Day, engine 491 was killed and drained, and we made it to Osier through the now calm storm by about noon.

January 2 Rotary OY, from Alamosa, was at MP 315 and running low on food. So were we at Osier. But the wind had died. Norman Kramer, a Colorado pilot and legend in his own time, bombed both outfits with food. At Osier where the diet for four days had been unflavored, unsalted beans and flour tortillas and nothing more, the food drop was especially welcome. Alamosa Lion Club members who had brothers at Osier included a large bag of Christmas candy and six bottles of brandy for us. Lions shared with non-Lions, and before eating the first good meal for four days, we all sat down where space was available and washed down quantities of candy with brandy.

January 3, in late afternoon, DUKs of the Mountain and Cold Weather Command of the Army, reached Osier with more food and fresh train and engine crew members. Next morning the DUKs transported relief crews to Rotary OY. Crew members from the rotary and from Osier who desired to be relieved were taken to Antonito by the DUKs.

Rotary OY reached Osier January 4, and the following day rerailing of derailed equipment began. The job was completed on January 5. Engine 491, dead in the drift, was reached and finally dug out and towed to Osier January 9.

In the meantime Rotary OM, from Chama, had reached the train in the slide west of Cumbres, freed it and towed it to Chama. After this chore was completed, the OM turned back east and plowed to Cumbres at 10:05 a.m. January 6 and beyond to the east end of Tanglefoot Curve. January 7 it had plowed to 2.5 miles east of Cumbres. But then it had to return to Chama for more fuel and general reoutfitting. Shortly after starting to plow again on January 9, it had to return to Chama for some repairs. These made, it started east again.

With engine 491 no longer an obstruction, Rotary OY continued plowing westward. At 8:15 p.m., January 10, the two ugly brutes, covered with snow, icicles, and cinders stood side by side at Los Pinos. Those two hunks of iron and wood pushed by a bunch of mountainbred railroaders once again had kicked the Hill in its teeth. Cumbres Pass was open.

BACK AT ALAMOSA

Shortly before midnight January 12 all the equipment, including both rotaries, was back in Alamosa. Rotary OY was cleaned of its accumulation of ice and snow, and minor repairs made. Rotary OM had to go into the backshop for some major repairs. However, no effort was made to move the backlogged freight while the OY was being reconditioned and supplied. Then, on January 17, the second generation of the snow of 1952 was born. The baby was a big, brawling brat, meaner and trickier than its sibling.

We had advance warning of the coming birth and tried to be on hand. Rotary OY left Alamosa at 3:45 a.m., January 16, with Joe Dalla at the OY's throttle and Jim Stephens on the wheel. Stephens was suffering from feet that had been frostbitten while in the slide west of Cumbres but refused to lay off. Engines 493 and 494, pushing the OY, had enginemen Ben Hindelang and Charley Firm with Frank Young as the skipper. All of these had been involved in the

West leg of covered wye snowshed at Cumbres after a storm and before first train. *Author's collection*

LEFT. Eastbound train below Windy Point. *John Krause/Dr. Richard Severance collection*

earlier battle with the mountain. Officials with the train were: T.J. Cummins, Road Foreman of Equipment, Herb Taylor, Water Service Supervisor, and myself.

As Trainmaster, I was with the clearing operations all during the first and second battles then was assigned to open the Silverton Branch, closed by snowslides and a dead, derailed engine.

We called out the coal chute operator at Antonito and topped off the bunkers and proceeded to Lava Water Tank without any difficulty. Just after taking water at Lava, we reached the cuts through the lava escarpment west of the water tank. They were full of snow mixed with dirt and sand and compacted to a consistency of concrete. The fan blades of the OY took a beating drilling through this. Upon arrival at Sublette, an inspection of the blades showed it would be necessary to turn to Alamosa to have the damaged blades replaced. While these repairs were being made, the storm levelled its full fury on the Pass.

The OY was started west again on January 20. There had been some crew changes. Charley Groshart was the OY's engineman with Ed Donaldson on the wheel. Pusher engines 493 and 495 had Jim Stephens and Ben Hindelang at their throttles and Leroy Shell was conductor. The same officials were with the train, and we had added a communications line man named Reddy.

THE SNOW GOD

The lava cuts and the cut through the moraine just east of Sublette were full, but not compacted. We reached Sublette without difficulty, and we tied up there for the night with some hope of a fairly easy trip. The Snow God had different ideas. At about 9:00 p.m. he unleashed an all-out killer attack on the three-foot gauge over Cumbres Pass.

We were fortunate we had not gone beyond Sublette this day because of a short delay enroute involving a broken water glass on one of the engines just west of Antonito that caused us to return to Antonito for a replacement brought from Alamosa by a machinist. Had this not have occurred, we would have been caught in more unfavorable terrain when the storm's fury broke.

During the night the storm never abated a bit. A check of conditions at 4:00 a.m. showed that almost a yard of wet, heavy snow had fallen and it had drifted. At daybreak, on snowshoes, I made a reconnaissance trip east to the lava cuts. What I found was sort of frightening. There was no way to get back to the Valley without a rotary plow ahead of us. The OM was at Alamosa with an indefinite repair date and the next wye west was at Cumbres. Old King Winter had outflanked us, cut off our retreat and set up a situation where we would be fighting a go-for-broke battle.

Upon my return we tried to start our advance, but the wind intensified to the point that the pilot on the wheel of the rotary had zero visibility. We tied up on the main at Sublette and awaited a lull. This came about 8:30 p.m. and we moved out. Progress was excellent for about two hours and we had reached the old Toltec section house when the OY was derailed.

During the next eight hours, those of us destined to go to hell had a preview of conditions there. To set frogs for rerailing we had to dig a 15 foot shaft through the snow alongside the derailed truck, then an adit to set all the frogs. Finally they were set, and each of us said a little prayer to whatever Power we believed in. There must have been a few Christians among us as the OY came back on the rails at the first pull.

NO INJURIES

After 22 hours of unceasing work without rest, we arrived at Osier at 6:30 p.m. and tied up for the night. Snow and the derailment were only part of our problems. In the earlier battle there had been no injuries or sickness. This trip was different. By the time we reached Osier, one section man had pneumonia and another older one could not urinate. We set up sick bay and assigned two men as nurses. The pneumonia patient was placed in a tent of blankets and a makeshift vaporizer devised to make a Vicks VapoRub steam. This, plus aspirin, eventually cured him.

The old one with the plugged plumbing posed a more complex problem. We tried towels saturated with hot water on his lower abdomen. Between towel changes the pubic area was anointed with Vicks to try to relax the muscles and organs by irritation. The patient was given enough hot tea and coffee to float a destroyer. The only result being that when his capacity was reached he threw it up. Nothing we had tried gave results and the man was suffering. We could find nothing to devise a catheter from.

Finally, one of his brother section men said his father had been treated for the same problem by a doctor who massaged the prostrate gland with his finger. He volunteered to do the same for the patient. He thoroughly cleaned his hands, and the patient's rectum, with hot soapy water. Then both were well lubricated with clean lard. A finger was inserted and the massage started. Within a few minutes copious streams of urine were flowing from the sufferer. When the flow stopped, the old man gave a few sighs of relief, turned on his side and fell asleep.

We took a 12 hour break at Osier. We were still on our own as the OM was not expected to be ready for service for at least a week. It was go to Cumbres or tough it out at Osier. We had adequate food supplies, but fuel could become questionable if the fight was prolonged and the drilling difficult, but more about the fuel situation later.

Twelve hours after we left Osier, we had only cleared about two and one-half miles west. We backed into Osier and tied

Eastbound train at Tanglefoot Curve. ***John Krause/Dr. Richard Severance collection***

Antonito, Colorado circa 1900. This is Main Street on the west side of the tracks; there was also a rival Main Street on the east side. ***Museum of New Mexico***

A westbound extra makes an air test before it descends the four percent grade into Chama in 1967. Engine #493 is ex-1005, rebuilt in 1928. The K-37's were formerly Class C-41 standard gauge 2-8-0 locomotives that Baldwin built in 1902. *Museum of New Mexico*

up for rest, refueling and water. The snow on the level had averaged 10 to 12 feet. In drifts, some a thousand or more feet long, the depth ranged from 20 to 25 feet.

NO FOOD WORRIES

This night an inventory was taken. We did not have to worry about food and, if it became necessary, Norm Kramer could bomb us with additional supplies.

Tom Cummins was concerned about the fuel. We had used a lot in the day's boring and the closest supply was at the top of Cumbres where the last Cumbres Turn had set out four cars of coal. Cummins laid the law down to the fireboys and enginemen, promising he would personally neuter anyone whose smokestack belched black smoke and the pushers would work one at a time except in extremely hard going.

January 24, a calm, cloudless day, found us at MP 321 by 7:00 a.m. Snow continued heavy and deep. The OY's fan kept turning and a beautiful plume of snow kept arching away from the strack. Approaching the telephone booth just east of Los Pinos, MP 323, I was looking from the OY's cab when I saw Lineman Reddy entering the booth which was blown clear of snow. It would be buried when the rotary passed it and Reddy would be entombed.

I threw my snowshoes out of the window and scrambled down to buckle them on to go warn Reddy. What he had done was thoughtless: What I did was sheer stupidity. I should have told the pilot to stop movement or, at the very least, told him where I was going. I did neither and was to suffer for it.

Just as I reached the booth, the first snow from the rotary hit. I barged through the door and closed it. Reddy looked at me flabbergasted. The noise of the OY diminished and it became silent in the booth. Fortunately the door opened inward and I opened it. Snow was packed deep around the

NEXT PAGE. Engine #492 is eastbound at Lobato. *John Krause/Dr. Richard Severance collection*

Rio Grande

The licensed trading post of Emmet Wirt at Dulce, New Mexico, today is a historical landmark. Posing in front of it is a Jicarilla Apache man and his wife. ***Museum of New Mexico***

booth to a depth no light came through. We were in deep trouble.

The interior of the booth measured about five by five by seven feet. Reddy packed and stomped down the snow as I dug and drug it into the booth using a snowshoe for a shovel. After 15 minutes of digging (it seemed like that many hours) we were running out of space in the booth for more snow but a tinge of light began to show. Soon I broke out of our snowy tomb and we both crawled out with little to say to each other as we walked the track to the train, mulling over our plight. It was not hard to picture ourselves as frozen carcasses to be found after the thaw. Back on the train we did not talk about what we had been through. You don't brag about being stupid fools.

Another stupid decision was made soon after. Without stopping to melt snow for water, we took a chance the curve at MP 324 and the approach to the bridge over Los Pinos Creek would be windswept and easy going. Neither was true and at about 6:00 p.m. we found ourselves low on water and reluctant to use fuel to melt the amount of snow to make the needed water, neither could we back all the way to Osier.

AT HIGH BANK

We stopped at a high bank above a deep hole in the Los Pinos kept open by the swiftly running water. Herb Taylor, the Water Service Supervisor, assisted by section men, went to work rigging a monkey-tail jetting system from the steam dome so water could be jetted from the creek to the rotary and engines. The rigging went smoothly until it was discovered we were short about 10 feet of the hose. Our hopes fell.

Taylor just said a few damns, then started walking around the extra equipment cars; the rest of us stood around and moaned. After awhile Herb came trudging back with a load of spare airhoses, coupled them together for the necessary extension and we soon had water pouring into our tanks.

The section men not working with Taylor were busy levelling a platform on the snow at dumpcar height and shovelling coal from a car to the platform. When watering was completed, the coal was transferred from the platform to the tenders of the OY and engines. The fireboys used the time to clean their fires and found a broken ashpan on engine 493. Repairs would be necessary.

A pit under the engine would be required and the roadbed was frozen solid. Taylor to the rescue again—he rigged a steam hose to thaw the frozen ground. Repairs made, fueled and watered, we were ready to move once more. But it had been nearly 12 hours since our last meal, so we took time to eat a hearty one and got moving close to 10:00 a.m.

While we were eating this meal and enjoying a last smoke and cup of coffee, there was a lot of cheerful talking but then a silence fell, the kind that comes when there is an imminent conflict in the air, when one man challenges another.

Ed Donaldson's fireman, a young man, had taken issue with Donaldson's instructions about the way the fire should be kept. He got out of line with his remarks, and it was apparent a violation of Rule "K" was about to occur. It was no place for officials to be, so Cummins, Taylor and I filled our coffee cups and went back to the cupola of a caboose. Under the conditions we were working under, it was better that the rules be overlooked and the air cleared.

From the cupola we watched Donaldson, 60 years old, and the young fireman move from the cook car to the ground. There they stomped down a ring in the snow and squared off. Donaldson may have been old, but behind him were a lot of years of heaving coal over Cumbres. The fireboy was young and cocky and confident. He had also had some boxing instruction in school. He came to the line like he had been taught while Donaldson just stood there flatfooted and arms relaxed. The fireman moved in. There was a blur of movement where the young challenger stood and then he hit the snow packed ring hard. Donaldson had struck just one blow, a sucker right to the fireman's chin.

FALLEN GLADIATOR

The victor rubbed some snow on the fallen gladiator, picked him up and carried him to the cook car. The air was cleared and it was time to go to work. No one made any comments as the three of us returned to the cook car and allowed it was time to get to work. Donaldson and his fireman went to their engine, and as far as I know, lived happily ever after.

At M.P. 327.5 the OY whistled for a back up to clean the fan's hood. In this movement the 493 derailed on ice. It took three hours to rerail her. Fifteen minutes later the 495 was on the ground but left clean flange marks in the ice. One pull and she was rerailed just like she was walking up re-railing frogs.

Five hours later, after drilling through 10 to 12 feet of mostly ice, we had moved only one-half mile. Still two and a half miles from Cumbres, we were down to our last car of coal. We tied up for rest after having been on continuous duty 40 hours and 45 minutes; the 16-hour law had been disregarded. The rest break started at 10:00 p.m., January 25.

Early the 26th I snowshoed to Cumbres while the last car of coal was being transferred and snow converted to water. At Cumbres, Alamosa advised me it would be at least five more days before the rotary OM would be in operation. A request for an air drop of food supplies was made and fulfilled later in the day.

Including about a half ton of coal taken away from the cook, our final supply of fuel was on the rotary and engines when we started moving. The supply would be insufficient to reach Cumbres, but Tom Cummins figured by using every firing trick we could make a point where the lower loop of Tanglefoot Curve would be separated from the top of the upper loop by only about 50 yards of clean snowclad slope and 25 yards below the upper point.

Norman Baughman and his bulldozer, along with a section crew, were at Cumbres having been stranded all this time. There were four cars of coal and several cars of lumber at the east end of the siding snowed in. The dozer was fired up and used to move lumber to the point where a chute could be built about where Cummins figured we could make. This was constructed on the base of packed snow, then Norman started tramming coal to the top of the chute.

COAL DUST LEFT

The rotary outfit did make the rendezvous with hardly more than coal dust left in the bunkers. Using the dozer blade to shove coal onto the chute, and gravity to lower it to the fuel-starved equipment, after several hours everything was fully fueled. During the refueling the cook's supply of coal was returned to him and he cooked up an oversized meal that was eaten in relays by the workers at the coal chute and the snow melting operations.

The rotary and locomotives fueled and watered, and all the men fed, we started boring out Tanglefoot Curve. At 8:30 p.m. the pilot shut off the rotary fan in front of the Cumbres telegraph office. It was cut away from the train to allow the remaining coal, previously cleared of snow by Baughman and the section men, to be picked up for use on the balance of the trip to Chama. While this was going on, I snowshoed around Windy Point and to Wolf Creek bridge. There were seven slides down and heavy drifting, but now we were on the downhill side and the rest of the chore would be kid stuff.

It was not to be quite that easy. Before starting the downhill pull we cut one of the engines out of the consist, turned it on the wye to follow behind us as we would not need its power to keep against the downgrade working face. It took all day to bore to the east switch at Coxo so we quit work at dark and let the engine following us pull us back to Cumbres where we tied up, refueled and took water.

Going on duty at 6:00 a.m., January 29, the water supply was replenished from the spout and we took off for Coxo and the working face of snow.

At day's end we were wasting coal and water like there would be no tomorrow as we rolled across the Chama River bridge just east of the entrance to Chama yard. Bells were ringing and the whistles were tied down on the OY and engines 493 and 495. Those whistles were shrilling defiance to that old devil, Snow, and Cumbres Pass as much as to say, "Baby, you just ain't got what it takes to wear the pants in this family."

Came spring at Osier and there was one mystery, never solved. While we were snowbound there on the first trip, we were made much by a large black female cat living at the sectionhouse. We never saw another cat, or tracks of one, all the time we were there, but when the section gang was moved back in along in March the old pussycat was still there and she had a fine litter of kittens.

Another evidence of our sojourn was when the grass came up there was belt of grass around the sectionhouse much greener and faster growing than the native grass. During the storm the outhouse had been buried under 30 feet of drifted snow. The house, due to some vagary of wind currents, sat completely free of snow in the shape of a steeply sided bowl. Anyone having a call of nature loosened his belt and got all prepared for action then bolted to a clear side of the bowl, evacuated, and returned quickly to the warmth of the house to rearrange his clothing. The fertilization did wonders for the grass.

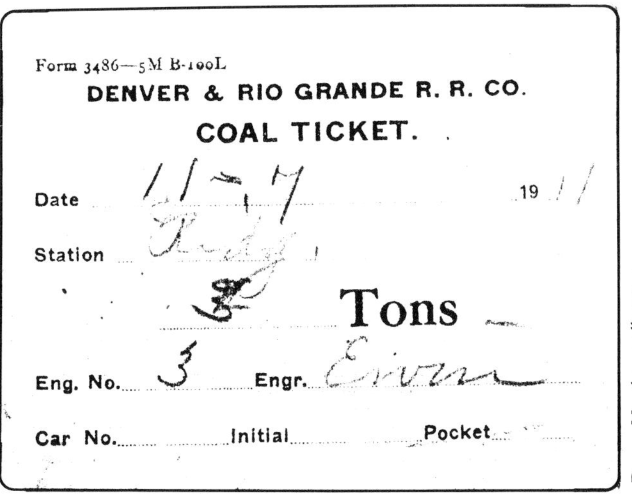

Form 3486—5M B-100L

DENVER & RIO GRANDE R. R. CO.

COAL TICKET.

Date .... 19 ....

Station ....

.... Tons

Eng. No. .... Engr. ....

Car No. .... Initial .... Pocket ....

Doug Hartley collection

Saguache snowslide, 60 feet deep. Animas Canyon, near Silverton. *Ruth Gregory collection*

Two Rio Grande locomotives make a run toward the snow slide near Silverton. ***Ruth Gregory collection***

Chapter 5

Slide Clearance on Silverton Branch 1952

The arrival of Rotary OY back at Alamosa after clearing Cumbres on January 29, 1952, marked the end of snow troubles that year over the Pass, except for improving clearances in deep cuts and drifts, and some later light snowfalls that were easily handled.

On my return with the rotary, I found my wife planning a dinner party for my 37th birthday, February 6th. The plans had to be cancelled when I was ordered to Durango to open the Silverton Branch, blockaded by snowslides.

Earlier in January an effort had been made and aborted when the lead engine of the snowtrain derailed and jacknifed in a slide. During the rerailing attempt, a severe snowstorm swept in and slides began to run. The derailed engine was killed and drained and the outfit fought its way back to Durango.

A Schenectady-built 2-8-2 #476 edges toward Rockwood with a passenger train on the Silverton branch in May of 1955. ***John Krause/Dr. Richard Severance collection***

Slide clearance on the Silverton Branch was an operation dependent on the use of bulldozers. Two were with this train and were used to clear the way behind the train as it backed up to Rockwood, the first wye. While working on one slide Henry Hotter, one of the dozer operators, was buried with his machine. As the slide struck him, he put his nose under an armpit and stayed in his seat.

When the slide quit running, rescuers went to the rescue with shovels. The dozer was still running and was easily located. After five minutes of frantic digging, Hotter was released from the slide, cold, but otherwise not injured.

Returned to Durango, it was necessary to hospitalize Joe Selby, trainmaster, who had been with the train for a severe case of pneumonia. The derailed engine, the 476, would have stayed at M.P. 486.5 until the sun released it in the spring, but the Colorado Public Utilities Commission got in on the act.

CONTINUE LOADING

Each winter the Rio Grande left all available tracks at Silverton set up with empty boxcars so the Shenandoah-Dives zinc operation could continue loading concentrates when service was interrupted by the weather. This was the case in 1952 when the derailment occurred and Shenandoah had a large number of cars loaded and ready to move when the market price for zinc jumped five cents per pound. This meant a good profit was represented by the loaded cars. Shenandoah petitioned the P.U.C. The Rio Grande was reminded that it was a "utility" and responsible for giving service. The order itself was more explicit: it simply said get the ore out of Silverton.

It required 94 days of brutal snowfighting and an expenditure of $90,000 to comply with the order.

The first chore after the order was issued was to rerail the 476 and get it back to Durango. A rerailing train, with bulldozers, reached the site February 7. Rerailing was completed and back to Durango at dark February 8. Repairs were pushed, for the 476 would be needed for the work ahead.

On February 13, with the 476 not ready, we made an effort using engines 464 and 478, but the 464 was in such a condition she could hardly move herself, so we returned to Durango. The 476 repairs were completed late February 15, and we scheduled a fully equipped work train to leave Durango on February 16.

Our outfit consisted of engines 476 and 478; two flatcars, each with a bulldozer; a well-stocked cook car; two cars of coal; necessary bunk cars; a fuel and supply car; and a couple of extra crummies for the train and engine crews to sleep in. The first day we were able to clear to a couple of miles west of Tacoma without having to unload the dozers. By the afternoon of the third day, we were almost to Elk Park when a real buster of a storm drove us back to Durango. One good feature of snowbucking on the Animas that differed from Cumbres Pass was that, barring a few slides that could be cleared by dozers, you could always retreat to return later.

While we waited in Durango for the storm to abate, we replenished our food and fuel supplies and hired a third Cat-skinner to work relief. This was necessary because the contractor with the dozers, Henry Potter, had one skinner, Lynn Brown, who had been badly whittled on by North Koreans during the so-called "police action" in Korea, and could only work about six hours per day.

The relief skinner was nicknamed "Tex" and as could be inferred, he was from the Lone Star state. He came on the job in his Stetson and high-heeled boots. Before his first day on the job was finished, the hat was replaced by a woolen cap and the boots were covered by a pair of overshoes bought from one of the section men.

Leaving Durango this trip our skipper was R.S. Murray; Steve Connor and John Dieckman our engine drivers. Late the evening of the 20th we reached Elk Park, dozed the snow away from the tracks, including the wye, and got set for the heavy work ahead.

EIGHT SLIDES

On the 21st I left the work in charge of Murray and Hotter and made a reconnaissance trip on snowshoes into Silverton. My notes from that inspection show that I found eight major slides from 100 to 500 feet long and 10 to 40 feet deep between Elk Park and the Twin Shed slide at M.P. 492.5. Snow depth between slides averaged six feet and the snow was of a granular texture like sugar, later to give us much trouble because it would not compact.

Twin Shed slide was always the largest in the canyon. It had run several times and filled the canyon from wall to wall to a depth of about 50 feet. The river had drilled a hole through the slide but before doing so had been backed up some, leaving a layer of ice over the tracks on the upstream side.

From M.P. 492.5 to Silverton there were numerous slides 50 to 100 feet long up to 25 feet deep with an average snow depth between slides of six feet. These conditions prevailed for about 10 days, but then Twin Shed slide ran again and the Cleveland and Jumping Jenny ran and many of the lesser slides had second or third runs. It was apparent the Shenandoah's zinc was not going to move to market anytime soon.

Excluding multiple runs of slides that had to be cleared more than once, the greatest handicap on the Silverton Branch in winter was the extremely low, constant temperature. High peaks surrounded the narrow canyon and the weak rays of the sun touched the rail line only between about 11:00 a.m. and 2:00 p.m. when the sun shined, and that was not every day. Rarely did the daytime temperature

A northbound Silverton Branch passenger train approaches Rockwood in Animas Canyon with #478 at the headend. *John Krause/Dr. Richard Severance collection*

reach 30 degrees, and at night we had between minus 20 and minus 50 degrees.

Such temperatures made it difficult to start the dozers' diesel engines each morning. Down to about 30 below they could be started by injecting the pony starting motors with ether. Lower than that, we often had to resort to spotting the dozers opposite an engine to use steam to warm the cylinders. After one extremely cold night we had to use the degree of ease in starting the dozers as our temperature gauge. Our thermometer only registered 40 below and on this one especially cold night someone forgot to put a bucket under the thermometer. The mercury fell so far it dropped out of the bulb and was lost in the snow and could not be replaced in the thermometer.

Clearing snowslides is different from clearing snow with a rotary plow. On the latter it seems there is constantly something happening that has to be taken care of by active men. At snowslides, once the dozers are moved to the face and unloaded, there is little for anyone except the skinners to do. Train crews and section men are only support troops.

Each morning, with the dozers loaded on flatcars in the lead, we moved from Elk Park to the current working face and unloaded the dozers. Before they began removing snow we stationed two teams of slide watchers high on the canyon wall opposite the slide. These teams consisted of two men each supplied with shotguns to be fired as warning in case the slide began to move. They were heavily clothed and had large metal cans in which they maintained a fire for heat. One

shot was notice the slide was moving and for the Cats and men to retreat to a safe place; two shots if a mass broke loose rapidly in which case forget the Cats and get out.

ONE INCIDENT

We only had one two-shot incident. This was at the Twin Shed slide toward the end of a working day. A watcher saw a black object fall from a tree to the surface of the snow high up the slide. Through binoculars he saw it was a porcupine and when it struck it started rolling downhill gathering snow in a ball. Soon the surface cracked across the face of the slide and the slide began to move. One shot was fired and a retreat started. Before the Cats were entirely in the clear the watchers fired a second shot. When the slide quit running, all our work was wiped out. Fortunately, the dozers were only lightly buried at the edge of the slide.

A trainload of railfan-passengers fill the windows and doors as Bakers Park appears. Engine #473 pulls a mix of cabooses and coaches on this fine day. *John Krause/Dr. Richard Severance collection*

During its run, a spruce tree with a trunk about six inches in diameter was observed bending toward the running snow. The vortex of the suction set up by the slide was so strong the tree finally cracked and fell into the slide. At the termination of the run, the slide's surface was covered with small spruce boughs that had been torn from trees on the walls bordering the slide path. In the slide were other full trees and rocks that made snow removal later much more difficult.

Elk Park was our tieup point at night. Until we cleared to the Whitehorse Water Chute before tieing up, we backed down to the bridge over Elk Creek and used a gasoline powered pump to water the engines. Above Whitehead Creek we could water as we returned to Elk Park by using a wooden trough out of the creek as it flowed in a series of cataracts close to the rails. The last chore of the day was to spot the engines on the main opposite the cars of coal to transfer coal by muscle and shovels.

We had to make a trip to Durango February 25 to get a new lap-and-lead rod for the 476. It had become inoperative by the granulated snow flowing around the plow as the engine moved through it, melting some and compacting from the heat from the cylinders until enough accumulated in a hard mass that caused the rod to bend when it formed enough hard ice.

For awhile we had been able to repair this rod at night by removing it to be heated in the firebox to a red heat. Engineman Dieckman and fireman Connor did this then, using a coalpick, straightened the rod and threw it in the snow to temper. They were careful in straightening to try to prevent excessive peening that would lengthen the rod. Several of the rods on the two engines had been worked on successfully, but finally one on the 476 gave way. We needed both engines working, so we returned to Durango for repairs (and some spare rods).

Newt Spearman and the roundhouse force worked all night, and we returned to Elk Park the 26th. We brought a third dozer back with us, a heavy Allis-Chalmer. Less than a day's work was obtained from it before it threw a rod and knocked out a cylinder head. It was maneuvered onto its flatcar by the other Cats and taken to where Highway 550 crosses the Silverton Branch to be unloaded to a flatbed truck. The roundtrip was made without having any snow trouble.

LEAP YEAR

1952 was a Leap Year—on February 29 we finally holed through Twin Shed Slide and hoped it would not run again.

Up until this time I had been making reports using a box-relay and Morse key cut into the telegraph line, but a slide finally wiped it out, so I skiied into Silverton to report.

The snow and slide situation found between Twin Sheds and Silverton other than the overall average that had settled to about four feet, was: 1,500 feet, six feet deep; 1,800 feet, 12 feet deep; 800 feet of slide, 35 feet deep; 2,000 feet, 15 to 20 feet deep. The Twins and Cleveland slide had run again and were deeper as had numerous small sidehill slips.

My return from Silverton was made in a light snowstorm that by morning had turned into a full-fledged blizzard. Radio weather reports said it was a major front, so we high-tailed it to Durango to let it blow out. Three days later there was a lull and we started back to Elk Park. The lull was deceiving. A second stage struck before we reached Elk Park, a storm worse than the first stage. We returned to Durango.

Late March 5 we were back at Elk Park and the next morning found the Sheds slide had run and piled up more snow

The Silverton train pulls around the wye at Silverton in this September, 1955 scene. ***John Krause/Dr. Richard Severance collection***

and debris than any earlier slides. A snowshoe trip to Silverton on March 7th disclosed conditions worse than before. Slides were deeper, numerous slips were down and the average depth was six feet between greater accumulations.

At Silverton I was instructed to bring the outfit to Hermosa the following day to pick up an inspection party. I demurred strongly to stopping work but was overruled.

We left Elk Park at 6:00 a.m. and had an easy run to Hermosa. And we waited—and waited. The party did not show and Durango did not know where it was. We tied up at Hermosa. The next morning the party was still unreported, and nobody could give any information. I told Durango we were returning to Elk Park to work and would return to Hermosa after work on March 10.

Finally, March 11th the party showed, and we took them to Elk Park. There we had lunch and went to the Sheds slide. At least we started for it—three nasty slides had run near Whitehorse Water Chute—and it began to snow. One of the inspection party was the Superintendent, C.E. McEnany, an office type who definitely was not a snowbird. Two others were the Chief Engineer and the System Engineer of Track.

A couple of hundred snowflakes fell while looking at the first slide. The Superintendent decided he did not want anymore of the Animas Canyon. He wallowed through the snow back to the crummy and said, "Come on. Let's get the hell out of here before we get snowed in."

Those were sweet words, and we had no objection to getting rid of our visitors. We had them back in Durango soon after dark. The Superintendent's hunch was right. Another storm moved in as severe as any up until then. We did not get back to Elk Park until March 18 and had to clear snow and slides to get there. Just east of Tefft, at M.P. 477, there was a large slide down and the Red Young had run.

March 19 I skiied into Silverton and met Ed Haase, our Division Engineer. We made arrangements with the County Highway Department to furnish county bulldozers and operators to start working eastward from Silverton. Haase was to stay with them and domicile at Silverton.

The last snowfall was a moist one and a Chinook wind blew in. The snow could now be compacted and "rolled" by the dozer blades. Tex went back to wearing his Stetson and put away the wool cap.

With better weather and dozers working from both ends, we had the Silverton Branch snow problem by the tail with a downhill pull. We pulled into Silverton at 3:00 p.m., March 24.

CELEBRATION NEEDED

Some kind of celebration was called for, so I skiied ahead and bought a T-bone steak for each man and took them back to the cook so he could have a big steak dinner ready when we tied up at Silverton.

The majority of the outfit had different ideas about how to celebrate. Food was the least of their desires. What they had in mind was liquid refreshment. (Even the cook took off uptown after setting the fine steaks on the table; most of them were uneaten and went into a pot of hash the next day.)

Next morning I had to roust out the cook to prepare breakfast, but there were no complaints about it being late. Only the sobersides and those with cast iron stomachs wanted anything to eat anyway, although the cook had to boil up a second go-round of coffee.

A section foreman and two or three others who had stayed

A 10-car passenger train led by engine #476 clanks along the rails near the wye at Silverton in 1954. ***John Krause/Dr. Richard Severance collection***

on the outfit with me were awakened about midnight by a commotion in one of the bunk cars. Investigating we found two inebriated section men sitting on the floor facing each other while they struggled to take off their overshoes. They were so befuddled they were having difficulty sorting out whose feet belonged to whom. We picked them up, one at a time, and, without removing their overshoes, rolled them into their bunks and covered them to sleep it off.

A bit later there was a second disturbance that took us outside. Another celebrant lost his footing on the ramp dug from the surface of the snow to car level and went under the car. His buddy trying to help him out slipped also, and both were wedged under the car and yelling bloody murder.

There was not much sleep that night as first one then another stumbled their way into the cars and their bunks.

Removing snowslides and snow with bulldozers lacks the aura of railroad romance that opening Cumbres Pass with the rotary plows has. But there were some sights and sounds any bona fide rail fan would pay good money to experience.

There was the staccato of squarely set valves echoing between the canyon walls; the belch of black smoke when the throttle was widened just as the fireboy heaved in a scoop of coal. Then there was the sensuous comfort of heat from a red hot flat-topped stove, and the smell of coffee steaming in a pot on that stove.

SNOWSHOE RABBITS

In 1952, on the Silverton Branch, when it was clear and the moon shining, there was the flash of snowshoe rabbits in the willows. In the daytime, coveys of black-eyed ptarmigan in winter white in the same willows. And, on a knoll at the tail of the wye at Elk Park, a herd of elk led by a six-point royal bull waiting for us to finish scattering their ration of hay and pellets that had been furnished by the Colorado Division of Wildlife. The herd never became tame enough to approach as we scattered the feed, but as soon as we walked away, they moved in, calves first, then cows, and finally that royal master of the harem.

When it was dark, in the headlight rays, frost crystals glittered like a million sequins. On clear nights the stars were a brilliant band across a piece of sky visible between the high canyon walls.

Then there was the sound of the blower as the engine watchmen freshened the fires and the clang of the firebox door as he added coal. Or, from the table in the cook car, a card player saying, "I'll raise you three matches and stand pat."

In every group such as this there is always one master story teller. Ours was "Buck" Buchanan. He never ran out of tales of the narrow gauge he had heard or experienced as an old-time engineman. But, Lord, he was aggravating. Some of his best stories, told in his slow drawl, he would keep us spellbound as he built up to the climax, then when we were awaiting the conclusion he'd often get up and say, "Well, boys, it's time to turn in."

Before retiring there was always a last duty to perform—one that, under the circumstances, could be classed as hazardous. Our outfit cars were not equipped with indoor toilet facilities and the outdoor latrine we built was not heated. At minus 30 degrees you knew your fingers and toes were going to get cold visiting the latrine, and you prayed that another important appendage would not be frostbit or frozen.

Those people who have never watched a large snowslide run cannot imagine how awesome the sight is. No two slides are alike, although they may run year after year at the same location. Some slides moaned, some groaned, some roared or rumbled. Then there were those that whistled or sounded like sandpaper rubbing a hard surface. A few were as silent as a cat stalking a bird. The Silverton Branch had all of these and the worst ones were full of rocks, trees and other debris. Some ran for a mile or more after starting at a point many hundreds of feet higher than the railroad. They carried many tons of snow that had to be removed.

One of the silent ones, fortunately not a large one, ran and hit our outfit while taking water at Whitehorse Water Chute. The length of the slide was from the lead engine to the rear end. A piece of rock in the slide jammed the valve of the whistle of engine 478 open. The unceasing blast was nerve wracking. Everything stayed on the rail except a caboose in which the cook was napping in the cupola. The slide ran under the caboose, started it raising, then following snow tilted it. Snow pressure broke windows and shoved one door open and filled the interior. The cook was thrown from the cupola and was partially buried.

After enough snow was shoveled from around one dozer, it was started and unloaded to clear snow along the train. When snow was cleared away from and under the caboose it fell back on the rails.

SHENANDOAH

Back to the freeing of the Shenandoah concentrates. March 25 and 26 were spent digging out the snowbound loads and in making up a train. We tied up at Elk Park the night of the 26th, and by 7:30 a.m. next day were Durango bound, for a little while. Just east of the Elk Park bridge over the Animas is a small side stream. The culvert was plugged by ice and water flowed over and froze on the track. The lead engine, the 476, derailed on the ice and came to rest against a jutting outcrop of rock.

The 478, behind the 476, could not shove the heavy train back to give us working room. The snow-covered willow growth made it necessary to cut several carloads of trees and brush to build a mat and roadway before we could unload dozers to go to the 476 for rerailing work. Once the dozers got in place, rerailing was simple and the 476 was undamaged.

Shortly before the end of March 27 the first of the zinc was in Durango. It would be almost 4 weeks before the balance was out of Silverton.

March 29, still carrying our outfit cars and dozers, we returned to Silverton. Until we moved the last of the zinc, we ran all the trains with this equipment. Coming out this trip at M.P. 463.5, old Pinkerton station site, a 20 to 30 ton rock rolling down the hillside broke a rail. Engine 476 hit the break and derailed. This was at 9:45 p.m. A car flanger was trained behind the 476, and the broken rail was picked up by a flanger wing. This taken together with the heavy train behind the engine back of the flanger, the 478, made it impractical to use it in rerailing the 476.

The dozers were unloaded and work started, but it was almost noon the next day before the 476 was on the iron again and we could proceed. Both engines were almost out of water when we reached the Hermosa tank.

A successful roundtrip was made April 2. The next one, April 5, lasted 13 days before we reached Silverton. The spring type slides had run and while not as large as the winter ones, carried great quantities of wet snow. It was of a consistency that worked well, but there was a lot to move. The air was warm, birds were nesting and small rivulets ran off the rocks playing merry tunes. It was a pleasure to be working then.

Silverton was reached April 18, and in the afternoon of the 19th, the last of the zinc was in Durango. Shenandoah was happy (It should have been. The price of zinc had gone up another nickel). The PUC had showed who was boss and cost the Rio Grande $90,000. Thankfully, the Commission

never ordered us to do it again. The Rio Grande received some financial benefit from this, but it took the fun out of winter slide removal on the Silverton Branch.

Engine #268 on May 21, 1955 rattles around Sargent, Colorado, presumably on special assignment. Note flanger at right. On July 14, 1881, the D&RG reached the old stage coach stop at Sargent's ranch at the bottom of the west side of Marshall Pass. Sargent or Sargent's (spelled both ways) was a helper station for the 20-mile-long grind up and over the Pass. *John Krause/Dr. Richard Severance collection*

It snowed—heavily—on Cumbres Pass during the winter of 1918. It was no place for the timid or weak. ***Colorado RR Museum/R.W. Richardson***

Chapter 6

1957 Snow Troubles

The big snows that gave the narrow gauge trouble on Cumbres Pass seemed to occur in cycles of five or seven years. Five years after the Granddaddy Snowstorm of 1952, another one caused a blockade on the Hill. I was Assistant Superintendent of the Colorado Division, stationed at Denver at the time, and Cumbres Pass was part of my responsibility.

Superintendent Ed Waring sent me to Chama to take charge of operations. For several reasons, mostly man-made, this was one of the worst foul ups ever experienced on Cumbres. Many of the old timers had retired, and their expertise was lost; management, lulled to sleep by five seasons of light snowfall, had economized too much, and we got caught with our pants down.

The morning of January 25, 1957, the snow gauge at Cumbres measured seven feet of snow on the ground. The new snowfall started late that afternoon, and in the next 24 hours laid down an additional four feet. About 10:00 a.m. of the 26th a spreader train with engines 481 and 489 left Chama to keep the fall under control. It took this train six hours to buck through to Cumbres, and under these conditions, the outfit would have returned to Chama and operations let rest until the storm, increasing in intensity, blew itself out.

But while turning on the wye at Cumbres, the 481 was badly derailed. After frogs were set, the 489 could not make enough of a pull to rerail the 481.

The fury of the storm increased and in hopes of at least getting the crews and section men off of Cumbres, a spreader-flanger train with engines 487 and 490 was called at Chama for 7:30 p.m. This outfit, after much difficulty, made it to within one mile of Cumbres and could proceed no further. One of the crew members struggled into Cumbres and reported the situation and advised only a rotary could open the line.

At Chama, only one engine, the 495, was left available, and no train or engine crews. Crews, with engines 482 and 488 were dispatched out of Durango, and upon arrival Chama, were enroute with rotary OM by 1:30 p.m. for the Hill. This outfit made it to Coxo with no difficulty, but the OM derailed there, and it took all night to rerail it. The 495 ran out of water and had to be cut out of the rotary combination and killed. (Three engines, 482, 488 and 495, were on the rotary power lineup.) Engines 482 and 488 were kept alive by melting snow in the tanks, as also was the case with the OM.

START FOR CUMBRES

Monday, the 28th, engines 482 and 488 pushed the OM to the flanger outfit and all backed to Coxo where the two engines from the flanger were lined up behind the rotary outfit. Then the combination started for Cumbres, but just east of Wolf Creek bridge a large slide had run. (This was the same slide that stalled the spreader train in 1952.)

Water was too low to permit clearing this slide and a decision was reached to return to Chama. This would not be too difficult ordinarily, for when the rotary outfit left Chama, engine 488 was headed in a westerly direction to be used in just such a situation. But a huge drift had formed near the Coxo highway crossing and while putting all the equipment together, it became stuck and could not move.

During the night because of a lack of water, engine 488 and rotary OM were killed. The balance were kept alive by melting snow. However, the men were becoming exhausted and by afternoon of the 29th, only the 482 was still alive.

On the morning of the 29th, engines 480 and 497 with their crews arrived Chama from Durango with bulldozers to be taken as far as possible by train, then started clearing the way ahead. In the meantime, a team from the Mountain and Cold Weather Command, Fort Carson, was attempting to reach the stranded equipment to evacuate the men. An Army helicopter took out four men who were seriously ill. After two flights into the hole at Coxo, this form of evacuation had to be abandoned because of danger involved under the conditions. In addition to the men at Coxo, there were 23 more at Cumbres using the section house and crummies for shelter and eating rationed meals.

LARGER OUTFIT

At 12:30 p.m. the following day, the 30th, a larger than usual rotary outfit left Alamosa. Engines 494, 492, and 499 powered this train. Engine 484 ran light to Antonito, turned and backed up following the rotary in case it would be needed to pull the rotary train backwards. A plentiful supply of coal, two bulldozers and a refrigerator car with a two-week supply of groceries were in the train in addition to the usual line up of outfit cars. The Army snowcats reached the stranded train and spent the night there and took out part of the men the next morning (the 31st). The balance were taken out February 1st.

The rotary OY found hard going and had to tie up for the night at Big Horn. It reached Phantom Curve about dark the 31st and backed to Sublette for the night.

On the 31st, engine 482 was finally killed at Coxo and the first contingent of men was taken to Chama on cargo sleds behind an Army "SEEP" (Seagoing Jeep). The bulldozers from Chama had to be unloaded east of the high trestle near Lobato from which point they began dozing snow eastward. The storm stopped, and there was not a cloud in the beautiful

#492, ex-1021, now part of the Cumbres & Toltec Scenic Railroad, marches a freight train on the Cumbres Pass line in winter. Note the high snow fences to the right, most of which have been allowed to deteriorate over the years. ***John Krause/Dr. Richard Severance collection***

Snow was taken very seriously on the Rio Grande narrow gauge. Here snow fences and a snowshed at Marshall Pass attest to that fact. *Colorado RR Museum/R.W. Richardson*

Colorado blue sky. It was calm but extremely cold, with subzero temperatures, especially at Coxo.

February 1st, the last of the men from Coxo were taken to Chama. The dozer train, engines 480 and 497, following the dozers reached Cresco. Rotary OY did not quite reach the tank at Los Pinos and was pulled back to Osier for the night. It reached Cumbres February 2nd and engine 481 was rerailed (and the 23 men at Cumbres made up for missed meals in the cook car of the rotary train).

February 3rd the bulldozers from Chama reached Coxo and rotary OY reached the slide below Windy Point. It was deep and frozen and the OY almost stuck in it. After much difficulty the outfit backed up to Cumbres and bulldozers were moved to the slide.

February 4th the rotary OY outfit and the bulldozer train from Chama were together at Coxo. After much maneuvering, thawing of frozen cylinders on dead engines, relaying across the high trestle at Lobato and sundry other minor delays the OY, alive, the OM dead and various engines dead or alive reached Chama.

CUMBRES OPENED

Rotary OY was conditioned, re-supplied and started back east and reached Alamosa February 6th as the sun came up over the Sangre de Cristo range. Cumbres was again open and backed up freight started to move.

Hubert Meek, Roadmaster, and a Mechnical Foreman named Winkel, were with the crews stranded at Cumbres. Pueblo Roadmaster, Johnny Ball, and Durango Roundhouse Foreman, Newt Spearman, were with me during the operation on the west side of Cumbres. Soon after I reached Chama from Denver, I talked to Hubert Meek on the telephone and was advised the only serious trouble he was having (other than snow, short rations and a derailment) was Winkel, who had either panicked or wanted to play hero, stirring up a storm trying to incite the stranded men as to the dangers they were facing and making an effort to enlist them to break a trail through the snow to Chama. I told Hubert to get Winkel somewhere off alone and tell him the facts of life. Then, if he still persisted in inciting the men and causing dissension, to take a brake club and beat his brains out.

When it became apparent we had a real mess building up on Cumbres, Superintendent Waring told me to get my winter clothing on and get going to Chama since it looked like any operations would be focused there. In the meantime, while I was traveling, he would ask assistance from the Mountain and Cold Weather Command and follow up activating a rotary operation out of Alamosa. Johnny Ball, Pueblo Roadmaster, was told to get to Alamosa to meet me. Both of us had hellish trips driving; between Pueblo and the top of La Veta Pass, the highway was a sheet of ice with a sleet storm still on.

We made connections at Alamosa and were informed that a team from the Command would soon leave Fort Carson with two SEEP's, small Jeep landing crafts that the Command had used successfully recently on a mission across the Greenland ice cap (they were to prove that the San Juan Mountains had a type of snow they were not built for).

DROVE TO CHAMA

I drove to Chama via Espanola as Wolf Creek Pass was closed. It was a long, lonesome trip, for I had left Johnny Ball in Alamosa to meet the SEEPs and guide them to Chama from Alamosa. Arriving Chama, I checked what was being lined up and found it satisfactory, talked to Hubert Meek and collected all the information available. Then I made hotel reservations for Ball and the Army men when they arrived and went to bed, leaving instructions that I be called when the SEEPs arrived.

They arrived late the 28th and were unloaded, fueled and made ready to start out at first light next morning. We traveled the snow-covered highway from Chama to the first crossing of Wolf Creek and intended to strike the rail line above that, but soon found the snow drifted and cornices of such magnitude we had to use a route up Wolf Creek valley to again strike a general rail route at Cresco. On this first day we came early to our first near-mishap.

We were moving in a whiteout, and it was necessary for me and one of the snow troopers to scout ahead on snowshoes to guide the SEEPs. We were maybe 50 yards ahead of the machines when we discovered we were walking over a smooth drift that ended at a cornice that topped a sheer drop of nearly 50 feet. The machines were stopped in time and we detoured around the danger. By this time we had learned that Artic snow, that is of a sugarlike granulation and packs hard, is different from our snow that is flakelike and does not pack the same way. The SEEPs were noseheavy and kept digging in at the front.

While it was uncomfortable for the driver, we were able to offset this tendency by moving in reverse. Speed was not decreased much, for the SEEPs had a total of 21 gears in forward and reverse. It did mean, however, we were moving into our exhaust fumes so had to keep the protective canvas windows open, and it was cold. One of the Command, the youngest and least experience, got SEEP-sick, which is worse than carsick. He had to be left at Chama when we returned that night and was sick from the fumes for the rest of the tour.

And we did have to return to Chama the first night. One of the SEEPs, just before we reached Cresco, developed transmission trouble and became inoperative. We used a nylon climbing rope doubled to tow it back to Chama. There, Sargent Jones, the Army mechanic, said it would require a new transmission for repairs. So he checked out the remaining SEEP carefully and readied it for the next day's activity. And we all had a big supper and went to bed for sleep and rest. All except a snowtrooper from Finland named (or called) 'Fin'. At supper our waitress was a vivacious, boastful young New Mexican girl. Somewhere in the ribbing the troopers were giving her, some remark was made that led her to brag she was more woman than any of them were men—she could wear out a half dozen of them. They all looked at Fin, and

A Sargents-Marshall Pass turn leaves the snowshed on Marshall Pass to run a caboose hop to Sargents. ***Colorado RR Museum/R.W. Richardson***

These are the buildings near the snowshed at Marshall Pass. Open door, left center, is operator's privy. ***Colorado RR Museum/R.W. Richardson***

he nodded his head. I had no idea what was in the wind as they made up a sizable pot of money and negotiated an all night stand with the chiquita for Fin. Next morning a subdued, unboastful, waitress served our breakfast. Fin, none the worse for wear, ate a double steak and egg breakfast and was ready to go when we moved out.

THE TOUGHEST

I have been associated with many men under a great number of conditions, but I never any time enjoyed a group more than I did these troopers of the Mountain and Cold Weather Command. They were the toughest, most competent men I ever saw, raunchy but well-behaved and clean. In some way, as part of a team, each was a specialist and snow and cold to them meant nothing.

One I especially liked was Sargent Jones, a middle-aged black too old for actual snow work, but traveled with the team as their expert mechanic, and he was more than just an expert. We had a D-8 Caterpiller setting at Chama waiting to load on a flatcar to move to our shops because our on-line mechanic could not get it to run. While we were up the mountain the first day Sargent Jones got it started, made some adjustments so it ran and sounded like a Rolls-Royce.

I looked him up to thank him and offered to pay him but he said, "Naw, sir. The Army pays me. But I ain't got much money with me, and I surely would like a drink or two and something to warm my bed tonight. Just as a little gift between friends understand, not pay."

I bought him a quart of gin and gifted him with a $20 bill. All of those boys respected their duties; Sargent was on hand to check us out when we left at daybreak. (When we returned to Chama with our first load of men from Coxo, Jones wanted to know if there was something else he could do for me as a gift for a gift.)

Late January 30th we reached the stranded train at Coxo and had to spend the night there. Next morning we took the first sled load of strandees to Chama. To allow more men to be moved, the troopers ski-jored behind the sled. I tried it a couple of miles but, while exhilerating, my old knees simply would not take it. We returned to Coxo early the morning of February 1st and transported the remaining men to Chama.

Going into Coxo from the end of our beaten trail at Cresco January 30th, we ran into terrain and snow conditions that were enough to make strong men cry. It was impossible to follow the rail line, and we had to take to the timber on and along the route of the highway. Snow depth was about 15 feet and drifted into patterns with steeply angled slopes so that for hundreds of yards at several locations we had to dig out trenches on the uphill side of drifts to level up the SEEP enough to keep it from sliding sideways. And all our movements with the machine had to be made in reverse. Fortunately, coming out over a packed trail we could operate normally.

The evening of the last trip out I arranged a big steak-and-drinks-supper for the troopers, and we had a fine old time. (The Army never did bill us for the Command's service and all it cost us was that I paid all the board, room and refreshments charges. I often wondered what the troopers did with their travel vouchers.)

There was still a lot of widening and cleaning of cuts to be done and Johnny Ball was riding the rotary to Alamosa. I stayed at Chama until the rotary arrived Alamosa, then took off for the long, lonely drive to Denver. It was February 6th, 1957, my 42nd birthday, and I wished several times on the drive I was young, footloose and with the Command boys getting ready to go to their next assignment, Alaska, to establish a training base for use of dogsleds, rock and ice climbing and survival.

For several years, each Christmas I received cards and notes from members of the team that worked on Cumbres. Sargent Jones, especially, kept in touch and never failed to again thank me for the pleasures he enjoyed at Chama. But, eventually as is usual, we all lost touch, and, for me, only memories of a time spent with an outstanding group of men are left.

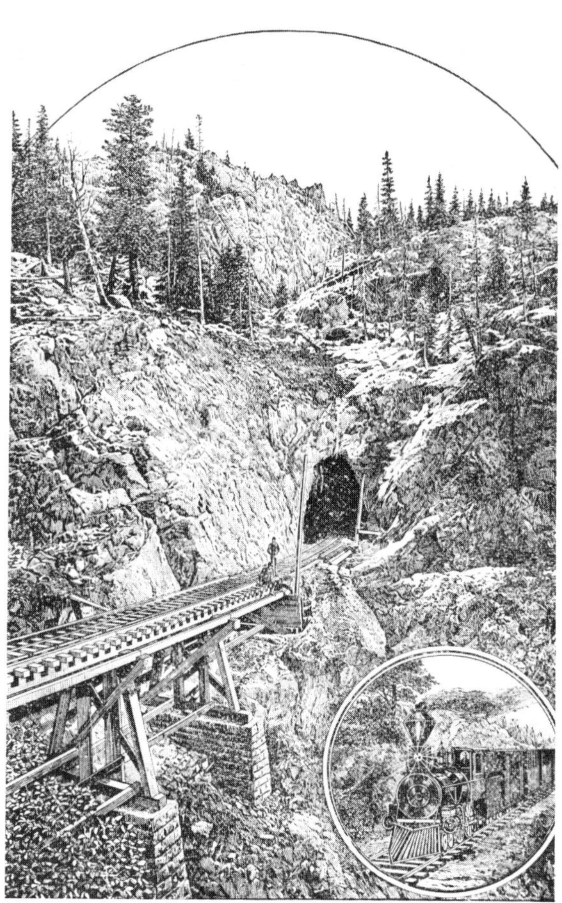

Old woodcut of west end of Toltec Tunnel in 1883. Trestle was later replaced by solid masonry wall. Tunnel was dug with black powder, not dynamite. ***Museum of New Mexico***

5

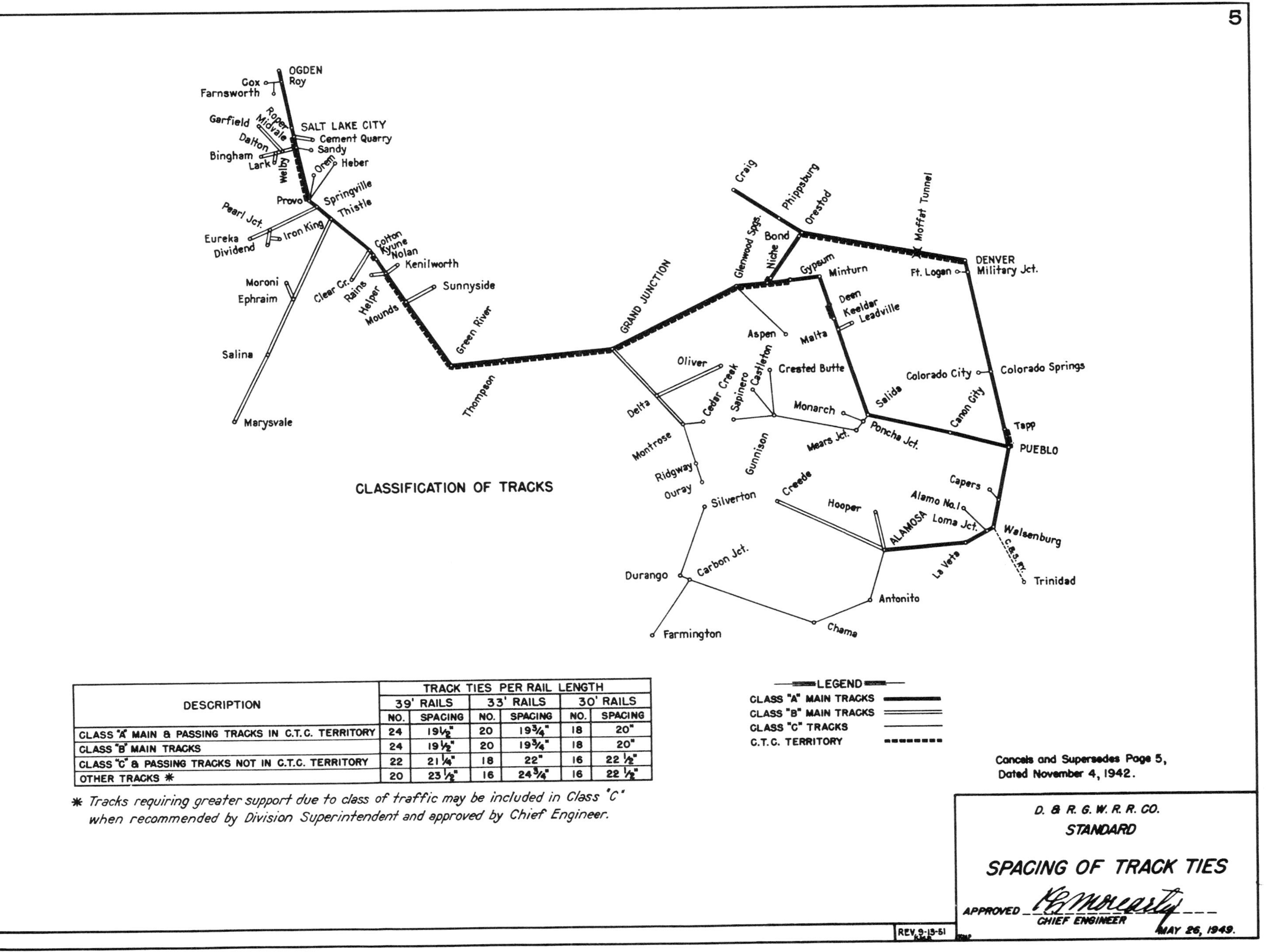

DESCRIPTION	TRACK TIES PER RAIL LENGTH					
	39' RAILS		33' RAILS		30' RAILS	
	NO.	SPACING	NO.	SPACING	NO.	SPACING
CLASS "A" MAIN & PASSING TRACKS IN C.T.C. TERRITORY	24	19½"	20	19¾"	18	20"
CLASS "B" MAIN TRACKS	24	19½"	20	19¾"	18	20"
CLASS "C" & PASSING TRACKS NOT IN C.T.C. TERRITORY	22	21¼"	18	22"	16	22½"
OTHER TRACKS *	20	23½"	16	24¾"	16	22½"

* *Tracks requiring greater support due to class of traffic may be included in Class "C" when recommended by Division Superintendent and approved by Chief Engineer.*

Cancels and Supersedes Page 5, Dated November 4, 1942.

D. & R. G. W. R. R. CO.
STANDARD

SPACING OF TRACK TIES

APPROVED K. J. Moriarty
CHIEF ENGINEER
MAY 26, 1949.

REV. 9-13-51

Chapter 7

Cumbres Pass Joint Railroad-Highway Survey

1964

When the snow accumulated on Cumbres Pass in 1964 to a depth it was not economically feasible to continue operating freight service for the small amount of business in sight, we petitioned the Colorado Public Utilities Commission for permission to close down for the winter. We were told we must first make a reconnaissance trip and submit a report to justify our petition.

We were also advised that the State Highway Department was considering such a survey to gather information to use in a study being made to determine if an all-weather road over Cumbres was justified, and the probability of being able to keep the pass open during winter months.

A few telephone conversations resulted in setting up a joint survey. The highway department would furnish a 4-man Sno-Kat, a highway engineer and a driver. We were to furnish transportation to the foot of La Manga Pass west of Antonito, supplies (including food and sleeping bags) and two railroad employees. You can better believe I was not going to let an opportunity like this go by, so I selected myself as one of the railroad employees (I was then the Operations Coordinator). R.E. (Bob) Davis was the second man for the Rio Grande.

Our party gathered at Alamosa, double-checked the Sno-Kat and other equipment, plus food supplies. The following morning early (before dawn), we headed for La Manga Pass. We began to run into snow on the road in Conejos Canyon, but our 4-wheel drives got us to the unloading point as the sun came up. The sky was an eye-shattering blue—it was too

Locomotive #484 was assisted into Cumbres from Chama and now is going around the wye to run light back to Chama. ***Colorado RR Museum/R.W. Richardson***

cold to be otherwise, the temperature being well below zero.

CROWDED KAT

The Sno-Kat started easily and was soon warm enough to be run down the unloading ramp. So, we had one last cup of coffee from our Thermos bottle, answered a last call of nature and climbed in the Kat. It was rated as a 4-man vehicle, but the designer had not considered the people in it would be taking winter equipment along; we were crowded. The heater was superb. In fact, too good. After only a short time it had to be shut off and some windows opened.

The Kat's tracks just kept rolling along up the La Manga grade leaving the Conejos valley. The snow was deep but not too badly drifted due to a good stand of timber along the route of the highway we were following. That is, until we reached the elevation where a summertime highway camp is located. For several miles beyond this, the roadway was not as well protected, and drifted snow between the hillside and the dropoff into La Manga Creek was on a slope. The angle was not too great for the Kat's hydraulic system for levelling the tracks to operate, but we had to move slowly and carefully.

The first six miles from starting to the top of La Manga Pass took almost two hours, but the next lap to the Los Pinos water tank required just a bit more than an hour. There was a great deal of snow, drifted and sculpted into fantastic shapes. The views and scenery under the blue, blue sky were poignantly beautiful.

At the water tank we paused long enough to eat a candy bar and shed a little of our heavy outer clothing, for by now the temperature was about 10 above zero. Climbing back into the Kat, we headed off down the railroad grade eastward. I knew, and Bob knew, there was a railroad somewhere down there under the snow. The highway men would never have guessed it. And that Sno-Kat could not have cared less. It carried us to the bridge over Los Pinos Creek and we knew it was there for the wind had swept all the snow from it. Progress was good until we reached the phone booth where the line curves to start into Los Pinos Canyon. There was no booth to be seen under the deep snow, but we could approximate its location in relation to the curve.

From here, until we turned back from where the engine 491 had been buried under the snow in 1952, the sloping angles of the drifts required constant manipulation of the Kat's tilt adjustment mechanism. Returning, we had our going-in tracks to follow and soon were back on the wind-swept Los Pinos bridge. Here, we just lazed awhile in the sun and ate a lunch of hard rations.

CAN GO ANYWHERE

Turning toward Cumbres from Los Pinos, we soon began to find sidehill slopes that made us begin to wondering if we should leave the line of the railroad and drop down into the valley of Cumbres Creek. The driver just manipulated levers and changed gears while he pooh-poohed the rest of the crew as being old women, scary ones at that. Like most drivers of tracked machinery, including Sno-Kats, he was crazy. "Didn't we know that tracks are proportioned to weight so that a caterpiller tread can go anywhere a man can?"

I had been told the same thing numerous times when I was remonstrating with one of our Catskinners telling him to be more careful. Theoretically, maybe, they were right, but their actions while working on snowslides were scary. A few times in the Animas Canyon in 1952, while we were clearing slides, I just could not take it. When that point was reached, I went back to the crummy for a cup of coffee and told someone

May 6, 1965 in the yard at Cumbres. No spring yet.
Museum of New Mexico

to call me when it was time to dig the crazy driver out from under the turned-over Cat. To prove to myself I was not a scaredy-cat, I rode with them a few times. But I never got over being scared and squeamish when the dozer blade was lifted to drop its load of snow over the dump, and I could see the blade and a couple of feet of caterpiller treads with nothing but empty space below them.

The slope at the curve and hill where we had the last big derailment on the narrow gauge was a smooth contour with almost a 45 degree angle from the top to where it touched the valley about 200 feet lower down. The tilt controls were set for maximum tilt, and we went onto the slope at slow speed. At about the halfway point across the slope, the driver turned his head and says, "See, I told you."

Then, that rig started slewing downslope. Later, after I quit being scared (when we were off that slope) I took a heinous pleasure from the startled, scared look that came on that driver's face—yeah, he was as scared as his passengers. But, he kept his cool, went to his lowest, slowest gear and jockeyed the nose on an angle upgrade. The Kat quit sliding and slowly, slowly, ground itself off the slope.

Off this slope was a stretch of level snow. The driver just barely pulled on it, cut the motor and we all piled out. Each of us pointing our bodies to break any breeze blowing, fumbled with our flies until we got them open and did what came naturally. Personally, there was an instant when that Kat started sliding and I saw the look on the driver's face, I almost lost momentary control of my bladder.

TANGLEFOOT CURVE

We rolled along, finding nothing as bad as that one slope, until we reached Tanglefoot Curve (Cumbres Loop). The upper leg of the Loop was buried under snow that had been drifted up through Sheepherders' Gap. The cornice at the edge of this drifting was 40-50 feet in vertical depth. The spruce tree grove that has survived on the eastern edge of this constant draft through the gap was flocked with snow and icicles on each tall tree. The sun striking them, the gentle breeze barely moving them, together produced tens of thousands of ever-changing prismatic flashes. The Kat was stopped, and we unloaded to spend long minutes, simply awestruck. Not a word was spoken; each of us worshiped in our own way, silently.

Construction train on Marshall Pass. Note water tank under construction just in front of headlight on down grade. *William H. Jackson photo/Museum of New Mexico*

Arriving at Cumbres, one of the party walked over the snow covering the sectionhouse and removed the board from the chimney, placed there to keep it from filling with snow. Luckily, the direction of the wind had kept snow from drifting over the front of the building. With some difficulty we got the door open and walked into an unoccupied, very cold shelter. While the others were unloading our paraphernalia, I got a fire going in the cast iron, flat-topped caboose stove and the room began to warm up.

With melted snow, a pot of coffee was soon perfuming the air. Then, while four 16-ounce T-bone steaks sizzled in the skillet and a pot of chili beans bubbled, we broke out the jug and mixed measures of its contents with snowwater and used pieces of icicles for ice cubes. Our highball glasses were enameled mugs, our dinner plates were beat up pie pans and the silverware a miscellany of knives and forks. Nonetheless, we did full justice to the repast, sopped up the bean and meat juices with chunks of Italian bread, and sweetened our coffee with small amounts of Kentucky's best product. Canned Melba peaches was the dessert, then we lay back against our sleeping bags and enjoyed good cigars. That is, three of us did. We made the driver wash the dishes as the penalty for scaring the hell out of us on the one hillside.

Pads belonging to the absentee owners were appropriated to go under our sleeping bags in the one warmed room. Sleep came easily, and I slept well. A couple of times I was disturbed by having boots thrown at me to stop my snoring. It was still dark when we awakened and by kerosene lamps ate a hearty breakfast of ham, eggs, leftover chili beans and stove top toasted bread, washed down with cafe diablo. The driver warmed up the Kat while we waited for daylight.

HEADED FOR WINDY PT.

Just as the sun came up, he made a test run up the hill and on his return, we loaded our gear and headed for Windy Point. On the snow burying the track at this large outcropping of rock, we found the tracks a snowshoe rabbit had made moving from a wind-cleared bunch of wild roses back to the protection of the rocks of Windy Point. These tracks were the only sign of any wildlife found on our trip.

We did not deem it necessary to go beyond Windy Point, but we did make detailed observations with binoculars and took some telephoto shots. Turning homeward we followed our ready-made tracks, leaving them at Los Pinos to go directly to La Manga Pass instead of back down the Los Pinos drainage. We did not even have any difficulty on the slope that had given us such a scare the previous day.

The highway engineer did have us detour at a few points to look at some locations he thought new alignment of the existing highway would be needed. Some of these detours were through growths of trees where the snow was not wind packed, and in these groves the Sno-Kat had a difficult time.

In midafternoon we were back at the four-wheelers and loaded up to return to civilization. There was some delay getting started because the batteries of the trucks were cold, as was the lubricating oil. We had to again unload the Kat and run it up to each truck to be used to jumper the trucks' batteries to get enough power to start them.

Back at Alamosa we went to the Grand Cafe for another steak. It was not nearly as tasty or tender as the one eaten at Cumbres. And the highballs we had at the Walsh Hotel bar were weaker than the melted snow water we used for mixer the night before.

The last train to Cumbres — December 6, 1967 — is headed by #493. The train of lumber is at the west switch of Coxo. ***Museum of New Mexico***

Our report got the desired permission to shut down for the winter, and not many years later there was a paved highway over La Manga and Cumbres passes kept open most of the year.

This is what happens on a four percent grade when a trainman fails to set the retainers. The runaway is on Barranca Hill, Chili Line. In the mishap, the engineer died and a number of passengers also died or were injured. ***Author's collection***

Chapter 8

No. 16 Is In The Gorge

I was Chief Dispatcher in 1948 when the eastward *San Juan* narrow gauge passenger train was struck by a snowslide that carried two of the cars into Toltec Gorge.

On February 11, 1948, I had been home from the office for only a short time when the phone rang. The callboy was on the line and told me the dispatcher was busy but they wanted me back at the office muy pronto. He continued, "No. 16 (216) is in serious trouble on Cumbres. Part of the train is in the gorge and some people are hurt."

Before I let him off the phone, I instructed him to get a train and engine crew on a short call while I was on the way to the office. Also, before leaving home I phoned the Yardmaster to put a train together of two coaches and the toolcar and a caboose for a train crew. Next, I told the roundhouse to get an engine ready on short call for this train. The last thing I did was to call our company doctor, Dr. Sidney Anderson, told him as much as I knew, and requested him to get to the depot to accompany the relief train with supplies he anticipated might be needed.

Activities were well under way by the time I arrived at headquarters. The cars were being pulled from the Coach Yard and the engine was about ready on short call for the hostler to bring it to the depot. The crew members were beginning to show up and the dispatcher had got an order to a crew member of the *San Juan* who had come on the phone to report the wreck annulling No. 216's schedule to Alamosa. Of course, the annulling order had not been handled strictly according to the rule book, but in an emergency what has to be done is done. He was putting out a work order to the hospital train when I walked into his office.

I returned to my own office, raised the section foreman at Antonito and Big Horn (we still had a gang there then) and instructed them to meet the relief train and go to the wreck with it. It was not necessary to remind them to pack a lunch and dress warmly; those men had been through the mill before. Both the Trainmaster and Road Foreman of Equipment were on the Durango end, but A.P. (Primus) Pearson, Alamosa General Car Foreman, was in town and went with the train. Someone with savvy and initiative, I later learned, had appropriated coffee and pots along with some emergency rations from the rotary outfit cook car and put them on the relief train.

READY TO GO

Within an hour after the first information was received, the train was ready to depart. Dr. Anderson showed up only minutes later and relief was on its way.

There was little left for me to attend to. I called the Chief Transportation Officer in Denver and gave him as much dope as I had, asking him to try to put a brick on any news to the media until we had more definitive information. I was just wasting my breath. The press is always looking for news, especially if it smacks of catastrophe.

I have always suspicioned that the media bribed the telephone operators to tip them off to any unusual news. I believed then, and always, this was as true of public operators as it was of our own. Anyway, in this case, I received a call from the *Denver Post* news room in Denver asking for details even before the relief train whistled off. I told them "no comment" and hung up. Next, a reporter from the *Alamosa Courier* barged into the office and started demanding (!!!) information. I gave him the "no comment" bit also upon which he became very insistent. So I blew up, got out of my chair and told him quietly (?), "Get out of here and don't come throwing your weight around with me."

A few more encounters with the media in which I followed the same tactics and I learned better. A "no comment" response, followed by throwing them out, is tantamount to getting a scorching, inaccurate, report of an incident. It is the same as putting fire to a short-fused bomb, then sitting down on top of it. In this case, nearly every morning edition in the state carried stories about the terrible wreck of a Rio Grande passenger train on Cumbres Pass, alleged injuries, possibly deaths, etcetera, etcetera, etcetera. What little information they had was misconstrued, then embellished ad infinitum.

A couple more experiences, and I became versed in the art of appearing cooperative and open with the press. Adept at feeding the press a line consisting of a few incontrovertible facts, just a little reasonableness and a lot of ambiguity and evasiveness. The point being that no reporter was going to admit you had him(her) so confused he did not know what you were talking about, so the story was buried off the front page and had it set in small typecase without a headline. (Years later, I found the same principle worked when testifying in court cases or in hearings before various public utilities bodies. In these, however, you had to keep an eye on the judge or hearing commissioner, and if he showed any indication of also being confused, you better back away and start over.)

LIFE PHOTO

Life Magazine rushed a photographer-reporter to Alamosa. He chartered a plane and took some aerial photos. By the time they were to be published, we had been able to report there were no deaths and only two minor injuries. The photo used was a masterpiece, and was a full two-page spread. But, then *Life* always did treat us well. We were photogenic and an anachronism that had reader appeal.

Until the relief train had returned to Alamosa, all I had to do was answer telephones and start lining up a train and equipment desired by Pearson to return to the scene the following day to pick up the pieces. The description of what happened, and persons involved, is put together from members of the crew of the passenger train, and one or two passengers I talked to.

Before starting their story, I am going to make a statement that will brand me as a traitor to the class of on-line railroad officials and supervisors. Of course, the second class, the corpulent, sedentary chair-polishing headquarter-assigned-bunch will approve what I say, and hopefully if we meet, buy me a few complimentary drinks. I operated on both sides in both classes a lot of years so what I'm going to say is gospel.

If you are a railroad officer, the softest, easiest, least stressful place to be during an emergency situation is at the scene. I would rather spend 48-72 hours at the scene, without taking my shoes off, cold, sleepless and hungry, than one shift at headquarters compiling and dispensing information, rescheduling around the blockade and other related duties. Being cold, sleepless and hungry is maybe stretching it a little. I've been on numerous jobs where this was true but, factually, if you were with a derrick outfit, at a washout, earth slip, or in a snow-bucking outfit, if you did not eat fairly well and often, or caught a few cat naps on the caboose cushions, it was because you were playing hero, hoping your superiors would get word of what a jewel they had out on the site.

That, to be truthful, was the name of the game. Your superiors, who had achieved warm offices and slept at home, wanted no part of the on-line work, while admitting some officer had to be out there. So what the hero in the field was expected to do was to stand around where he could be seen constantly, looking important and in charge. There were competent, trained people (usually on overtime whose checks would be bigger than the officer's) to do the work and get blisters on their hands. At my first emergency show, I was with the section gang with a shovel in my hand when my superior, K.L. Moriarty, came along. He motioned me away from the job and says, "Get rid of that shovel and act like a boss. You aren't paid to shovel dirt. You are here to let the hunkies know they have a 'brain' in charge." Good advice; I never was guilty again of actually working.

Ed Morgan was conductor, Sid Skirvin the trainman and "Sunny" the parlor car chief-attendant (I can't recall his last name. He was relieving the regular attendant, but he was to prove to be one of the heroes of the catastrophe). Snow was falling on Cumbres and some wind blowing, and the varnish was doubleheaded out of Chama. The lead engine was the regular sport model equipped with a bullnose (pilot) plow. Dan (Dang Shoe It) Holly was the engineman. The second engine was manned by a freight service engine crew. The consist from the engines was: mail car; baggage car; two coaches and the parlor car.

BEST ACCOUNT

The best account I received was given by the fireman who shoveled coal for Dan Holly. He was the only one in a position to see the drama unfold in its entirety. It is written as a quote to the best of my ability to recall his story:

"It was real cold as we left Chama, with just a little wind and snow. Taking the snow reported at the top into consideration, we topped off the tank at Cresco, but had very little difficulty knocking some small drifts out, until we hit MP 331 on Windy Point. There was a drift there complicated by a small slide. Dan widened on her and the helper did the same. We broke through with a little steam left, and pulled to a stop at Cumbres station. A warm chinook was blowing and the old snow under the new was settling, cracking and popping like a string of firecrackers. Icicles were breaking from the eaves.

"The car toad lifted the blue flag and Dan whistled off. The chinook did not last. Within five miles of Cumbres it was cold again, the snow had almost stopped, but it was drifting. At about 330 we had hit a heavy drift where the wind from the west side of Cumbres always blows through Sheepherder's Gap and leaves a drift at the top bend of Tanglefoot Curve. With a downhill advantage there was no sweat getting through, but both engines came out of carrying a lot of snow.

"At 327 there was the usual drift on the inside of the curve under the hill. (Note: the last big pileup on the narrow gauge in which two engines and some cars of a freight train were laid on their sides occurred here.) We blared right through it, adding some more snow to the load we were already carrying. Then since we had again topped off our water at Cumbres, we rolled right by the Los Pinos tank, hit a medium drift at 322 and a bigger one at MP 321. (Note: this would be the location where, in 1952, engine 491, engineman Joe Dalla and fireman Johnny Lira were buried for four days.)

"The drift at 321 hardly slowed us down, and soon we were on the shelf and rolled down to the tunnel without hitting anything. The snow had quit and the sky was almost clear. We rolled right along, just drifting and broke out our jugs of java.

ENJOYING BREW

"I was enjoying the brew at Phantom Curve and admiring the view of the hillside and canyon wall as we passed the Phantom. My eyes wandered to the skyline and with a shock I saw a big crack starting in the snow near the top.

"Doing what came naturally, I slammed my cab window shut and screamed at Dan, 'Slide—widen on 'er!!!'

"He did, and that 470 took off like a turpentined cat as I moved to the driver's side of the cab, shoved the curtain aside and looked back along our train.

"The tank of our engine was just being hit by the first of the slide, and we were still moving. The second engine came through and the mail car. Looked like the baggage would not make it as snow began to run under and over it. I thought it was a goner, but it finally cleared.

"Now it was the front end of the head coach being assaulted. The slide handled it like a mad bull with its head down and goring. The coach starts raising and its knuckle climbed out of the baggage car's rear coupler. The cars separated with the train line and steam hose broken. Brakes went to emergency and the steam from the steam line made a fog as it hit the cold air. I told Dan to shut it off and he did.

"The pressure of the slide shoved the front end of the coach around, and riding the breast of the slide, it started downhill toward the canyon's bottom. The second coach begins to turn as the coupling is broken, and it performs the same moves as the first car and starts tobogganing down hill. Then the parlor car turns and begins to follow the first two. The weight of snow in the slide is pushing them from above and raising their rear ends a little so that in front the cars are pushing piles of snow ahead of them that the trucks are digging out.

"The parlor car is the first to stop. It hits a protruding rock and is anchored there with its rear platform just off the grade. The front end caves in some when the rock is struck.

"Below, the two coaches are still sliding side by side, but the slide has quit running as they begin striking trees in a grove of pines, spruce and aspens. By this time both cars have turned on their sides. Behind them is a plowed trench.

"I don't know how much time passed until the cars stopped while I was there in the gangway holding onto the handrail and staring. Maybe only seconds that I watched. Suppose after movement stopped on the front end of the train the engineer at least of the second engine saw some of it, maybe his fireman, but I know the baggage and mailman did not.

"Anyway, I just hung there, paralyzed and wondering sickly how many were dead. I never want to go through a thing like that again."

The balance of the story is put together from the accounts of others on the train.

MAKE REPORT

Without taking time to check for details (he realized it was a major wreck), he had his fireman uncouple their engine and they ran about two miles to a phone booth to report to the detainer. The fireman went to the phone and gave the first report and the detainer asked him to copy an order annulling their schedule on to Alamosa so a relief train could run against them. The fireman told me later he was not about to write out an order, but he did listen to it, and then repeated it back from memory and assured the dispatcher they sure were not going anywhere. Back to the train they went to assist where needed.

While they were gone all able-bodied men on the grade, including the second engine crew, the baggage and mailman started down to the other cars. From the parlor car came the local traffic department representative, the conductor and two or three male passengers. The attendant, Sunny, had a lot of lacerations below the knees of both legs that were bleeding, but that did not deter him. Ed Morgan, conductor, had lost his cap and his face was bloody from a wound caused when his head struck something sharp that tore a 3-inch triangle of his scalp loose from the forehead back into the hair. The others on the parlor were shook up but with no wounds.

RETURN TO TRAIN

Returning to their train and seeing so many others climbing down to the cars and around them, Dan Holly and his fireman began gathering whistle cords and anything else resembling rope to make a line for those coming back up the slope.

Morgan was only a short ways down when a train whistled west of the slide. With the loose flap of scalp bouncing, he struggled back up to the track and started running toward the cut and curve back of his train. As he ran he cracked a red fusee (on the narrow gauge every crew member always carried one or more fusees somewhere in their clothing). He had just got well into the cut when a small slide ran at the west end. Possibly it was brought down when the approaching engine acknowledged the red fusee. (The whistle came from an engine that had helped a Chama-Cumbres Turn and was cut off at Cumbres to run light to Alamosa). Anyway, it stop-

The westbound four-car *Shavano* on the grade west of Poncha Junction. Note front numberplate and two side numberboards on locomotive. *Colorado RR Museum/R.W. Richardson*

ped before it hit the small slide. Morgan told them what had happened, so the engine crew tied down their engine and returned with Morgan. The cold air on Morgan's bare head had just about stopped the bleeding from his wound.

The press in followup stories said it was a fine example of the type of people who rode trains through the wilds of the mountains. Everyone remained calm and collected all during the episode. Oh, yeah!? Wasn't that way a'tall.

When the men from on top reached the two coaches, they found pandemonium, screams, hysterical laughter and moans from both. As the cars turned on their sides, those on the upper side were tumbled into those on the lower side, and the only way to get to the doors was to crawl over the arms of the seats laying on their sides. And some of the stronger had reached the doors to crowd around them so they could not be opened. Quiet and calm being restored, the doors were opened and the rescuers entered the cars.

In the lead coach, they found the emergency circulator heater had broken loose and careened halfway down the aisle to lodge between the seats. (This was against all the laws of gravity but had happened). Enough calm restored, it developed, aside from fright, shock and bruises, there were no injuries. Except to Sid Skirvin, the brakeman. He lay on one of the rear seats of the first coach unconscious, and at first glance dead, for he was pinned to the cushions of the seat by the trunk of a dead aspen that had speared through the coach's exterior to fasten him to the seat.

LITTLE HARM DONE

Closer examination showed the trunk had not punctured his body. His clothing torn loose from the wooden lance, it was discovered it had done nothing more than crack some ribs without breaking the skin. A liberal application of snow to Sid's head brought him back to consciousness.

The rescurers finally convinced everyone to stay calm, and a few at a time struggled over the upturned seats to the doors so that a few at a time could be taken to the top. The remaining people stayed put where it was halfway warm until their time came. And that was the way it was.

Up on top, Dan Holly and his fireman had cut in the steam from the second engine and plugged the line at the rear of the baggage car so that the baggage car and mail car were getting warm. They had also built a fire in the stove of the baggage car. As people reached the top, they were loaded into the warm cars. There was a short duration of resistance from the mail clerk when they started loading passengers in the mail car. He told Morgan that no one, *repeat no one*, except himself could enter the mail car. Ed very quickly straightened him out, among other things telling him to get out of the way or he would be neutered.

The injured trainman, Sid Skirvin, ambulatory but assisted by others, reached the top and was laid out in the baggage car. A little New Mexican darling (the kind to drive men crazy) while standing to get her turn to get on the warm car, was crying about how cold her feet were. Some guy, inconsiderate of her feelings, says, "You dumb #?!#, why don't you put your galoshes on?" She was standing there with a pair of furlined galoshes she had carried in her hand all the way up the hill.

Another group that came up later had a well-built redhead in it. She stood waiting for someone to help her into the baggage car, complaining about how cold she was. Draped over one arm was a fine fur coat her live-in boy friend in Chama had just bought her. She was reminded maybe she would not be so cold if she put it on.

Oh, well, it looked good in the papers to tell the world there were people in the Rocky Mountains who could go through a life-threatening situation and remain calm and collected.

The relief train arrived to take the passengers on to Alamosa, followed by the light engine. Dr. Anderson examined the brakeman, Skirvin, and decided he would be okay to Alamosa. Ed Morgan he decided needed some trimming up and stitching. Ed was calm and collected at the beginning of the Doctor's attention, but when Doc Anderson started to cut away a few pieces of torn scalp, the Irishman came alive and mean. He yells, "Doc, why in hell don't you ever sharpen your scissors? Them ain't fit to work on a sick dog with."

The track at the slide had not been damaged, and the westward *San Juan* ran on time the next morning. A wrecking outfit was put together and four or five days later the three cars were back to grade, re-trucked as necessary, and moved to the Alamosa shops for repairs. Until the regular attendant returned, "Sunny" continued serving T-bones and drinks on the parlor car, wearing some bandages applied by Doc Anderson, and basking in the stories the rails told the passengers about what a hero he was.

#268 and train on Sapinero Branch along Gunnison River. *John Krause/Dr. Richard Severance collection*

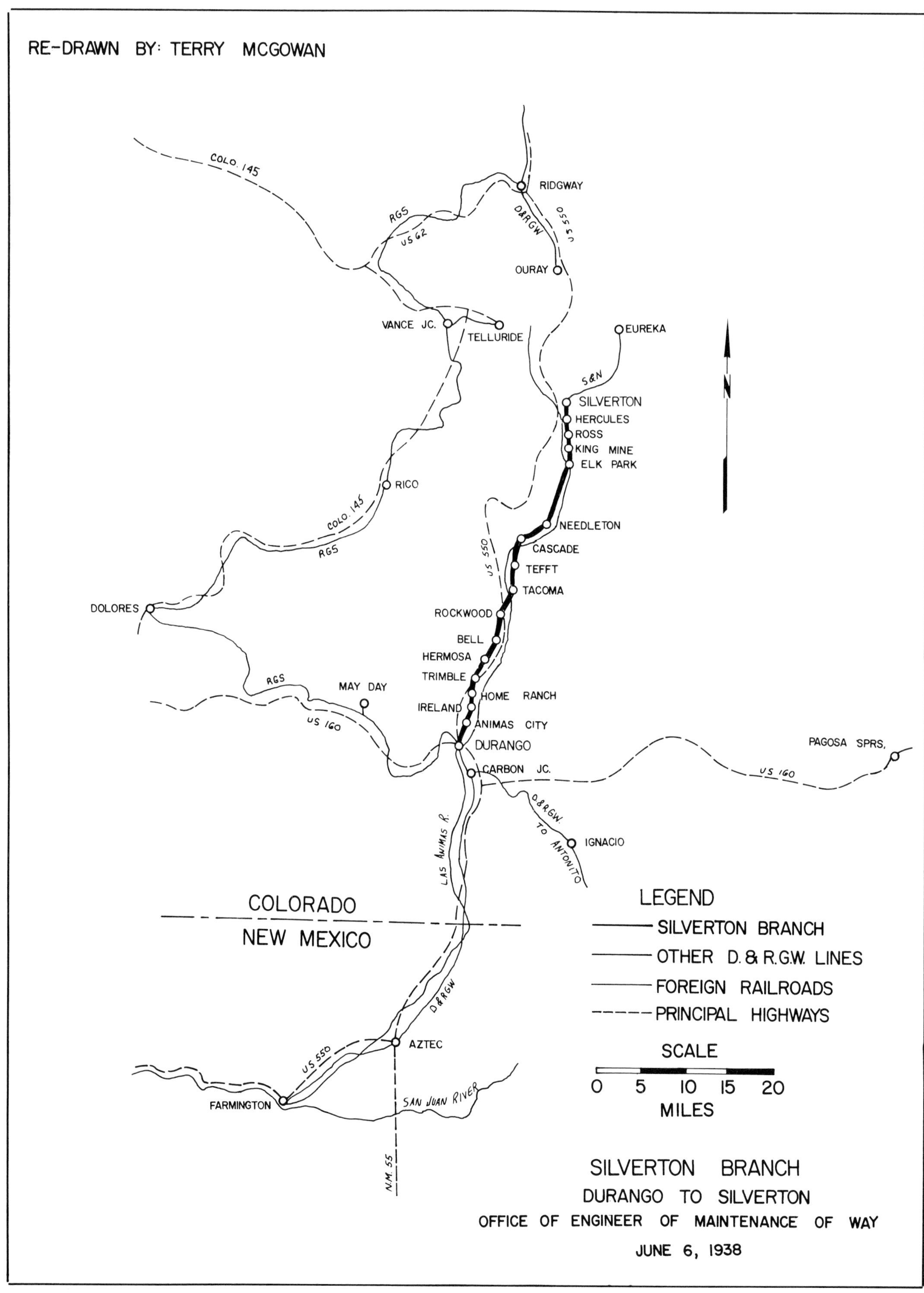
RE-DRAWN BY: TERRY MCGOWAN
COLO. 145
RIDGWAY
RGS
US 62
D&RGW
US 550
OURAY
VANCE JC.
TELLURIDE
EUREKA
S&N
N
SILVERTON
HERCULES
ROSS
KING MINE
ELK PARK
RICO
COLO. 145
RGS
NEEDLETON
CASCADE
US 550
TEFFT
TACOMA
DOLORES
ROCKWOOD
BELL
HERMOSA
TRIMBLE
RGS
MAY DAY
HOME RANCH
IRELAND
US 160
ANIMAS CITY
DURANGO
PAGOSA SPRS.
CARBON JC.
US 160
D&RGW.
TO ANTONITO
IGNACIO
LAS ANIMAS R.
COLORADO
NEW MEXICO
LEGEND
SILVERTON BRANCH
OTHER D.& R.G.W. LINES
FOREIGN RAILROADS
PRINCIPAL HIGHWAYS
D&RGW
SCALE
0 5 10 15 20
MILES
AZTEC
US 550
FARMINGTON
SAN JUAN RIVER
N.M. 55
SILVERTON BRANCH
DURANGO TO SILVERTON
OFFICE OF ENGINEER OF MAINTENANCE OF WAY
JUNE 6, 1938

The Animas River runs alongside the Durango-Silverton Branch line. This 1954 passenger train is northbound toward Silverton. ***John Krause/Dr. Richard Severance collection***

Chapter 9

Silverton Branch High Water

The Animas River is not the largest or longest river in the area the narrow gauge once served. But what it lacked in size, it made up for in meanness.

Except for a couple of miles out of Silverton, and about three miles through Cascade Park where Lime Creek dumps into the Animas, the river is tightly constricted between high walls. Numerous sidestreams besides Lime Creek are tributary to it, and from Hermosa upstream there are no locations where the river can spread and be relieved of overflows. When a heavy snowmelt, heavy rains or flash floods occur, the runoff must follow the canyon.

Over the years since the line was first opened for service, it has been severely damaged at times by these facts. Segments of roadbed have been completely wiped out, bridges damaged beyond repair, while rail and ties have been washed away.

Most of these catastrophes have struck without warning, Colorado high country weather being what it is. The latest such happened in September, 1970.

To fully understand how so much damage can be done in such a short period of time we have to look at characteristics of the river. Besides being constricted to such a narrow channel between precipitous canyon walls, the river has very few meanders. Factually, it is almost a straight gut, and it drops rapidly in grade, flowing between and over boulders that have fallen from the canyon walls.

OLD SAVAGE

From Silverton to Cascade, a distance of 19 miles, the fall is 1,500 feet. At old Savage, on the High Line just west of Rockwood, the river is approximately 300 feet below the rails in a gorge. This point is seven miles downstream from Cascade and has dropped an additional 800 feet for a total fall to this location of 2,300 feet. The tracks leave the Animas here to return to it at Hermosa, 35 miles from Silverton, and becomes a relatively slow flowing river on to Durango. However, in its course of 35 miles until it flattens out, the river had descended 2,700 feet.

There are no highways running through the canyon, so there has been no problem of automobile traffic. The residents are few and far between, almost entirely at resorts, so there has been no water-connected fatalities or destruction of private property. Destruction has been restricted to loss by the railroad.

In September, 1970, I was working at our Denver headquarters when word was received that the heaviest flashflood for decades had struck the Animas below Silverton. Fortunately, the two trains for the day had reached Durango shortly before the wall of water came rushing out of the canyon to flood the Hermosa flatlands. I was instructed to buy film and rations, load my packsack, and get to Durango to walk through the canyon as quickly as the flood quit running to evaluate damages.

I flew to Durango and arrived the afternoon following the flood and found the crest had passed and the river was falling fast. I made arrangements for the Roadmaster to take me to Rockwood at daybreak, from which point I would walk what we surmised would be a sorry looking sight with many segments of roadbed washed away. Our "surmise" understated what I found during the next two days on foot in the canyon. (I was always grateful to our president, "Gus" Aydelott, that he let me take on chores such as this alone. Traveling and working under hazardous conditions, at least for me, is best done alone without being hobbled by an inexperienced companion.)

The Roadmaster dropped me off at Rockwood as the sun was coming up over Lake Shalano. My pack carried a shelter half, a sleeping bag, a few cooking utensils, and enough rations for three days, plus a couple of cameras and a big supply of film. My stomach was full of a breakfast big enough to carry me for the day. Aspen leaves, just turning, reflected a sun that was shining in a clear blue sky and a small breeze promised that walking the canyon would be a pleasure.

Leaving Rockwood I took time to go out on a point to view the vista toward Durango and to see if the Mermaid of Lake Shalano was basking in the shallows. Must have been just a bit too chilly as she was not there.

The first evidence of the flood was at the high trestle over the river just beyond the High Line. Driftwood, logs and other debris had been deposited 20-25 feet above the normal water level. However, I could find no indication that the trestle had incurred any damage.

At Tacoma, water had come up the sides of the power plant buildings several feet but had receded rapidly enough to have caused only minor damage. About two-thirds of the siding was badly scoured but was in place and usable. The upper switchstand had a couple of driftlogs against it.

ROADBED GONE

A short distance beyond this switch there is a section of track built at the base of a sheer cliff. In the original construction, to obviate the necessity of heavy rock work, a crib was

Engine #476 smoke it up near Silverton on this September, 1954 da

John Krause/Dr. Richard Severance collection

Doubleheaded train with #478 and #476 in Animas Canyon. *John Krause/Dr. Richard Severance collection*

built the length of the cliff using green, native pine logs. This crib was then filled with boulders and small rocks and the roadbed of soil and gravel compacted over these. The roadbed was completely gone along here and scoured down to the original rock surface with the exception of a few remains of the old cribbing logs still in place. The rails hung suspended (a few points rested on large boulders in the river). Most of the ties had washed away from the rails although some did remain attached to the rails. The steel ribbons were bent in some bizarre shapes and twisted about each other.

Two other times over the years this segment of roadway had been destroyed by high water but never so completely. In portions of the section that were somewhat protected by the old crib, I found artifacts of earlier work and track building. Some rusted small spikes of the type used in the 1880's; remains of the first small, thin fishplates that were used before our present heavier tieplates; pieces of 45-pound rail and old hand-forged spikes that were used in building the original crib. Near the upstream end where an eddy had been formed by a large boulder I found a rotted section of a pine tree with a piece of 45-pound rail about 10 feet long. The tree had grown around the rail.

Proceeding onward I found either scoured or washed out sections of roadbed one after another. Culverts and short timber bridges that provided drainage at sidestreams or other runoff points were uniformly either filled by rock and debris carried by the flood or washed entirely away. There were numerous locations where the roadbed had been undermined and washed away leaving the rails suspended. Ties were missing at many locations where the track had been lifted in the air by the water and, when the ties were washed away taking away the buoyancy, dropped back to the roadbed. Where the force struck at a curve, rails were broken and grotesquely twisted.

And over and over I found piles of driftwood, trees and other flotsam jammed along the right-of-way. Every side drainage had brought down a burden of cobbles, boulders and gravel to deposit them in huge heaps over the rails. At Cascade Water tank the bridge had held, but the channel of the creek was so full of outwash the stream that supplies the tank had been filled and relocated so that no water was going into the tank. The new channel was tearing over the rails and cutting out the roadbed.

The bridge over the Animas at Cascade was not damaged, although it was piled up with a lot of flotsam. The roadway through the park incurred some scouring but was basically sound. Willows and small growth had been flattened extensively and a lot of drift left behind where the park had formed a relief valve for the racing water.

LIME CREEK

Above Lime Creek the damages continued to be frequent and severe. Between there and Needleton two sections were gone, lock, stock and barrel, rails, ties and roadbed. The hardware was buried somewhere downstream in new channels under rock and gravel. One location had about 1,500 feet gone; the other nearly a half mile.

At the point of rock just east of the east switch at Needleton (the same point where engine 473 hit a sunkink and went into the river in July, 1951) the railroad was missing without trace, as was part of the point. The river, after washing away the roadbed, undercut the cliff so that it fell into the flood leaving a sheer wall of rock. The water was still running in its new channel against the cliff too deep and too strong to be negotiated.

Rio Grande Southern RR layout at Ridgway, Colorado, from the depot looking toward the roundhouse around 1910. The RGS was controlled by the D&RGW. ***Museum of New Mexico***

LEFT. Mill concentrates from the North Star Sultan operation are being loaded at Silverton in 1934. Concentrates were loaded wet, and by the time they reached Alamosa, were often frozen and caused great expense and car damage during the transfer. *San Juan County Historical Society*

A compressor for the Aletha Tunnel on Sultan Mountain at Silverton was transferred from a standard gauge car at Alamosa to a narrow gauge car, No. 6000. Mine machinist Arthur Berkey gets ready to unveil the load and make an inspection. *San Juan County Historical Society*

I could not climb the cliff with my pack, but was able to do so unencumbered, then pulled up my pack with a 50-foot length of rope from my pack. The same rope was used to let my pack down terrace by terrace then utilized for roping down myself. By the time this making like a goat was finished, and I was in the pocket of flatland at Needleton, I was ready for camp and two or three ounces of Kentucky Dew mixed with Animas river water, although it was still a bit murky. It was so comforting, I had a second round.

A fire of aspen burned down to glowing coals while I pitched my shelter and smoothed a place for my sleeping bag. Then there was a thick T-bone steak broiling directly on the coals, a can of chili beans and a can of coffee heating at the edge of the coals. The evening down river breeze came up as I enjoyed my supper and topped it off with a half-bottle of good red wine and a pipe of tobacco. For me, Heaven was right there at Needleton.

Sipping the wine and inhaling the pipe's aroma, across the river about a dozen does and their fawns came to the edge of the river, drank, then browsed awhile on the riverside shurbbery before moseying off up the hill, and the evening was almost perfect. Perfection came when a coyote, maybe more, yodelled a Requiem for the dying day. (You never can tell from the sounds how many coyotes are involved or from the location. They are Nature's ventriloquists.)

THEN TO SLEEP

Then it was only a matter of dousing the fire and into the down for a night's sleep. The wind in the trees whispered lullabies that overrode the coyotes but did not keep me awake.

Southbound daily on Chili line delayed by washout and rocks near Embudo in 1932. *Museum of New Mexico*

Sometime during the night I had a nightmare of slipping and tumbling down the face of the cliff trying to rescue my pack which was tumbling into the river. The action was vivid but did not awaken me.

There is a chill near a river just before daybreak. It is an efficient alarm clock, and I crawled from the sack to start a fire to cook breakfast. A big one: an orange, bacon, eggs (three of them), hard rolls and lots of coffee. (Something learned from experience backpacking is how to carry eggs and breakable potables safely. Wrapped in the sleeping bag there is no worry about breakage. Fresh meat can be carried in the middle of the pack and, insulated from exterior heat, will keep for a couple of days.)

Across the river from my camp, about the middle of the Needleton siding, Needleton Creek had built a new delta at the junction with the Animas. The course of the river had been changed and had damaged, was damaging, the banks on the railroad side. This change of current was also what has contributed the most to washing away the rocky point at the east end of the side track.

At Needleton Water Tank, approximately two miles west of the siding, the usually peaceful rivulet that flows off the hillside to supply the tank by gravity had gone wild. Its channel had been swept clean while being widened and deepened. All of this outwash was deposited across and above the track in a pile some 100 feet wide and 25 feet high. It consisted of boulders and cobbles; all small stuff had washed away. The same type of situation existed at locations where two other sidestreams usually flowed through culverts into the main river. All embankments along here were undercut with long sections gone, leaving the rails hanging, although the ties had mostly stayed attached to the iron.

The type of destruction found in this two miles was in evidence to a greater or less degree all the way to the steel truss bridge over the Animas approaching Elk Park. The abutments and piers of the bridge had been scoured and undercut badly. In lieu of repairs, later this bridge was replaced with an open deck, girder type bridge.

The wooden bridge over the brawling stream at the east end of Elk Park was buried under a burden of outwash from the stream, and water was flowing over the top of this with the old channel, above and below the bridge, filled almost to the river. Banks of the main river paralleling the tracks through the park were badly damaged and undercut. The park itself was under more than a foot of muddy water and silt, the water slowly draining away or drying.

DECREASED DAMAGE

Continuing from Elk Park to about MP 43 from Durango where the Silverton Tank (no track) stood until it was demolished a number of years earlier by a snow slide, track and roadway damage, while still extensive in overall lineal dimensions, decreased in cubic yard displacement. The numerous sidestreams east of Elk Park had yet to contribute their waters, and the roadway was higher above normal river level and built more on solid rock. Culverts and small timber bridges still continued to be plugged or washed out.

From MP 43 on into Baker's Park (Silverton), track and river bank damages decreased more as Silverton was approached. Numerous locations would require work in the upper three miles, but most could be handled by using a bulldozer to shove new fill back up to grade from the river, surfacing and relining the track. The wooden trestle over the Animas, the last before reaching Silverton, was undamaged except for the possibility a piling or so might show damage after the accumulated river flotsam was removed.

At least, the upper portion above Elk Park was not the scene of havoc found down river to Tacoma. In fact, upon seeing it in midafternoon, I was tempted to make camp close to the old water tank site, cook my remaining steak and consume my other half bottle of wine. It was a sore temptation, but I was never too proficient at lying to "Gus" Aydelott, our president. I knew he was in a hurry for a report and would be unhappy if it was delayed while I lazed, ate and drank.

So on to Silverton to be picked up by the Roadmaster to be conveyed to Durango and a lousy restaurant-cooked meal. The bar drinks were not as good, either.

Chapter 10
Narrow Gauge Trains

In the Standard Rules Book a train is defined as: "A train is an engine, or more than one engine, coupled with or without cars, displaying markers."

But a train is much more than that. In a newly developing section during pioneer days, and later when the road system for off-rail means of transportation is still not perfected, trains are the lifeblood of communities along or served by the railroad on which trains are run. Up until highways were built that made trucking feasible, the trains on the narrow gauge were the primary means for moving the commodities to the communities required by them and products and produce from them to market.

Smaller in size and hauling fewer tons per train, they were not as economically efficient as trains on the standard gauge. But, there was an aura of romance, nostalgia for the past that the big brothers never had. Railroaders involved in all aspects of railroading required to run a narrow gauge train were more closely in touch with, and took a greater professional pride in, each train than on the standard gauge.

As an agent and operator, I had a part in receiving the waybills for hundreds of shipments inbound, and as many for outbound ones. Thousands of messages were copied and sent relating to trains and freight and almost as many train orders copied and delivered to trains. Then, from terminal

Baldwin-built #318 on Ouray Branch in 1952. ***John Krause/Dr. Richard Severance collection***

Engine #268 delivers a train of cattle from the Powderhorn Pool just west of Gunnison. ***Colorado RR Museum/R.W. Richardson***

points, there were consists sent to the next standard gauge junction.

An abbreviated consist was sent from terminals to Alamosa, Montrose or Salida to permit transfer forces to plan in advance for standard gauge transfer cars, and to line up and assign transfer forces and machinery. These consists were transmitted by Morse telegraph and showed train handling, departure time from terminal, car number, contents and destination. While I was telegraphing on the narrow gauge, we did not have teletypewriters. When sending these in the still of the night you could fantasize on how and where the load originated, where it was going and the kind of people involved. Each train then became, in a sense, an individual story.

ONE COMMODITY

On the narrow gauge, trains tended to be made up of only one commodity. That is, the train might be a lumber train, coal train, ore train, wool train, pipe train, stock train (when carrying cattle they were always called a bull train), fruit train or bean train. For many years we operated a daily westward L.C.L. (less-than-carload) merchandise train running on a second-class timetable schedule. On the main line of the narrow gauge the term "mixed train" referred to a train carrying several commodities; on the branch lines, a mixed train was a train carrying both freight and passengers.

We were able to operate solid trains of one commodity due to the inherent factor of small power handling small gross tonnages. Until the production of tonnage from frontier resources

began to decline, many of the sawmills or mines could produce enough of their product to make a train. Sheep and cattle ranchers could to the same when ready to ship to market in the fall.

Narrow gauge cars had a tare weight of 10 to 12 tons each and a maximum load capacity of 25 tons. Thus each car had a gross weight of 35-37 tons, and it did not take many of these to reach the tonnage rating of a narrow gauge engine. Each train was given cars up to the maximum tonnage for the easier grades and helper power was dispatched to meet the train where the grade became heavier.

A double-header stock train was usually made up of 40 carloads which, with helpers, could be moved over Falfa Hill out of Durango; over Cumbres; Marshall Pass and Cerro Summit. The grade was favorable from Cumbres and Marshall Pass and helper power was cut off at their summits. The same applied at the summit of Cerro Summit, but if the power being used was C-class in this territory, the train was double headed through or given a helper at Sapinero or Iola.

Several sheep barons regularly shipped from 25,000 to 100,000 head each fall. On the Cumbres end there were: Ed Sargent, the Gomez family, the Sanchez and Gonzales clans. On the Gunnison end, the Fitzpatricks were the single largest shipper. On the Rio Grande Southern, that connected to us at Ridgway and Durango, there were also several such large shippers.

Until farmers no longer found them profitable, we ran a weekly Pig Special from the Durango-Allison district to Santa Fe. A trainload was normally 18-20 carloads and made passenger train time from origin to Santa Fe.

Again, finally stopped when there was no longer a demand or profit, we ran Fruit Specials in the fall from the Farmington-Aztec districts and the Espanola area on the Chili Line. We did not have enough refrigerator cars to care for a heavy fruit movement, so the product, mostly apples, was loaded in boxcars which were insulated with straw. Fruit Specials were light tonnage trains and made passenger train speed.

CATTLE TRAINS

Cattle trains were thought to be the acme of representation of the romantic Old West; reminders of the Texas cattle-drive days; of the plains black with longhorns and diamond stack engines hauling beef to the meat-hungry Eastern markets. To us they were a pain in the posterior, destroyers of a profitable operation and disrupters of train movements.

On train sheets dispatchers usually identified them as BS Spls, or Bulls. However, the only bulls on these trains were old, worn out ones that could no longer cut the mustard among the heifers. They were called "cans and cutters" by the meatpackers and went into hamburger, corned beef and bologna. A few old cows were shipped under the same classification but most of the animals were surplus bull calves neutered soon after birth and grew up as fat, juicy steers.

Shipping trainloads of cattle through Alamosa were the Crowleys, Shehans, Grahams and Fitzhughs. From the Gunnison range the largest shipper was the Powderhorn Pool, a combine of cattle ranchers that "pooled" their fall market offering and moved as a "pool." Trainloads of cattle moved through Ridgway and Durango from the Rio Grande Southern, but no one rancher rounded up enough head for a train in his own name.

As redolent of the past as the cattle drives to the narrow gauge loading points were, there was also vitality to the sheep movement, and what a smell! Nothing in the world smells quite as high as a large flock of sheep that has been on the trail for days subjected to a fall rain or snow and confined in the pens awaiting shipment. Before the sheep movement is finished everyone involved, including trainmasters, train crews and sectionmen, is impregnated with the smell on their clothes and bodies. It never took less than three months to get rid of the smell. My wife often lost hope she could wash it all out, and simply discarded the clothing (occasionally I think she even considered discarding me, also).

One of the big headaches in hauling livestock was the Confinement Law. Livestock could be confined in the cars for only 28 hours before they had to unload for feed, water and rest. A shipper could sign a 36-hour Release which allowed the stock to go 36 hours before being unloaded. Nearly all the shippers we dealt with understood narrow gauge operations and signed this release. A few, thinking to force a more rapid transit, were recalcitrant and would not sign. If the train carrying their stock met with unexpected delays, making it necessary to unload enroute where feed, water and rest were available (the shipper had to pay the expense) when they were billed, or missed the best market days, a squall was raised to the high heavens. The sound that came from such shippers under these circumstances sounded just like the sound of pain that came from their rams or bulls as they were transformed into wethers or steers.

Handling of lumber, ore, coal, oil, beans and other dead freight was prosaic and routine in nature. Trains going west set out empties as required at loading points, switched out and lined up east loads for pickup later. Sometimes a Branch train would deliver a tonnage train at the junction point and in this case a caboose hop would be run to pick it up. From terminals, when tonnage for a train was ready and engines and crews available, a train was called.

NO GLAMOUR

Essentially, that was the sum and substance of it, no glamour, no romance, just the day in and day out commonplace chore of moving something a shipper wanted to sell to a place where a buyer wanted to buy. Year in and year out, it was coal smoke in your lungs and nostrils; cinders in your eyes and down your shirt collar; sunburn in the summer and chilbains in the winter; and bruised heels and sprained ankles from a train moving too fast. (A lot of today's railbuffs, who have never been there, say, "Boy, oh boy, I would have loved to experience all that.")

But, no matter how you dreaded it, each fall the stock shipping season came around. For three or four months nobody had any satisfying rest. Train and engine crews worked as many trips, as many hours as possible under the Hours of Service Act. Other employees worked long shifts as long as they could stand it. The edict against overtime went into limbo until the last neutered bull or stinking sheep was moved for the season.

There were two stock movements I have nostalgic memories of. The Farmington Navajo sheep one was almost Biblical in its atmosphere, considering a difference of about 2,000 years in time. The Powderhorn Pool cattle loading was like a scene from the days at Abilene, Dodge City and such. That is, as it really was, not as motion pictures, books and television tell it. I feel privileged that I once saw them and took part in them.

The Navajo movement included all the tribe's gathering of sheep destined for the feedlots of northeast Colorado where they were fattened on sugarbeet pulp, then sent to market for butchering. It was dependent for a loading date after enough snow had fallen on the reservation to provide water (snow) during the drive across the arid stretches of Navajo land. For the most part, these were spring lambs about as big as jackrabbits. We referred to them as Navajo jackrabbits.

Other sheep we loaded each fall averaged 90-100 pounds, but not the Navajo ones. These scrawny animals reached Farmington weighing in at seldom more than 60 pounds, their wool was thin and matted with burrs, and their lips were ulcerated from their diet of tumbleweed and thorny brush. After 90 days on the beetpulp dumps they attained a different look and had a ready sale in Eastern markets.

The part I remember best was the picture of the flocks arriving in Farmington herded by the Navajo men and boys. After the long drive, their long hair was as matted as the sheeps' wool. They were dressed in rainbow hued shirts and

Half a dozen humped-back stock cars trail #318 as she puffs proudly southbound along the Ouray Branch in June of 1952. At this point in time, the narrow gauge portion of the D&RGW is coming to a fast close. The year before the tracks between Mears Junction and Hooper were abandoned. The Ridgway to Ouray branch was closed in 1953. *John Krause/Dr. Richard Severance collection*

Engines #459 and #478 are hauling a mixed train, but mostly livestock going to the summer range. Here the train is leaving Whitehorse water chute. *Colorado RR Museum/R.W. Richardson*

faded Levis; some were Navajo-style moccasins, some boots with runover heels. The women who followed the herds in wagons were dressed in the traditional Navajo squaw-dress (later made popular by hippy girls) usually of purple or brown color ornamented with silver conchos and other beautiful silver and turquoise jewelry of tribal manufacture and design.

The Navajo is of extremely clean nature. Almost immediately after the last sheep was loaded, came cleanup time. The men made a heavy suds using yucca root and washed their hair. Sweathouses, prepared in advance, had fires burning outside in which stones and bits of old iron were heating. After the hair washing, the men lined up at the sweatlodges and two or three at a time rid themselves of dirty clothes, entered the lodge where there was a pail of water and bundles of willow withes. Hot stones were passed in to them to have water sprinkled on them to make steam. Having sweated until they were parboiled, they rushed out of the lodge to be doused by a bucket of cold water, or to roll in the snow if there was enough. I never figured out how the women got clean for, even after the sheep drive, they still were clean and their hair was well-combed, glossy black and braided.

COLD AND WET

The Navajos were tough, and seemingly disregarded cold and wet. Upon arrival at Farmington, once the pens were full for the first train and overflow sheep bedded for the night, the herders ate a frugal meal of "pica" bread (Navajo tortillas), pinon (pinyon) nuts and squash seeds with a little mutton jerky. That finished, each individual would build a small mesquite or cedar fire in a protected nook, curl around the fire and fall asleep. There were no bedrolls and seldom even a blanket—at most a sheep pelt between them and the ground.

At daybreak they were awake and (sometimes having to brush off some snowfall) went to the fires the women had going where they drank coffee, ate warm "pica" bread and boiled mutton. I often wondered how much sleep the women got considering the time spent preparing the morning meal. Breakfast over they attended to the horses and checked the sheep, then went to the pens to await the arrival of the first train of empty cars. There was not much conversation while waiting.

Finally, the engine and a string of 40 cars drifted to a stop at the water tank, took on water and moved to the stockyards.

Sheep dogs barked, the tribal singer (boss) lined up where individuals were to work. The first car spotted, the exasperating, stinking job began. Each deck of sheep was led from the pens, up the plank and into the car by an old long bearded, trained "helper" billygoat called a "chivato." As the chivato reached the doorway of the car, he stepped to one side, and when the last animal was aboard, stepped out and walked down the plank for the next deckload.

It was hard, dirty and stinking work, even with the assistance of the chivato. By the time the first train was loaded and ready to go, there would be a second string of cars from a following train ready. During the years of the pipe movement, we had real problems shuffling cars around the Farmington tracks to find room for both operations. Two trains a day were the best we could do, and only then by closely scheduling trains and the empty car return. Sometimes toward the end of the loading days we had to substitute single decks for doubledecks, which meant a train of singledecks (if all singledecks) could load only the equivalent of 20 doubledecks.

Watching the Farmington annual sheep loading you saw the scenes of the Bible re-enacted; at the Powder Horn Pool, loading it was like a bunch of Texas trail drivers loading at Abilene, in a hurry to get the job done, receive their pay so they could start their tour of the saloons and pleasure houses. And it was not a scene from a Matt Dillon or John Wayne picture.

SUMMER GRAZE

Down from the high summer graze of Cebolla Creek, the Powder Horn and Lake Fork areas, across the rolling grass and sagebrush flats the cattle streamed. Riding point, rear and on both sides of the herds rode the males (and a few females) of the Powder Horn—every male old enough to have put away his three-cornered pants during the summer. There were very few 10-gallon Stetsons, no wooly chaps, and the neckerchiefs were everyday cotton bandanas. Some wore work shoes instead of high heel boots. No large-rowelled spurs chimed a tune. Six-shooters were scarcely to be seen and scabbarded Winchester carbines were few and far between. These were *working* cowboys, but they knew cattle, and they did not need fancy trappings to tell the world they did.

They were in high spirits, for loading out the season's crop was their time of the year to whoop it up, spend their summer wages in town and forget the toilsome, lonesome days in the saddle.

The herds were brought in the night before loading and held on good grass along a creek. At daylight the herd was brought to its feet by yelling cowboys. Just as the eastern sky began to lighten, the cook served a big breakfast of thick steaks, warmed-over beans and fresh Dutch-oven biscuits. It was all washed down with a barrel of paint-remover-strong coffee. Some may have just left their mammy's breast, but for this time they were men, and they ate like there would not be another meal. A quirley or two, hand-rolled using brown papers and Bull Durham, with the last cup of coffee and they were raring to go.

With the pens full and the holding herd bunched to await more room, the men had time for spinning yarns while waiting for the train. And God help the engineer who used his whistle blowing for the station. These were wild range cattle reared where they had never heard such a sound. A blown whistle would have meant a stampede, and the engineer guilty of starting one could expect, at the least, to be given the surgical treatment involved in turning a bull into a steer.

A tradition of the loading of the Powder Horn Pool could be observed when the train came in sight. Each cowboy went to his saddle and from it removed a bottle, and it did not contain water. By the time the first car was spotted, on the top of each square-topped post of the pens was a bottle with the cork pulled. It was a marvel to see how a cowboy could ride by a post, take a drink and replace the bottle on the post without spilling a drop. Loading cattle at Iola was not like loading sheep at Farmington. Instead of a chivato there were yelling cowboys who knew their business. Some of the younger boys, for the hell of it, would drop astride a steer in the chute and ride it up the plank as far as the door. It was fast, loud, dusty, lusty work. The quicker the last steer was loaded, the quicker they could ride into Gunnison and celebrate.

The last steer loaded and door closed, there was a hiatus toward the bright lights. The cowboys always beat the train to Gunnison, a distance of 10 miles.

I am glad I was privileged to be in on these two movements, my only regret being that at the time I had not yet acquired the habit of carrying a camera with me constantly.

Sargent depot sign with mileages and elevation. ***Bob Sloan photo***

LEFT. A train of cattle with four—count'em—four locomotives heading east to tackle Marshall Pass in October, 1954. ***Colorado RR Museum/R.W. Richardson***

BELOW. Engine #489 was retired in 1962 and went to the Cumbres & Toltec Scenic RR in 1970. Here, Engine #489 heads a train of empty coal cars down the west side of Marshall Pass. ***Colorado RR Museum/R.W. Richardson***

268

Chapter 11

Narrow Gauge Train Density

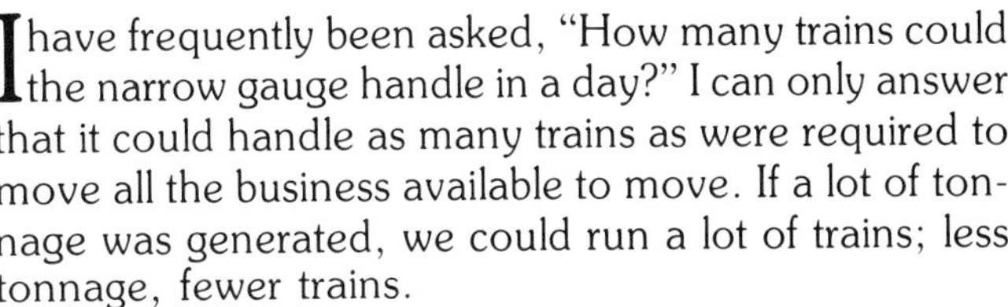

I have frequently been asked, "How many trains could the narrow gauge handle in a day?" I can only answer that it could handle as many trains as were required to move all the business available to move. If a lot of tonnage was generated, we could run a lot of trains; less tonnage, fewer trains.

As on the Rio Grande's standard gauge, or any railroad, each day was different. To the non-railroader it appeared to be the same over and over. But to the initiated, each day, each season, each locality differed—never did the same set of conditions seem to appear twice.

A second question has been, "When did the day begin on the narrow gauge?" The answer, with no intention of being facetious, is that the operating day of the 3-foot gauge began at the end of the day. It was accepted on the Slim-Gauge that the moment you hired on, you traded your bed for a lantern. This was true on all of the narrow gauge.

During the period of small engines there was no "day" of operations. Train and light engine movements had neither a beginning or an ending, the wheels just kept turning as fast as crews were rested and engines readied. There were always cars to be moved, for the days of the small engines corresponded to the peak years on the narrow gauge.

Once I asked one of our veterans, D.H. "Henry" Hines, who had put in most of his years in passenger service west of Alamosa, how many trains he estimated were run during the heyday over Cumbres.

He replied, "I have no idea. But this I can tell you. I have been the flagman on a passenger train when everything cleared the main for us. It seemed there was a train or light engine in every passing track for us to meet or pass all the way. Sometimes there would be two trains at the same siding waiting for us. So, when we arrived, we would be stopped between switches. One train would pull through and proceed and the second would follow him. If it was a pass, one would back out of the siding to let the other occupy the siding. I wouldn't even guess, but there were a lot of them every day."

A veteran on the Gunnison line could say the same thing for Marshall Pass. Those who only have knowledge of train movements after the coming of the mudhens, K-36's and K-37's have no way to picture the density, except through old stories what it was like. A lot of tons of freight were moved over the narrow gauge before the demand and presence of frontier resources began to dwindle.

On the branches, the sawmills, mines and agriculture produced enough business to require six-day service. The Santa Fe Branch had a daily mixed train each way with an occa-

An eastbound clean-up train on the Sapinero Branch (Gunnison to Sapinero, 25 miles built in 1882)) with #268 in the lead sends up a nice plume of smoke as she rolls along the line. The tracks were removed the next year. *John Krause/Dr. Richard Severance collection*

Tripleheader eastbound, east of Lobato. *John Krause/Dr. Richard Severance collection*

#318 and train are being loaded with sheep at Ridgway, Colorado, in August, 1952. Note tent at right. ***John Krause/Dr. Richard Severance collection***

sional dead freight, fruit or livestock special. The Silverton and Farmington branches required daily service with some clean up trains. On the Silverton Branch, if metal prices were high, two, or sometimes three, trains might be required to move all the ore being produced.

SIX TRAINS DAILY

A fair estimate is that on both segments, Cumbres and Marshall Pass, not less than six trains per day in each direction were run. This does not include the trains that shuttled loads to the summits, nor light engine helper moves. Or Lumberton-Chama turns run because of the grade over the Continental Divide at Azotea.

The Pagosa Springs Branch, a mixed run, six days per week, usually arrived at Pagosa Junction with from 10 to 20 carloads. Then, when lumber was in high demand, a second train handling only lumber would be run, and in the stock season, solid trains of stock.

Between Mears Junction and Alamosa until coal use declined, there was a fairly consistent heavy movement. This was handled by eastward trains setting out at Mears Jct. to be picked up by a train out of Salida for Alamosa. Not infrequently an eastward train would make a side trip from Mears Jct. to Roundhill with Valley loads to be picked up by the next through train.

The Gunnison area coal mines produced enough coal to make tonnage for three or four trains daily. Heavy trains could be run on the flatland between Gunnison and Sargent. Sargent-Marshall Pass Turns shuttled cars to the Summit frequently, similar to the Chama-Cumbres operation. The Sargent-Marshall Pass Turns were all three-engine trains so there were a lot of light engine movements. Between Gunnison and Montrose, for the most part except during stock season, one train per day in each direction sufficed. Because only small power could be used on this district, there were times when additional trains were required. The Lake City Branch operated a daily mixed train up until it was abandoned.

For many years our timetables carried some second-class regular schedules. These schedules carried odd numbers westward and even numbers eastward. Some of them are:

441-442 between Alamosa and Chama
451-452 between Chama and Durango
461-462 Silverton Branch mixed
471-472 Farmington Branch mixed
425-426 Santa Fe Branch mixed
427-428 freight between Antonito and Santa Fe
431-432 Pagosa Springs mixed
423-424 La Madera Branch mixed
343-344 Parlin-Pitkin mixed
325-326 between Salida and Gunnison
327-328 between Gunnison and Montrose
323-324 between Salida and Alamosa
349-350 Lake City Branch mixed
329-330 between Montrose and Ouray
347-348 Crested Butte Branch mixed
341-342 Monarch Branch mixed
345-346 Baldwin Branch mixed

These schedules were in the timetable for operating convenience to the train dispatchers. The "mixed" identification did not mean that mixed trains were actually operated on each segment shown. If the dispatcher desired to make use of the schedule he could issue an order for a specified engine to assume such schedule. Or, if he wanted more latitude in controlling movements, he could annul the schedule and run his trains as extras having inferior rights but moving on train order authority.

OLD SCHEDULE NUMBERS

Right up to when the last trains were operated over the Alamosa-Durango territory, Chief Dispatchers when putting out the daily program still stated, "Run No. 441 when Transfer is pulled and ready." West of Chama the program read, "Run No. 451 to connect with No. 441 on crew's rest." This was the case on each segment of the narrow gauge where, even after the timetable no longer carried these schedules, the westward or eastward freights were still identified by the old schedule numbers. Callers would call crews for: No. 441, 442, 451, 452 or as the case might be.

So when the day's work of the transfers at Alamosa, Salida, or Montrose was completed and the miners and sawyers had gone home, the work of the narrow gauge began. This had always been, and remained so, up until the end.

The first freight out of Alamosa or Salida usually departed about midnight. If needed, a second train left about noon with empties released from the rip tracks, team track loads and any early releases from the Transfer, and any left from the earlier train. Other trains were interspersed as required. Trains from the west end of each segment were run so as to reach Chama or Gunnison in the evening, so that the crews would be rested to run close connections with the westward trains. An effort was made to run as many eastward as westward

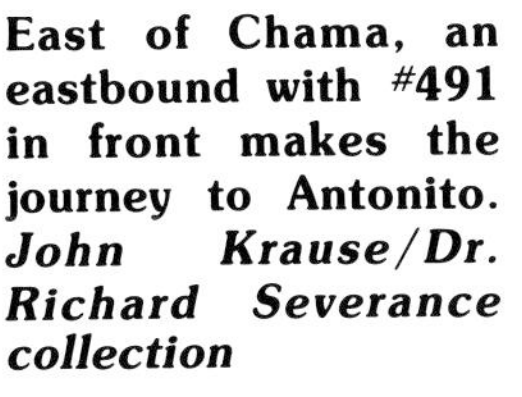

East of Chama, an eastbound with #491 in front makes the journey to Antonito. *John Krause/Dr. Richard Severance collection*

Locomotive and mid-train helper east of Lobato on their way to Cumbres. ***John Krause/Dr. Richard Severance collection***

trains in order to balance off crews. Otherwise, it was necessary to deadhead deficit crews, and the Rio Grande had a phobia against paying out deadheads.

Rio Grande management was never altruistic. It believed in getting a full dollar's value for every penny of wages and pound of coal burned. Only such tight regard for expenses kept the various segments in operation as long as they were.

Barring adverse weather conditions or uncontrollable tieups due to derailments or such, every effort was made to program and operate an organized, balanced operation. Because the narrow gauge was completely dependent on its supply of locomotives and cars, this was mandated. There was no possibility of calling on other divisions, or other railroads, for assistance. Speedy unloading of cars to be returned for more loads was as important as moving the loaded business. This was just as true in the matter of turning and conditioning locomotives.

Early in 1928, had anyone been paying heed to the signs, it became apparent we were running fewer trains because there was less business to care for and, consequently, fewer empties to be provided. The fall off was spasmodic, and when the Big Depression finally descended, there was a marked widening of train density. Although the narrow gauge on the whole weathered the Depression better than the standard gauge, except for seasonal spurts, it finally came down to where one train a day in each direction could handle all the tonnage available, coal from the Gunnison area being the exception, although even here demands were gauged by the demands of the Colorado Fuel and Iron Corporation's steel mill at Minnequa (Pueblo).

But in 1936, when the country as a whole began to improve, the narrow gauge territory failed to follow suit. Thus, for four or five years, demand for freight service was light. First there was cancellation of trains on a day-to-day basis.

This finally resolved into a somewhat fixed tri-weekly program of operations.

IMPROVED CONDITIONS

Conditions improved somewhat starting in 1941 and during WWII there was some increased activity. Coal to make more steel was in demand, lumber to build homes for wartime workers, and lead, zinc and silver enjoyed increased production. Cutoff employees were recalled and new ones hired. Firemen began to get callouses on their hands again from swinging a scoop more often. Trainmen became acquainted with brakeclubs again. The Rio Grande had to purchase a large number of new lanterns because trains were again running at night as well as during the day.

The Farmington Branch came alive with crude oil shipments. More wells were drilled that required casing and other supplies. Then farmers found that the semi-arid soil around Aztec would produce pinto beans like crazy, and there was a meat-starved Armed Force, and civilians, who could get their protein from beans. We ran solid trains of pinto beans. Over on the Rio Grande Southern, other farmers joined the bean bonanza and gave us trainloads of them. The planer mill at Chama and a new one at Durango had such heavy orders they were working two shifts each day. Once again the narrow gauge was healthy. There were no engines in whitelead, and the rip tracks were working full blast. It was as though there had never been a Depression.

Came the discovery of gas in the Farmington area that needed line and well pipe, and cement and machinery. We had more business at times than we could move currently.

Then the debacle began. The mine at Crested Butte closed; the big rush on the Farmington Branch was over; there was little or no demand for metals; and the Pacific Coast took the lumber business. Highways (and trucks) were improved.

The effects were slowly felt, and day by day fewer trains were required. The active, prosperous, flurry diminished until the train density on each segment was down to one train a day each direction, then tri-weekly, finally weekly, monthly, seasonally.

And, at last....none at all.

#318 Northbound on Ouray Branch with nine cars and a caboose. ***John Krause/Dr. Richard Severance collection.***

Engine #268 plods along with its consist towards the next outpost of civilization. *John Krause/Dr. Richard Severance collection*

Chapter 12
Train Dispatcher

I saw the dean of narrow gauge train dispatchers, K.M. Jarrett, who broke me into the craft, utterly nonplussed one time. At a gathering, he was introduced to a lady as being a train dispatcher. The lady beamed at K.M.J. and said, "Oh goody. I've always wanted to meet one of those men who announce the arrival and departure of trains."

K.M.J. turned red, and finally got out, "Yes, m'am, and now you have."

The lady could be pardoned. There were a hell of a lot of people, including railroaders, who did not know much more about the duties of a train dispatcher.

I had been a railroader's kid a long time before, finally going to work for the Rio Grande. To me, the train dispatcher was a God-like figure way up in an ivory tower, and he was boss of the railroad. Long after I had been one, and promoted to better things, I still felt that way. The belief almost got me fired by A.E. Perlman and K.L. Moriarty, both of whom sat next to God in the hierarchy of the Grande at one time.

The Grande was in the throes of trying to teach the staff how the line of responsibility worked. L.B. Coleman, Alamosa Division Superintendent, took me (then Chief Dispatcher) to one of these seminars in Denver. In one of the classes, Perlman pointed to me and says, "Mr. Norwood, who runs the Rio Grande Railroad divisions?"

I had been tipped off by Coleman I would be asked this question and was supposed to answer that the superintendent did. Well, I always believed in speaking what was my honest opinion, so I answered, "From my experience, the train dispatcher." (Oh, man. All the way back to Alamosa, Coleman hardly spoke a civil word to me.)

On the three-foot gauge the train dispatcher was boss. He was respected as *the authority*, and everyone hated his guts. They had reason, and I was no exception while I was in the train dispatcher's chair. With a very few sporadic and momentary exceptions, every train dispatcher I knew was in some way cantankerous, bullheaded, quick on the trigger, sarcastic, high-handed and blasphemous.

They played a big game of chess, with sidings for chessboard squares, and a lot of rolling stock and crews for the chessmen. The working tools consisted of an accurate watch, a strong Morse wire, and competent train order telegraphers. (At Alamosa it was late in the game before telephones were put in service for use in train dispatching. Imposed on wires, many as old as the original stringing, they were not as dependable as Morse.) Also, at first, the train dispatchers, used to yelling into the old telegraphones, distorted transmissions by still yelling into the new phone transmitters.

I finally made a date as dispatcher at Salida on June 4, 1942 and worked a short while there on a temporary assignment. Next stop was at Grand Junction where I had a brawl with the Moriarty mentioned earlier. WWII made dispatchers inviolable to discharge, so I was transferred overnight to Salt Lake City. In mid-September I bid in a regular job at Alamosa,

A short train leaves Ridgway headed south for Ouray. Ridgway depot is visible in the background. *Ruth Gregory collection*

Southbound train on Ouray Branch in June of 1952. ***John Krause/Dr. Richard Severance collection***

and began to learn what old-time train dispatching was like.

ONLY ONE LEFT

By the time I bid in a job at Alamosa, it was the only dispatching office left on the narrow gauge. The set at Salida assigned to narrow gauge dispatching had been abolished. So had the Gunnison office. On the Rio Grande Southern the Ridgway office was closed and, under receivership, the dispatching was handled at Durango. One dispatcher handled this, so he had to fix up train orders so trains could continue to run during periods he was off duty. Soon after I started at Alamosa, we were also given the standard gauge trackage Alamosa to Pueblo, and from Walsenburg to Trinidad, to handle trains on.

Train order offices were being closed wholesale as economy moves. It was only due to the use of bigger power and decreased business that reduced the daily density of train movements we were able to keep our heads above water. But it was no sinecure, and standard gauge train dispatchers

sent to Alamosa on temporary relief assignments went back to the main line as quickly as possible.

Only those who had experienced it can appreciate what it was like. There were pounding out Morse, wires down, engine failures, high water, snow, earth slips, trains overdue and unreported. The gut-grinding stress, too much tobacco, too much black coffee, and too long between P-breaks.

The Alamosa dispatcher's office was located on the southeast corner of the second story of the combination passenger station and Division headquarters. The door to this office had a big sign that said "Private." The Chief Dispatcher could enter as could the "AS" relay operator and the crew caller. Everyone else, including the Superintendent and Trainmaster, threw in their hats first. If they were thrown or kicked out, the owners stayed out.

The office measured 16 x 16 foot and contained only spartan furnishings. One corner held a knocked together coat closet. The fastening was a wooden bar that spun on an eight-penny nail. The hangers inside were also nails driven into the wall. The worn wooden floor was oiled occasionally and the walls had received new paint, but infrequently.

Air conditioning was available, when the wind was not blowing, by opening unscreened windows. On windy days all you could do was swelter, because wind coming in the opened windows blew papers and flimsies all over, and the train sheet would belly like a sail causing ink inscriptions on it to blot and run. In the winter, a single steam radiator hissed and gurgled and kept the room at about 90 degrees. It could not be shut off because it was on a straight line, common-distribution system. If any single radiator was shut off, circulation stopped all over the building.

BRASS SPITTOON

If the heat, wind and dust were not enough, there was a gallon-size brass spittoon sitting in spitting range to the working table. It received cigar and ciagarette butts, pipe dottle, lunch remains and the spittle of tobacco chewers. A swamper brought in a clean one each midnight that had a couple of inches of Lysol in it to add to the effluvium. The smell was something you never forgot. No wonder the "Private" sign was respected. Nobody but a train dispatcher or a habitue of a skunk-works could stomach the odor.

The furniture consisted of two beat-up chairs, one on each side of the work table which was a huge heavy thing built to last until Eternity. It was the product of one of our early day carpenters, a Swede named Gus Linderholm. The table material was hand-selected, well-dried pine lumber that after construction had never been painted. The top measured 8x8 feet, built of 2x10's. Gus had fitted board to board so closely it looked like a single plank. The legs were of 6x6 inch bridge timbers. The whole was held together with nails applied on the basis that if one is good, two are better.

That table was built to outlast the narrow gauge, and it did. The leg to the left of the dispatcher's seat had been used as a handy surface on which to scratch matches in lighting smokes so much there was a deep gouge worn into the wood. The gouge was at least two inches deep, giving testimony to how many smokes had been consumed by the dispatchers.

Down the center of the table was a divider consisting of numerous pigeonholes opening to both sides of the table. On the dispatcher's side was a complement of Morse sounders, a relay, resonator and telegraph key. (Later, when telephones were put in service, there was a combination talk-receive box.) Except for the telephone, there was a duplicate set of instruments on the other side of the table. The duplicate setup had been used in earlier days when there were more train movements to issue train orders for. On that side a "copy" operator sat and copied the train orders being sent in Morse by the dispatcher. He also checked the repeat from the receiving operator. The dispatcher gave the "Com" (complete) and time.

Alamosa train dispatchers, like most of the craft, had some firmly ingrained foibles. They never trusted their memory and did not memorize timetable schedules. Train order No. 13 was never used. In the train order book this number was writ-

Main Street, Farmington, New Mexico just before the gas boom. No paved streets, street lighting or traffic signals. ***Museum of New Mexico***

ten down as a number then the word "Void" written below it.

Many other habits and eccentricities were part of the office and individual dispatchers. One of them being that when coming on duty the dispatcher, when putting his coat in the closet, would give the button used in lieu of a lock to keep the door closed a spin. If the elongated button came to rest in a vertical condition, he firmly believed he would have an easy trick ahead. The coat put away, he reached to the pigeonhole reserved for "bullets," criticisms of past performances and such. If the spin of the button was favorable and there were no "bullets" from the Chief or Superintendent, he took the transfer in a happy mood. If both signs were adverse, pity the poor operators and train crews while he was on duty that trick.

FRESH SMOKE

Move No. 3 involved getting a fresh smoke or chew going. After the transfer of outstanding train orders and train sheet, current instructions were ingested. The outgoing dispatcher got out of the hot seat and the new one sat down. And he was in the midst of chattering telegraph instruments, 90-degree heat and the smell of the spittoon. There was no warmup period or practice shots. When your bottom touched the seat of the chair you immediately went to work.

No dispatcher ever thought the man he relieved had done

After money was available from gas boom, Main Street was paved and traffic signals were installed. ***Museum of New Mexico***

a satisfactory job. So he made his first hour of work twice as hard by changing most of the meets and instructions to trains issued by the men he relieved. There was no rancor, and less reason, for doing this. He knew the dispatcher who relieved him would do the same with his work. It was just a bit of conceited vanity to get the word across the line that he was a better dispatcher than the one he had relieved. The changes never made the trains run any more efficiently, and all it resulted in was more work for the dispatcher and the operators out on the line.

On the narrow gauge, due to the shortness of sidings and other operating restrictions, trains were moved almost altogether by train orders specifying either meets or passes. The only trains that other trains "bucked" without train orders were the few first-class passenger trains which ran on schedules. A dispatcher on the narrow gauge had to acquire a mental encyclopedic knowledge of terrain, engine and engineman capabilities, length of sidings, water and fuel needs, work to be performed by trains, location of emergency forces, and had to keep abreast of current weather conditions.

It was only with the coming of the big power and the consequent reduction in the density of train movements that Alamosa dispatchers slowly and reluctantly began to make use of the Standard Rulebook Form S-C, "Giving a Train the Right Over an Opposing Train."

It was even much later before the Rio Grande quit using forms 19 and 31 train orders and went to a single train order form, using a signed clearance card in lieu of the older Form 31 which required a train, under certain circumstances, to be stopped and receipt of order acknowledged by signing for it. "MBs", Manifold Bulletins, covering track restrictions were abolished, and instead this information was issued in a bulletin book which each engineman and conductor was required to read and sign for when going on duty. After signing they then became responsible for their train complying with the bulletined restrictions.

CLEARANCE CARD

Each operator who had orders to deliver to a train, had to prepare a Clearance Card, addressed to the train and listing the orders to be delivered in reverse numerical order, and the order numbers to be delivered repeated to the dispatcher who gave an okay and time. After we went to the signed Clearance Card, an operator, unless instructed to stop the train and get a signature, could prepare the Card and deliver it without a check.

The dispatcher was also occupied in entering OSs, train arrival, by, or departure times as transmitted by on-line operators in the appropriate spaces below each train shown on the train sheet. Besides the train reports, there was a multitude of bits of information continuously coming in that had to be recorded, and a lot of information and instructions going out from the dispatcher at Alamosa in Morse. The hard rubber sending buttons and the switch on telegraph keys, often the entire key, had to be replaced at least once a year because of wear. Very few dispatchers used a "bug," a mechanical transmitting device, and each had his own preferred adjustments of the key. Consequently, because of so much use of the adjusting screws, the threads wore and contacts (dispatchers were furnished keys having platinum contacts) burned and battered requiring replacement.

No two Morse telegraphers sent alike. The individual's rhythm, spacing and overall transmission created a signature that was as easily identified as the man's voice or face. Some were good "senders," and some were lousy.

Aerial view of Farmington in 1957 shows construction boom as a result of finding natural gas in the area. Farmington went from a population of 3,600 to 23,700 in 10 years. *Museum of New Mexico*

Old-time operaters (and dispatchers) had a distinctive style of handwriting not taught in any school. It was a beautiful hand, rolling and easily read and it was also non-tiring. It was into the early '40's before dispatchers were allowed to use the fountain pens for entering data on the trainsheet. Up until then, the wooden pen ("stick") with a fine steel point was used. Each dispatcher had his own favorite "stick" and pen. The pen was dipped into an open-topped inkwell that contained a godawful type of copying ink. After fountain pens were permitted, it then became a chore after being relieved each trick to clear your pen by using a solution of water and vinegar. Four years after the ballpoint pen was introduced, we began to use them. By that time, copying of train sheets on a gelatin roll had been replaced by a photographic method. (If you thought the old spittoon stunk, you should have smelled a gelatin roll after a week's use in warm weather.)

The rules required that train orders being sent to more than one train, should be sent to as many as possible simultaneously, it being mandatory that the superior train receive the order (address) first. When ready to put out orders, the dispatcher cleared the Morse wire by opening his key and sending several Morse code 9s. As each station called answered by sending "I-I" with the station call letters, the dispatcher pounded out "19 (or 31) cy 4 W" (Form 19, or 31, copy 4 west). If there were two engines on the train, the operator was told to copy 5. Each engineman, the conductor and rear trainman of a train received copies. If it was to be a long order, operators were told to "Cy fn all" (Copy fine all). The poor lightning slinger who had to break and send "brk cy ov' was in for a masterly cussing spelled out in Phillips Code or other abbreviations.

Among those on the conductor's seniority list were three

ex-telegraphers. By cutting in the switch of a telegraphone they could read the Morse being sent over the telegraph wires by induction. When they thought they were being delayed at a siding for another train, they would listen in for OS reports for the expected train and those of others. If, from their calculations, it appeared the delay was too unreasonable, they frequently would buzz in the operator at the next open office in advance and reach an agreement for him to "hold the red" until the speaker and his train arrived. This in effect, was setting up a block system.

DID ADVANCE TRAINS

Though not strictly according to Hoyle, so long as the operator holding the red was dependable, it did advance trains that otherwise would be delayed. The dispatchers did not condone it, but neither did they put a stop to it. Two other methods of advancing delayed trains were used. They were covered by the rules. A delayed train could flag a first-class (passenger) train, and have it display green signals for a following section, then follow the green signals until the expected opposing and delayed train was met, or an open office was reached. A second method was to flag a train that had train order authority to keep moving and send a member of the delayed train on it as a flagman to hold the expected train when met.

#490, which was dismantled in 1963-64, discharges lots of black smoke in this September, 1954 scene. ***John Krause/Dr. Richard Severance collection***

Train crews, as well as the dispatchers, were anxious to get over the road. The narrow gauge never had any CTC (Centralized Traffic Control) that permitted a dispatcher to move trains by pressing a button to display an advance signal for trains. A superior train delayed by a hotbox, break-in-two or doubling a hill could start a chain reaction of delays that would sew up the line. Anything done by delayed trains, if no hazards were involved, was considered as being acceptable, even good railroading and expected of train crews. When such trains were able to advance and mitigate delays it was incumbent on the conductor of such trains to notify the dispatcher as to what had been done so he could revise his handling of other trains.

As an art, almost a science, train dispatching on the narrow gauge reached its zenith during the days of small power when it was necessary to run frequent trains to move the tonnage; the peak seasonal movements of livestock, and heavy market demands for lumber or ore rushing to smelters during a price increase. Big power, and the business decline during the Big Depression, reduced part of the stress and expertise required to dispatch trains on the narrow gauge.

Before the decline begain, however, a dispatcher had to be capable of keeping 40 to 50 movements advancing during his trick with a minimum of delays. He had to be without any nerves, have a computerlike mentality and an oversized bladder and the ability to work his full trick without eating. My kids thought it was a special treat to get into my lunch box when I came home without having opened it all day.

We all lived with one apprehension and fear—that of the *lap-order,* which means orders issued that caused a lap of authority for two opposing trains to be on the main track simultaneously, resulting in a head-on collision. Newly-made dispatchers loudly proclaimed it would never happen to them. Retired dispatchers lied in their teeth when they said they had never issued a lap-order. The working dispatcher just prayed he would not issue one. Or, if he did, some alert operator or train crew member would sense danger and get in the clear.

AWARENESS PRESENT

Because of the awareness by dispatchers, operators and train crews that the possibility was present, and efforts made to guard against them, hardly any were issued, and fewer incidents of collisions or near misses. On the narrow gauge the Operating Rule Book was our Bible. Especially that portion entitled "Rules For the Movement By Train Orders."

In my career as a train dispatcher, I was guilty of issuing two lap-orders. Neither caused a collision for, in one instant an operator called my attention to what I was doing. In the other, a conductor, before leaving the point he received the orders, came back to the station and had the operator advise me of the mistake so I could correct it.

One of the nightmares dispatchers, including me, were awakened by after a particularly heavy shift was to see two trains approaching each other with throttles open. For me, the locale was always on a stretch of shelf-railroad on a mountain side in curved territory. The collision always occured on the point of a curve, and the engines and cars after the collision just kept falling, and falling, into the abyss.

Our wives, when we started to sweating, thrashing and moaning, awakened us gently. Once in awhile the dream was so vivid the only way to clear the feeling of dread was to get up and return to the office to check the orders we had issued and ascertain that there had not been a wreck. The dispatcher on duty at the time never made fun of the worried man since he had been through the same experience himself.

Train dispatching by train order and Morse telegraph was an art, a science. Thank God for CTC, radios and all the other present-day things that replaced the older method.

Locomotive #278, a combine, and a couple pose for their photographic portrait at Sapinero in 1920. The #278 is now on display by the National Park Service near Cimarron, Colorado. ***Collection of Don Heimburger***

Sargent on May 21, 1955 saw #268 making lots of smoke, steam and noise. ***John Krause/Dr. Richard Severance collection***

Chapter 13

Home Terminals and Working Districts

Enactment of the 16-Hour Service Act, and the granting of working agreements (Contracts) to train service employees, resulted in a better way of life for these employees.

It was a change that made it possible to establish a home of more or less permanent nature, where he could be with his wife and children on a quasi-regular basis. Of course, the irregular calling times for trains (other than the passenger trains) and unpredictable time on the road, still did not mean they had a home life such as office workers did. But, at least, they knew where home base was. And the change not only made the men happier, it also made for more contented wives and the chance for children to become acquainted with their fathers.

Prior to the establishment of home terminals and defined working districts, on the narrow gauge where enginemen and firemen followed their engines and train crews their caboose and were paid by the month or trip, they had no way of knowing where they would be working. It was possible under the old practices for crews to be called out of Alamosa, go to Chama, where they might make a Cumbres Turn or two, then be dispatched to Durango, thence possibly over Rio Grande Southern trackage to Ridgway to Montrose, and return to Alamosa via Salida, days or weeks later. So, it is easily perceived the men liked the concept of home terminals and fixed working districts.

Establishment of home terminals brought other desirable changes. Working districts of defined limits were set where employees could use their seniority to advantage. The first-in-first-out at the away from home terminals became the norm rather than being called when an engine (assigned to an engineman) was ready. A by-product of this turning rule was to influence trains to make faster runs so they would be first in at the away-from-home terminal, and so catch an earlier train on the return leg of a trip.

Under the change, the home terminals were: Alamosa, Durango, Salida, Gunnison and Montrose (Gunnison was home terminal for certain branch operations). Sub-terminals, or fixed branch line assignments, were auxiliary to home terminals, such as Pagosa Springs, for the Pagosa Springs Branch; Lake City, for the Lake City Branch; Sargent, for Sargent-Marshall Pass shuttling crews; Cimarron, for Cerro Summit helper crews; Chama, for Chama-Cumbres shuttling service; and Antonito for Chili Line (Santa Fe Branch) crews.

Alamosa to Creede and Antonito service used crews with Alamosa as home terminal; crews to Crested Butte, Ruby Anthracite, Pitkin and Baldwin Branches called Gunnison their home. Montrose was home to branch employees working to

It's lonely at Sargent, Colorado, 15 years after the Rio Grande pulled up the rails there. ***Colorado RR Museum/R.W. Richardson***

Ridgway and Ouray and Durango for those working to Farmington or Silverton.

Occasionally, crews with Durango as home terminal, were used out of Lumberton on the Rio Grande & Southwestern to El Vado or Gallinas; or on the Rio Grande and Pagosa Springs. These lines were not acknowledged as belonging to the D&RGW, and when crews were used on them, it was sort of a lend-lease basis.

As nearly as possible, the recognized working districts were established on the basis that freight trains averaged 12½ miles per hour. Hence, based on an 8-hour day, the district theoretically was to be 100 miles long. Since this was impossible due to already established operating points, payment was based on a minimum of 100 miles (8 hours) with overtime being paid for miles over 100 miles on the district.

MULTIPLE TRIPS

Alamosa to Chama was 92 miles and paid 100 miles base; Durango to Chama was 108 miles and paid 8 miles overtime even though the trip used less than 8 hours. If the crews had time to work in shuttling service and not exceed 16 hours, they could be used for multiple trips and be paid miles, but not less than 100 miles. When this was done, the first-in-first-out rule did not apply.

Because the route over Marshall Pass ran via Gunnison-Montrose to Grand Junction and west, employees, seniority permitting, could elect to work either on the narrow gauge or west out of Grand Junction on the standard gauge or between Grand Junction and Montrose. Trains between Salida and Alamosa had to be manned by Salida crews. If no Salida crews were available at Alamosa, and it became necessary to operate a train Alamosa to Salida, it was required that Salida crews be deadheaded to Alamosa to man the train. (Crews deadheading over a district got paid the district rate.)

Crews jealously defended their right to go home first (first-in, first-out). Crew dispatchers had to be accurate record-keepers and knowledgable in figuring rest time, and average running time for the train to be called. If a crew at call time did not have required running time, it could be run around while retaining its position on the "board." First-in, first-out was based on arrival time; rested time on time tied up, often different because of putting the train away.

Next to train dispatchers, crew dispatchers and callers were the most maligned of railroad employees. In the long run, both were indispensable to operations. Without competent train dispatchers and crew dispatchers, the train operations would have been in a constantly confused, disorganized mess.

In early times (and even later), the crew board at Chama (a prime example of crew boards) really kept a crew dispat-

#268 waters up. *John Krause/Dr. Richard Severance collection*

cher and three callers humping to keep it straight and get crews called on time and correctly. The "board" was a wall-size blackboard in the ready room near the roundhouse foreman's office. It was divided into an east board, a west board, and a section for Hill shuttling crews, plus a small section for hostlers.

Headings at the top of the board read from left to right: Train Called For; Conductor; Trainman; Trainman; Engineer; Fireman; and Time Called For. Entries were written with chalk with the first out crew(s) at the top of the list. Upon the departure of a called train, the first out information was erased, which put the next out crew(s) in the first out spot. At midnight, the third trick caller had to clean up the board, keeping employees' names and calling status correct. Woe betide him if he omitted a crew or entered it out of order when making the new entries on the clean board. The same action was taken at each point where a crew board was maintained.

INFALLIBLE RECORDKEEPER

A crew dispatcher (and caller) had to be more than an infallible recordkeeper. He had to be better versed in the provisions of train service working agreements than the men themselves. God knows, he had to defend his interpretations often enough. Especially he had to be able to convince newer employees who, while they might not know much about the Rule Book, spent hours perusing the Agreement trying to find ways and means for euchering the crew dispatcher or in finding a possibility of collecting a "run-around."

The callers, beside having the wisdom of Solomon, the tactfulness of Ben Franklin, the charity of Christ, and meanness of the Devil, had to be at times blind, deaf and dumb. They

D&RG #266, a Baldwin C-16, glides across a bridge in Ouray, Colorado spanning the rushing Uncompahgre River. #266 was dismantled in March of 1926. *Ruth Gregory collection*

had to be able to take being cussed out, blackmailed, threatened, insulted and willing to take a bribe. In a terminal, nobody knew the weaknesses, foibles and transgressions of the train service employees better than crew callers. Going to call a man and finding him tied up in a hot gambling game, about to score with a willing town belle, or full of booze, he soon learned the proper action to take—silence and receiving the accepted bribe of one silver dollar.

He learned to mark the man off and annotate the call book as the reason being: "tomain" (ptomaine), for food poisoning; "trots" (diarrhea) where this was valid at a terminal having bad water; or "can't see" for snowburn. All reasons were acceptable, but never show the true reason. The man so marked off, in addition to the dollar bribe, lost his turn, and went to the foot of the board. Also, since wives could estimate about when he was due home, he had to think up a valid excuse for not coming in with his crew.

Chama, for many reasons, was the most active-away-from-home terminal on the narrow gauge. During the good years, it originated and received more train and light engine movements in a 24-hour period than any other. There are two lines in Cy Warman's poem, *Creede*, that could have been written of Chama: "It's day all day in the daytime...And there is no night in Creede."

During the years, the natural resources west of Chama were being exploited, and before the advent of truck competition, trains arrived in fleets. From the east were trains loaded with commodities and supplies for the mills operating around Chama, and for points beyond where there was activity. From the west came lumber, ore, coal, hay and livestock. And in both directions there were trains of empties being distributed where needed for pending loads. Then, there were numerous light engine movements returning from making helps up Cumbres, or going to Lumberton or Pagosa Junction to help eastward trains. During WWII the heaviest eastward movement was of pinto beans from the San Juan Basin. And, of course, there was the hectic period of the pipe movement to Farmington for awhile.

ACTIVITY HALTED

Struggling for space and the opportunity to work amidst inbound or outbound movements were crews putting away their trains, or making up trains and switching the lumber mills. Twice a day all activity had to pause, and the main track cleared for the varnish to go through.

The heyday of narrow gauge operations at all terminals, especially Chama, was a 24-hour madhouse of engines and trains moving. Behind all this, prior to most mechanical services being centralized at Alamosa, was a support force of about 125 people working on cars or locomotives around the clock. In addition, at least a score were working at the coal chute and cinder pit, and another dozen loading and unloading LCL (less than carload) freight at the freight dock and freight section of the depot. Gunnison, Montrose and Ridgway did not have as many employees doing similar work, but all were active—to the extent it was almost impossible to believe the impact of trucks could have made such radical changes.

Each time, when reading of the Klondike Rush in 1898, especially descriptions and photographs of goldrusher's supplies piled up at the foot of Chilkoot Pass and the long line of men, belly to back, heavily loaded with backpacks, struggling up the ascent, I regret there are not like pictures of the train movements up and down Cumbres and Marshall Pass.

Think what it would have looked like to have been a "spy-in-the-sky" and looked down on the 14 miles of four percent grade between Chama and Cumbres; or over the route between Sargent and Marshall Pass. Trains moving almost engine pilot to caboose platform, smoke boiling from smokestacks (fuel was cheap then) and a plume of steam above the popoff valves. Or, to have a super hearing aid to catch the staccato of square set valves. And to have been above the anthill activity in the terminals at the foot of the passes.

Chapter 14

Assignment with *Life* Magazine

The most completely enjoyable assignment I had in my entire connection with the narrow gauge was a two weeks tour with Wallace Kirkland, a *Life* magazine staff photographer in May, 1950.

Life, as it often did, had ferreted out information that the Rio Grande was hopeful of being able to obtain permission from the I.C.C. and Colorado Public Utility Commission (also N. Mexico P.U.C.) to discontinue passenger service between Alamosa and Durango. They requested permission and assistance to record the possible last days of the only remaining scheduled narrow gauge passenger train in the U.S.A. Permission was granted, almost eagerly, and I was assigned to accompany and assist their photographer. Dates were set, and we started at Alamosa.

Wallace Kirkland was the camera expert assigned. I'll refer to him as "Kirk" from now on.

Kirk arrived from Denver on No. 115, and I met him. Being from *Life,* I expected to meet someone very much different than the man who climbed off the Pullman car, carrying an old battered suitcase and a dented, beat-up metal camera case. Kirk was a man approaching 60 years of age, but still flat bellied. His gray hair was covered by a crumpled hat of Irish tweed and his large frame was clad in heather-colored rough tweed. The coat looked like it had never been pressed, and the pants were even more wrinkled. His face, also with wrinkles, was clean-shaven except for a perfectly trimmed, very black, military moustache (I later caught him dying it). But his eyebrows and hair were gray, the brows heavy and beetling.

I soon found Kirk had an enthusiastic personality with a young viewpoint and was exceedingly articulate. He had a magnetism that drew me to him immediatley. In the time I spent with him, I quickly became aware of the fact that this magnetism did not work on men alone. Without being a womanizer in the least degree, everywhere we went, on the *San Juan* passenger trains, in hotels, restaurants and bars, or any gathering, if a woman, or women, were present, regardless of age and marital status, they flocked around Kirk like bees to the honeycomb. A few got down to the nitty-gritty and were chagrinned when Kirk did not respond. For two weeks I sat on the side lines, admired, envied and tried to determine what he had, hoping all the while some of it would rub off on me. For all my life I had never had to carry a club to chase women away.

ANOTHER TRAIT

He demonstrated during our time together another trait that endeared him to me. In 1950 Rio Grande salaries had not yet started to escalate and expense accounts were closely audited. Kirk paid for most of the meals and liquid entertainment. In his left pocket he carried a money clip full of $20 bills that never seemed to get smaller. I soon noticed a peculiar habit he had of paying even the smallest charge with a new

Engine #492 in the lead, and helper at the rear, climb eastbound near Windy Point on the Cumbres Pass line with a mix of box cars, flats and gondolas. *John Krause/Dr. Richard Severance collection*

A work train is in the making as the crew chats about the job to be done. *John Krause/Dr. Richard Severance collection*

$20 bill taken from the left pocket. When he received his change, it went into the right pocket. Finally I asked him why he did this. His reply: "The left pocket is *Life's*; the right one is mine." (*Life* did not require an accounting of expenses.)

The first day we spent getting acquainted and outlining our program. Kirk took a number of pictures of equipment and facilities at Alamosa. He soon realized I knew little or nothing about cameras, composition, light or anything to do with photography. For the balance of our time together, he was a diligent and easily understood instructor. My interest and ability with a camera dates from this assignment. He taught me things about picture taking in a way I never forgot them. I studied many books later about photography, but they had but little to teach me Kirk had not already given me.

The second day, just as it turned light, we left Alamosa on one of the heavier motorcars. W.G. (Bill) Luebke, the Roadmaster, was the operator, and with a clear railroad we rolled right along. The sun came up over the Sangre de Cristos, and Kirk had us stop on top of the loop at Big Horn to get sunrise pictures of the morning coming over the San Luis Valley and the twin peaks, Ute and Kettle Mountains.

We rolled through the big moraine cut and headed up the canyon east of Sublette. Rounding the last curve east of Sublette, Luebke frantically pushed the brake lever forward and yelled. There, just yards away, was a two-man motorcar coming fast. I had a picture of the sun-lightened car with the operator turned facing the second man on it and talking, and a large cardboard box balanced on the deck behind them. I instinctively stood up and let our car roll from under me and hit the berm standing. Then, without any reason to do so, I pulled out my watch and saw it was 7:35 a.m.

The approaching operator looked up as Bill yelled, but it was too late for him to take action. The wheels on our car were sliding as the second car slammed into it at full speed. Our car was the heaviest, so that both Luebke and Kirk stayed in place on the deck. The passenger on the second car went high in the air off the back of the car and struck the roadbed stretched across the rails. Landing on his back, his head struck one rail, his coccyx the other, and he laid there without moving, unconscious. The operator slammed forward hard against the forward handrail of the car and laid there.

The cardboard box soared, and when it came down, it was ruptured. Two or three hundred baby chickens exploded like a pillow of feathers. Luebke came forward nursing his right hand. He was wearing a new pair of buckskin gloves and the right one had a tear on the palm. He had put so much pressure on the brake lever handle the buckskin had split, and the skin of his palm was red and angry looking. Kirk walked up, limping a little and carrying a camera.

EXAMINED OPERATOR

While Luebke examined the operator of the motorcar, I went over to the passenger, just knowing he was dead from the way he struck the rail. So, I pushed him over with my foot. Blood was streaming from his nose, and dead men don't bleed, so I handled him more carefully. After awhile he came to, and we got the nosebleed stopped. The operator had several broken ribs and his passenger a slight concussion and two beautiful black eyes.

Luebke walked on up to the Sublette section house to get the foreman and one more employee there. They came back to the wreck with the heavier section car and some tools. After a struggle, we separated the two damaged cars and towed them to Sublette.

While all of this was going on, those two or three hundred baby chicks (what was left alive) were busily scratching in the frontend cinders of the ballast and cheeping happily. A few had landed on the hot cylinder of the motorcar and there was a smell of burnt feathers (fluff). Kirk sat on a rock at the side of the track nursing his foot, with his camera in his hands and an innocent look on his face.

But I did not trust him, and asked if he had taken any pictures. He says, "My foot is hurting too bad to think about pictures." When the story did appear in *Life*, you guessed it, there was a full page spread of the two mangled motorcars, one section hand slumped over the rail, another supine on the ground with blood all over his face and cute little chickens, some scratching busily, others perched on the deck of the motorcar. Never trust a photographer. Luebke and I just knew we would be fired, but the picture struck the funnybone of all our bosses and we kept our jobs.

Espanola, New Mexico, was reached with Rio Grande rails on the last day of 1880. In 1936, film stars, extras and townspeople converged at the depot for the filming of *The Texas Rangers,* starring Jack Oakie. A more ambitious film, *The Light That Failed,* was made near here. A section of the Rio Grande River was made to look like the Nile and D&RGW engine and cars revamped to resemble the kind used in Egypt by the British. *Museum of New Mexico*

Diesels arrived on the Rio Grande in February, 1942. The #551A was an FT with standard drawbars between units. Whenever a locomotive set was separated, the suffix "A" was added to its number. Photo taken at Alamosa around 1947. *Museum of New Mexico*

We fired the two section men for operating a motorcar without authority and off-duty. They did not go to work until 8:00 a.m., but had taken the car to take the baby chicks to the head of a trail leading down to Los Pinos Creek where the parents of one of them had a ranchito.

Transferring our paraphernalia to the Sublette gang's car, we proceeded west and spent the better part of the day taking background pictures and putting both of the *San Juans* on film at photogenic locations.

Chama was reached about 4:00 p.m., and I noticed as Kirk walked from our set off to the depot, he was limping badly. I got Luebke off to one side and asked him if he had been shown a motorcar permit by Kirk. He replied he had just taken it for granted this had been taken care of in Denver when Kirk checked in with our publicity department. Personally, I had not given it a thought up until then. I got on the telephone and started checking. The answers were all negative, and I was told that was my responsibility—more worries.

After checking in at the Shamrock Hotel, Kirk admitted his foot was hurting quite a lot and would get it x-rayed at Durango. The only x-ray at Chama was Dr. Harry Huntington's dental x-ray, but he allowed maybe he could x-ray a foot if we could get it in a position the x-ray could be used. Kirk was game to try, so we went to the doctor's office, put Kirk in the dental chair upside down and got some excellent x-ray exposures. There was a greenwood fracture in one bone of the arch. "Doc" Dunham was called, and he applied a bandage of athletic tape and told us Kirk would live.

BOUGHT SCOTCH

While Luebke was taking care of the x-ray and bandaging, I returned to the depot and had the Chief Clerk in the Superintendent's office give me the form and wording for a motorcar permit. I typed this up and pre-dated it. Then I went to the liquor store and bought a quart of the best Scotch they had, to the Chama Mercantile to buy three of their best steaks, and so to Annie's Cafe and got her lined up to cook up a super meal.

This done, at the hotel I found Kirk and Bill, and we broke the seal on the Scotch. Two or three drinks, and we went to supper. A couple of more drinks, and I nonchalantly handed the permit to Kirk, telling him it was a paper we had failed to have him sign. Without demur, he signed it, and I took it back, feeling much relieved.

At the hotel we had a nightcap and prepared to separate to go to bed. Bill and I were at the door when Kirk says, "Fellows, I appreciate the good booze and fine supper to get me to sign what I'm guessing is a release, but all that skullduggery wasn't necessary. *Life* carries a big accident and life policy on each of us. Their policy is that no one is ever sued over anything that happens to one of us." That was a relief, but then I got to worrying about how I was going to get the booze and steaks on my expense account.

The following day Luebke traded the slower section motorcar for a better one, and we spent the day between Chama and Durango taking scenery and locale pictures, plus more shots of the *San Juans* at locations along the San Juan River. At Durango we checked in at the Strater Hotel and spent a quiet evening. Kirk's foot was giving him little or no pain. We laid plans for the next day for Luebke to go back east and relocate the borrowed motorcars; Kirk and I to spend the day taking location and equipment or facility shots locally.

Early in the afternoon I was given a message by the agent to call the chairman (chairwoman) of the "Save Our Trains Committee." I did so, and received an invitation for Kirk and I to have supper with the chairwoman and some of Durango's notables at the Strater. Naturally I accepted. And about 5 o'clock we went to the hotel and, the sun being over the yard-arm, had a couple of drinks before showering and getting ready to meet society. That consisted basically of putting on clean shirts. Kirk still wore his old wrinkled, romantic looking tweeds, and all I had was a change of knockabout pants. Both were acceptable; Durango doesn't go for white tie and tails.

We met the chairwoman in the lobby about 7 o'clock. She proved to be very well preserved, comely and nicely, even sexily, dressed. I judged her to be in her fifties (to me still being fairly young, I thought of her as an old lady). It did not matter, for after one long look at Kirk, I ceased to exist. He magnetized her, and she really poured it on about her committee's efforts to save the trains and other topics. She conducted us to a large, low round cocktail table in the bar (the Diamond Bell lounge had not yet become a fixture of the Strater). On the table was a splendid assortment of canapes and munchies; a bar girl had been assigned to her table. Guess I have forgotten to say that the chairwoman, besides being a very attractive woman and enthusiast for saving the *San Juan,* was a rather wealthy widow, a power in the community.

Other community bigshots and committee people kept gathering around the gal's table. Kirk was the center of attraction. I just sat back, raised a finger to the bar girl occasionally for a refill, and tried to get the committeewoman's daughter (just recently returned from a stint at a New York models' school) attention. All she could see was Kirk.

PHONE RANG

Kirk and I had adjoining rooms with a door open between. About 2:00 a.m. I was awakened by the phone ringing in Kirk's room. It was the chairwoman saying she would send her man for us about 8:00 a.m. to take us to her mesa-top home for breakfast. Just before she hung up she suggested Kirk bring along his camera equipment, just in case he found the view from her picture window photo worthy.

The gal's "man," dressed in pseudo-Western garb, picked us up and drove us to breakfast in an overdressed Ford station wagon. Her "little ranch on the mesa" was a sight to see. And the view from her 10x30 foot window, it simply was overwhelming. To the left was the Hermosa Escarpment in full view, to the right the headwaters of the Vallecitos, and down the middle Missionary Ridge. In the far background was the still-snowcapped peaks toward Silverton. I could have sat in front of that window for hours. Of course, all this time I was trying to get a whiff of bacon and eggs frying and the aroma of hot biscuits coming out of the oven.

We spent long minutes admiring the view, then the hostess finally told us it was her cook's day off so, we should relax while she fixed breakfast. We did, and waited for the smell of breakfast cooking. It never came, but finally the gal walks in with a big tray and on it are three wine cooler tubs full of crushed ice and in each is a 12-ounce glass of orange juice. Only when we took the first sip, we discovered it was a mixture of about four ounces of gin and eight ounces of orange juice, and no ice to dilute the mixture. Actually, it tasted pretty good. So good we accepted a second serving.

The *Silver Vista* trails the train in Animas Canyon near Rockwood. *John Krause/Dr. Richard Severance collection*

Then the gal suggested maybe Kirk would like to get some pictures from her windows. He went after his cameras and brought in a camera and tripod. The camera was a professional Rolleiflex, and he carefully set it up and adjusted it. Then he told the gal that while it was a beautiful view, he needed something in the foreground to give him depth of field so why didn't she sit in front of the window. What do you think she had been waiting for? Sure she would pose on the cushions in front of the windows.

So she got posed, and Kirk snapped a couple of shots, and I noticed the gin had got to him, and he had not removed the lens cap. I got up to remind him and he gave me a sign to stay put. He made a few more adjustments and snapped some more shots, then allowed there should be some cheesecake. He called me over to snap the pictures while he cuddled the gal a bit. They cuddled, and I snapped, and advanced the film for a few more shots. Kirk took down the equipment and her "man" drove us back to the Strater.

We took the camera equipment to Kirk's room, then went down and had beefsteak and eggs for a solid breakfast. While eating, I asked Kirk why he did what he had done—lens cap and no film in the camera—to the poor woman.

"Son, all she wanted was her picture in *Life*. Orange blossoms for breakfast ain't pay enough. She's a barbarian and deserves it."

The balance of our assignment we spent driving around and riding the *San Juan,* interviewing and taking pictures. Truth to tell, it was sort of a mailman's vacation for both of us.

But we did not go back to Durango, for we were afraid the gal may have gotten wise.

Locomotive #476 and train leaving Silverton. ***John Krause/Dr. Richard Severance collection***

Chapter 15

Herding Rail Buffs on the Silverton Branch

The most frustrating, aggravating, yet hilarious experiences I had on the narrow gauge were during the first year after we inaugurated our summer excursions of the Silverton train.

I was Trainmaster on the Alamosa Division, and soon after the train began to run, I started receiving complaints from crews on this train. A few times I was asked if there would be any repercussions if they used bodily force to restrain some of the passengers. I thought they were joking, but it finally reached the stage where it looked like the crews would all refuse to work the assignment. I went to Durango to ride a few of the trains to see if there was any validity to the crew's discontent.

Two or three trips convinced me there was considerable truth in every complaint I had received. In fact, most of them were understated. I soon had to admit that if I were either a trainman or engineman I would bust a head or two each trip. To this day, I do not know how ordinary humans took all the guff they did and not strike someone. The passengers we carried during the first season, were for the most part people, tourists, who had primarily come to the Durango area sightseeing, visiting Mesa Verde, or just traveling through and took the train ride as a lark. They were a far cry from the riders we had in following years.

I stayed with the train a week, then established a program of having some Division Supervisor on the train daily. By rotating this undesirable task between us, we at least that summer, kept the crews working and prevented any bloodshed. Happily, before the season was over, we had started to receive a better clientele among which bona fide rail buffs began to appear. Between our endeavors, the better educated passengers, and the lectures given by dedicated rail aficionadas to inform fans how passengers should act to encourage railroads to retain some of the historic trains, the atmosphere changed from rowdyism to acceptable behavior.

SAFETY FIRST

It was tough while it lasted. There was the constant necessity of making parents keep their children away from open windows where they were leaning out to grab leaves or flowers while the train was moving. Or, any time the train was stationary, rushing to the engine to assist the engine crew in keeping joyriders off the tender, pilot, or walks around the boiler when the train started moving again. Settling disputes between passengers over whose seat belonged to whom was a daily occurrence usually involving the necessity of, finally, telling some guy that it did not matter if he was the mayor of Podunk, he still did not have the right to keep changing his seat to suit himself.

Our water coolers had a limited capacity and the cups furnished were the small flat ones that opened to a cone when used for drinking. Periodically kids would start a water fight, filling cups and throwing them at each other while racing up and down the aisles. No matter how gently a stop was made of this childish fun, there was always at least one momma who took exception and promised we would be reported for manhandling her sweet little child. I doubt if any of the crews ever did lay on their hands, but I did once (fortunately the recipient's parents were in full accord with the action I took). A young redhead about 14 years old who looked like one of those precocious females designated as "quail" or "jailbait" finished a soft drink, then started to throw the empty bottle

· · SCENIC LINE OF THE WORLD. · ·

THE DENVER & RIO GRANDE R. R.

IN

COLORADO, NEW MEXICO and UTAH.

Traversing the Switzerland of America, the scenery along its route being universally acknowledged as the grandest, most varied and most beautiful on the continent.

"AROUND THE CIRCLE," a grand summer tour from Denver, Colorado Springs, Manitou or Pueblo, has been arranged, being a trip "Around the Circle," of one thousand miles through the Rocky Mountains, comprising more noted and magnificent scenery than is compassed in any other thousand miles of travel in the known world. Fare for round trip, $28.00.

For full information and for elegantly illustrated books, "Rhymes of the Rockies," "Tourist Hand-Book" and "Around the Circle," call on or address

S. T. SMITH, General Manager. A. S. HUGHES, Traffic Manager. S. K. HOOPER, Gen'l Pass'r and Ticket Agent.

DENVER, COLORADO.

From collection of Marvin Gregory

Beloved Narrow Gauge passenger Conductor Alva F. Lyons talks to patrons on a run between Durango and Silverton. ***Museum of New Mexico***

at the glass in the door. I was in the aisle only a few seats back of her when her arm went up to throw. With a couple of steps I reached her, took hold of wrist and squeezed hard until she dropped the bottle. There is no doubt I exerted too much force, for she began to cry in pain and her wrist turned red. If her father took the action he promised her, her bottom also was red that night.

Then there were those he-men who brought along a flat pint of redeye to enliven the trip. And the more effete who carried Thermos bottles loaded with Martinis or other exotic drinks. Or people who carried lunches and threw their scraps on the floor, including banana peelings that could cause falls. Lordy, you cannot believe what the first year's crop of excursionists could think was sport and tried to implement. Nor could you believe how the type of passengers changed by the next summer. Those who came then, and since, were real honest-to-God railfans riding the Silverton Train as though it was a privilege to be on it and acted with decorum and extended courtesy to fellow passengers, and the crews. Within a week the second year, we were able to do away with our program of furnishing keepers to keep the animals under control.

SWALLOWED WHOLE

We learned we had to be circumspect in what tall tales we told the passengers about points of scenic or historic interest along the route. They swallowed them whole and passed them on as true.

One story we had to quit telling was the legend of the mermaid of Lake Shalano. The legend was that Shalano was for generations a favorite summer hunting and fishing rendezvous for the Ute Indians. (This part was true.) One year the chief had an extremely beautiful daughter just entering puberty. She spent many hours on the shores of the lake watching and admiring the trout in the water. At last she became so enamored of the fish she decided she wanted to become one and spend her life in the lake with them. So, she inveigled the tribal medicine man into performing a ceremony that did turn her into a fish.

Thereafter she lived among her friends, still in the form of a beautiful maiden who never grew older. Of course she had to quit wearing any clothing because they would have made it difficult to swim as easily as the fish. During the summer months her special delight was to laze in the sun-warmed shallow water of a particular beach. This beach could be seen as the train moved along the rocky shelf above the lake approaching Rockwood.

For some time afterwards passengers, especially the men, would all crowd to the side of the train next to the lake and cause confusion among those who could not care less about ogling a beautiful nude Indian princess turned mermaid.

The trainmen also thought it was funny, at least for awhile, to announce to the passengers as the train moved through Rockwood that everyone should move to the left hand side of the coaches before they reached the "High Line" where the rails were laid on a narrow rock shelf a thousand feet or so above the raging Animas River. If this was not done in order to tip the cars toward the inside, they might tip toward the river and fall into it. Of course, word soon got around this was only foolery and passengers quit taking the announcement seriously.

Twice that season when I was on the train, I had two identical occurrences on the High Line that, when over, were hilarious. These instances occurred about a month apart but were, in the one instance, identical. In each case I found a camera fan down on his belly on the car platform stretched as far out as he could taking pictures vertically of the river below. The only safety he had provided was his everloving spouse sitting on the platform also with a deathgrip on his feet. Until these picture takers were safely up from their prone position all I could do was stand looking out the door and holding my breath. Both of them must have had trusting natures and faith in their wives.

The other incident involved a passenger who, besides being a camera fan, was a tape recording nut. While the train was running through the Cascade meadows, a passenger complained to me that the toilet marked "Hombres" was locked and he had need for its use. I got the trainman's key and unlocked the door. Inside was the recording artist, down on his knees in front of the toilet with his microphone hanging down through the tube recording for posterity the sound of the wheels as they clattered over the rail joints. Until the environmentalists forced us to put holding tanks on the excursion cars, the toilet design consisted of only an open tube that dumped the human excrement directly onto the roadway. For comfort, the tube was topped with a standard toilet seat. Until the environmentalists decided this method of disposing of passengers wastes was unsanitary, the only complaint we had ever received was from mechanical department people who had to clean the truck the toilet was situated over.

Sometime, if you are invited to listen to a tape recording of the sound of wheels on the Silverton Train, you can think maybe it was recorded by a really dedicated fan down on his

Eastbound passenger train several miles east of Lobato on the Cumbres Pass line with #492 pulling. Vacationer's cars at left. *John Krause/Dr. Richard Severance collection*

"The last run, excursion special at Espanola, New Mexico," reads the caption from this photo. No other information is provided. *Museum of New Mexico*

knees with his face buried in a toilet tube while he manipulated his microphone.

Now I can laugh at the many things that happened on the Silverton Train that first summer. At the time, except for a few instances, it was an exercise in being tactful, understanding and using the wisdom of Solomon.

One dozen cars, including caboose, plod along behind #268. ***John Krause/Dr. Richard Severance collection***

Chapter 16

Lonesome Operators At Hilltop Offices

I once drew an assignment as a telegrapher at one of our hilltop offices. It was in the winter at Cumbres and lasted only a month—but that was too long.

The snow was deep, the wind blew, and I was alone with the exception of the section men and a Swede carman who was a recluse. He later went insane. The only activity was to keep the fire burning and shovel snow accumulated during the night out of the trench kept open between the office and the outdoor privy. Weather reports had to be wired to the Alamosa dispatcher about every two hours and occasionally there was a train order to be copied. Those orders were almost always copied at night on overtime, and it was necessary to put on heavy clothing, light the kerosene lamp and climb the train order mast with it. There it was placed in position to light up the lenses of the semaphore signal. Then stand out in the cold and snow to hand up the flimsies.

The only diversion was the passage of Nos. 115 and 116, the passenger trains. You combed your hair and stood in the doorway hoping to see faces of young exciting females looking out of the coach windows. You were better off if there were none. If there were, you just suffered more from the libidinal fantasies a young man, not too long married, does. Walks in the cold down the track did not help, and there was no bathroom where you could take a cold shower to cool your ardor.

Passenger train service between Alamosa and Durango was discontinued February 1, 1951. This must be some passenger equipment moving in a freight train going by boarded-up station building at Dulce, New Mexico, in 1963, headed for Durango. ***Museum of New Mexico***

At night, coyotes serenaded each other and the moon, when there was one, and a lone horned owl perched on a snag behind the office and hooted, and hooted, with a cadence as regular as a metronome, hour after hour. A few nights of that regular hooting, and I was going nuts. On a clear moonlit night, using a rifle borrowed from the section foreman, I caught that disturber of my sleep in silhouette against the full moon and blasted it to eternity.

The only operators who took these jobs were those low on the seniority list; old men in whom the urgencies of youth were dead or someone wanting to make a stake, for you get enough "calls" during off-duty hours to produce good paychecks.

Or, as one operator who bid in Marshall Pass, someone who was at outs with his wife. He suffered from several other irrational traits, and it was not long after going to Marshall Pass he had more. He had not been there long before he was at outs with the section men and the carman, and train and engine crews were talking about some of his more bizarre actions.

I was Trainmaster and heard a lot of these stories and began to keep tabs on him. The telegraph office was inside the snowshed at Marshall Pass, but the privy was out of it and, as at all these hilltop jobs, in the winter they had to be kept shoveled out. Usually the section men helped the operator do this, but they did not do it for this one. One time in a tantrum, he pulled too hard on the door and it came off the hinges. The snow blew in and he had to carry a shovel each trip he made. He was not mechanically inclined and had no tools to repair the door even if he had been able to do so.

SUFFER LITTLE LONGER

Finally, he got me on the wire and asked me to order the section men to fix his door. I told him that he would have to handle that with the section men's boss, the Gunnison Roadmaster. Then I got hold of the Roadmaster by Bell telephone so the operator could not listen in, and told him to just let the guy suffer a little longer for he had really made life miserable for a lot of people who came in contact with him.

Later, both the Roadmaster and I would regret our actions. The operator became so frustrated and irrational one night while copying a train order for an eastward train he kicked his chair to pieces, and beat on the window over the telegraph table with his fists. The glass broke and gashed his forearm severely. The conductor of the train came to the office to see what was delaying delivery of orders and clearance card. Discovering the condition the operator was in, he got on the phone to the dispatcher and reported what was going on.

He completed the train order transaction, then was instructed to clear the order board and take the operator to Salida on his caboose where a car and employee would meet him to take him to the company hospital. The operator recovered and went back to Marshall Pass, but his disposi-

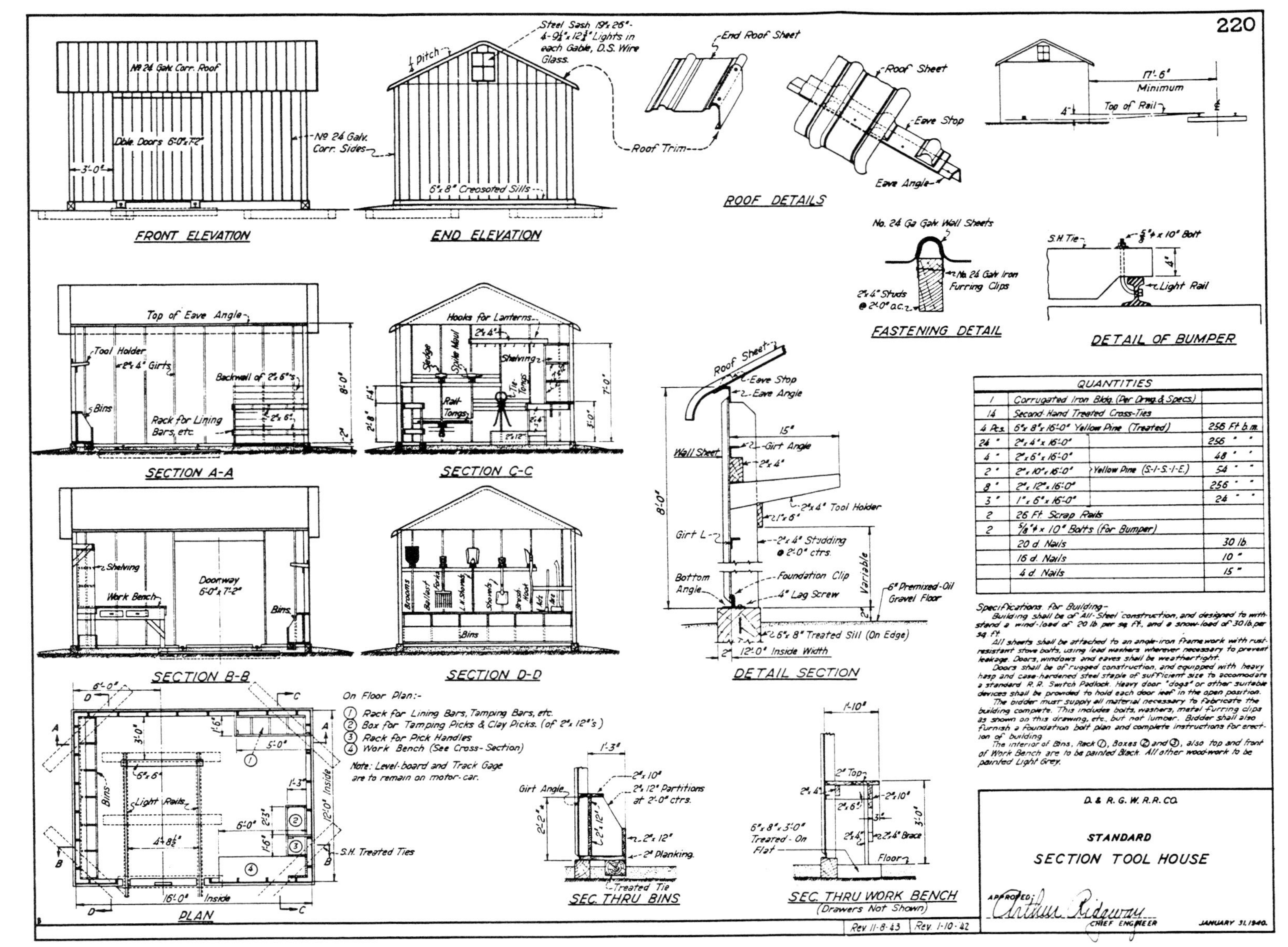

220
No 24 Galv. Corr. Roof
Dble. Doors 6'-0" x 7'-2"
No 24 Galv. Corr. Sides
3'-0"
FRONT ELEVATION
Pitch
Steel Sash 19½ x 26" - 4-9¼" x 12¾" Lights in each Gable, D.S. Wire Glass.
6" x 8" Creosoted Sills
END ELEVATION
End Roof Sheet
Roof Trim
Roof Sheet
Eave Stop
Eave Angle
ROOF DETAILS
17'-6" Minimum
Top of Rail
4'
No. 24 Ga Galv. Wall Sheets
No. 24 Galv Iron Furring Clips
2" x 4" Studs @ 2'-0" o.c.
FASTENING DETAIL
S.H. Tie
⅝" x 10" Bolt
Light Rail
DETAIL OF BUMPER
Top of Eave Angle
Tool Holder
2" x 4" Girts
Backwall of 2" x 6"s
Bins
Rack for Lining Bars, etc.
8'-0"
SECTION A-A
Hooks for Lanterns
Sledge
Spike Maul
Rail Tongs
Shelving
Tie Tongs
7'-0"
3'-0"
SECTION C-C
Shelving
Work Bench
Doorway 6'-0" x 7'-2"
Bins
SECTION B-B
Brooms
Ballast Forks
L.H. Shovels
Shovels
Brush Hook
Bins
SECTION D-D
Roof Sheet
Eave Stop
Eave Angle
Wall Sheet
Girt Angle
15"
2" x 4" Tool Holder
Girt L
2" x 4" Studding @ 2'-0" ctrs.
Bottom Angle
Foundation Clip
4" Lag Screw
6" Premixed-Oil Gravel Floor
Variable
6" x 8" Treated Sill (On Edge)
12'-0" Inside Width
8'-0"
DETAIL SECTION
On Floor Plan:-
① Rack for Lining Bars, Tamping Bars, etc.
② Box for Tamping Picks & Clay Picks. (of 2" x 12"s)
③ Rack for Pick Handles
④ Work Bench (See Cross-Section)
Note: Level-board and Track Gage are to remain on motor-car.
6'-0"
5'-0"
Bins
Light Rails
4'-8½"
12'-0" Inside
16'-0" Inside
S.H. Treated Ties
PLAN
1'-3"
Girt Angle
2" x 10"
2" x 12" Partitions at 2'-0" ctrs.
2" x 12"
2" Planking.
Treated Tie
SEC. THRU BINS
1'-10"
2" Top
2" x 10"
2" x 4" Brace
6" x 8" x 3'-0" Treated - On Flat
Floor
SEC. THRU WORK BENCH
(Drawers Not Shown)
Rev. 11-8-43
Rev. 1-10-42
QUANTITIES
1 | Corrugated Iron Bldg. (Per Drwg. & Specs.)
14 | Second-Hand Treated Cross-Ties
4 Pcs. | 6" x 8" x 16'-0" Yellow Pine (Treated) | 256 Ft. b.m.
24 " | 2" x 4" x 16'-0" | 256 " "
4 " | 2" x 6" x 16'-0" | 48 " "
2 " | 2" x 10" x 16'-0" Yellow Pine (S-1-S-1-E.) | 54 " "
8 " | 2" x 12" x 16'-0" | 256 " "
3 " | 1" x 6" x 16'-0" | 24 " "
2 | 26 Ft. Scrap Rails
2 | ⅝" x 10" Bolts (for Bumper)
20 d. Nails | 30 lb.
16 d. Nails | 10 "
4 d. Nails | 15 "
Specifications for Building-
Building shall be of "All-Steel" construction, and designed to withstand a wind-load of 20 lb. per sq. ft., and a snow-load of 30 lb. per sq. ft.
All sheets shall be attached to an angle-iron framework with rust-resistant stove bolts, using lead washers wherever necessary to prevent leakage. Doors, windows and eaves shall be weathertight.
Doors shall be of rugged construction, and equipped with heavy hasp and case-hardened steel staple of sufficient size to accomodate a standard R.R. Switch Padlock. Heavy door "dogs" or other suitable devices shall be provided to hold each door leaf in the open position.
The bidder must supply all material necessary to fabricate the building complete. This includes bolts, washers, metal furring clips as shown on this drawing, etc., but not lumber. Bidder shall also furnish a foundation bolt plan and complete instructions for erection of building.
The interior of Bins, Rack ①, Boxes ② and ③, also top and front of Work Bench are to be painted Black. All other wood-work to be painted Light Grey.
D. & R. G. W. R.R. CO.
STANDARD
SECTION TOOL HOUSE
APPROVED: Arthur Ridgway
CHIEF ENGINEER
JANUARY 31, 1940.

Ridgway, Colorado in earlier days. On August 2, 1893 the Silver Panic forced the Rio Grande Southern into receivership, with the D&RG gaining control. ***Ruth Gregory collection***

tion and actions did not improve noticeably, and he was told to move to another job at the first opportunity. Later he resigned and went to another railroad.

For several years following WWII, we were blessed with the presence of a few women operators. A few of the older ones who held jobs in "AS" Alamosa relay office were very competent and a pleasure to work with. Then there was one who bid in the job on top of La Veta Pass (Fir). About 45 years old, she was flamboyant at times, dowdy and depressed at others, and always a crybaby. She had an illusion (maybe it was true) that she was the "Lady in Red" of the Lindbergh kidnap case. She was an excellent Western Union type telegraph operator, but left a lot to be desired as a train order one. She absolutely refused to stand out and hand up orders to a moving train. And she was a cat lover.

She finally left our employment because of an incident involving one of her cats. One night when I was working as the night Chief Dispatcher, she came on the phone in hysterics and told me one of her poor little cats had, in some fashion, crawled up between the outer and inner walls of the office and was crying piteously. She just knew it was dying, and she wanted me to call out the section men to chop a hole in the wall to rescue her cat. She had already asked them and they had refused.

WHINING VOICE

I never could tolerate her whining voice and put-on airs, so I was not very tactful with her. What I did tell her was that the section men had better judgment than she did, and if the cat did die, since it was cold weather, it would not start smelling until spring. Next day she contacted the Superintendent and reported me for being brutal, inhumane, ungentlemanly, abusive, and guilty of using foul language to a lady. She also told him about the cat which was still in the wall. That fine old gentleman came into my office at the beginning of the next shift and allowed he guessed he was going to have to fire me for being abusive to an employee. He said this with a straight face, but when I showed concern, he grinned then laughed. Anyway, after the gal reported me he arranged to have the carman go and cut a couple of boards out of the outer wall and release the cat.

She stayed with us a couple more weeks, then transferred to another Division. Too many trainmen passing by Fir or going into her office to get orders were calling her "Poor Kitty," or greeting her with a loud "meow."

Two other female operators we had during WWII left the railroad on the same day, and left us in the lurch at a busy terminal during our heaviest perishable movement out of the San Luis Valley. Neither was entirely satisfactory on the job, but we took what we could get in those years. One worked the second trick, the other third. Both were under voting age and just a bit wild. One of them was married to a Marine fighting in the Pacific, the other single. She drove a heavy Buick that was on a quasi-permanent loan to her for favors given to one of our employees. (Both were putting out a lot of favors if rumors were to be believed.)

The Marine was wounded, and when released from a stateside hospital, was granted a leave. He wired his faithful little wife he could be coming to see her in a few days. That threw the gal, and her chum, into a tizzy. In addition to spending all their pay on parties, they had also spent all the allotment money the little wife had been receiving. The little wife had also got herself in the family way as a result of one of the favors she had bestowed.

Without giving any notice of quitting, they loaded up the Buick and departed to other climes. I do not know what became of them—they never did send any advice as to where to send them checks for time they had coming.

It was fun while it lasted. I wouldn't take a million bucks for the memories or give a thin dime to do it over.

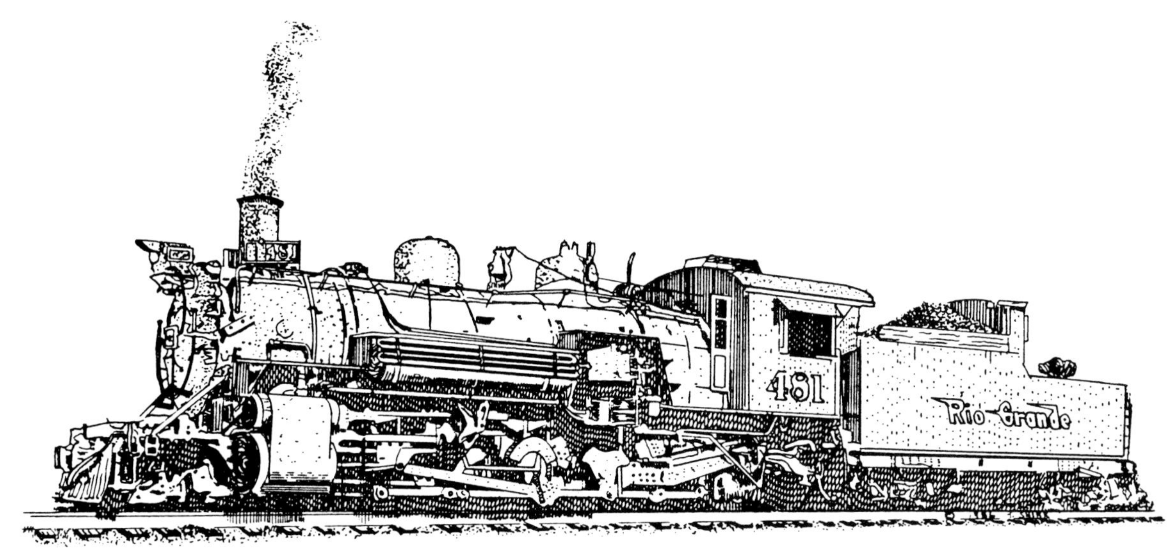

Chapter 17

Narrow Gauge Languages

Three languages were commonly used on the narrow gauge: American (quasi-English); Campesino (farmers') Mexican; and Railroadese.

It would have been helpful to have had command also of Ute, Apache and Navajo. But as languages are usually learned by daily usage and close fraternization I never became educated in the latter three. Railroadese I heard at home from the time I started talking.

A....

Alley—Clear track.
Anchor them—set the brakes on standing cars.

B....

Beanery—a railroad eating house.
Beanery queen—waitress.
Bend the iron—change the switch position.
Big Hole—emergency position of the air brakes.
Big Hook—derrick, wrecking crane.
Big Ox—freight or passenger conductor.
Black Diamonds—company coal.
Board—a fixed signal to display some governing indication. Train order board; slow board; clear board; red board.
Boomer—A drifting type of railroader (in some craft) who travelled from road to road and stayed a short time only on any of them.
Brainless Wonder—Conductor, engineer, trainmaster or travelling engineer (Road Foreman of Equipment).
Brains—conductor.
Brass Collar—members of the official family, the enemy.
Brass Hat—same as immediately above.
Break—a break in the continuity of service under the Hours-of-Service Act.
Break-in-Two—an undesired separation between cars, caused by defective equipment, slippery rails, incompetent engineers and a myriad of other causes.
Brownies—demerit marks given as discipline where firing was not indicated. An accumulation of 90 brownies resulted in automatic severance. It was easier to get them than to lose them.
Bull—Special Agent of railroad security force—cinder dick.

C....

Caller—the most despised employee in a terminal. He "called" the train and enginemen for trains.
Canned—fired, discharged.
Captain—freight or passenger conductor.
Car Toad—car repairman. Also: car knocker, car whack, etc.
Chasing the Red—going out to flag under Rule 99.
Clown—a switchman.
Club—a hickory club used to set hand brakes before the advent of fast-acting wheeled, windup brakes.
Cornered—what happens when a car is not quite in the clear at a switch and a clown gives a kick sign to his partner.

268
268

Repairs to bridge 393A are still under way as a passenger train moves across it. Bridge is one-quarter mile west of Jacona siding between Otowi and Santa Fe. ***Museum of New Mexico***

Corn Field Meet—a head-on collision of two trains caused by two trains occupying a section of track—one of them without authority to be there.

Cow Catcher—the pilot, necessary in early railroad days in the West to shove wandering cows and buffalo off the track.

Cripple—a defective car needing repairs.

Crummy—caboose, so-named from the days when sheepherders and cowmen were allowed to ride in cabooses as caretakers and left seam-squirrels, lice, behind.

Cupola—lookout addition on cabooses as a vantage point to see troubles along the train; also the gathering place where caboose riders aired complaints against the company, their wives, girl friends, etc.

Cushions—the sometimes comfortable seats of a passenger car, i.e., passenger cars.

D....

Deadhead—riding on a company pass, or on company business such as "deadheading" to relieve another crew (dog-catching) or when equalizing crews account a surplus at some point.

Deck—the floor section of a locomotive cab where the fireboy stood to heave black diamonds into the fire.

Detainer—a train dispatcher.

Diamond—a crossover.

Dick—a railroad detective—cinder dick.

Dinger—yardmaster.

Dog Catching—crews sent to relieve others account running out of time (Hours-of-Service Act).

Drawbar—goes back to days of link-and-pin couplers. A strong beam in center of car to which pockets to receive the link was part of car. Later, use of "coupler" became common to denote the coupling assembly, including the knuckle.

Drop—to cut a car away far enough back of the switch to let engine go beyond switch before bending the rail for car to roll in by gravity or momentum.

Dynamiter—a car with a defective air brake that puts car in full emergency when service application made from the engine. Brakes released by pulling the "bleed rod."

E....

Eagle-eye—locomotive engineer.

End Man—rear brakeman, an authority on women, run arounds, working agreements, when forced by the conductor went out to flag under Rule 99.

F....

Flagging—working under an assumed name to evade the "black list"; train protection under Rule 99.

Flimsies—train orders.

Flop—a bed; go to bed; hit the cushions for rest.

Flying Switch—a switching movement, essentially same as a "drop" but made at faster speed; sometimes engineer went in the hole and car rolled against train being made up.

PREVIOUS PAGE. #268 and train. ***John Krause/Dr. Richard Severance collection***

Foot-board—step on each side of couplers at front and rear of locomotive for trainman or switchman to ride while making switches, pick ups, etc. Outlawed for safety reasons a number of years ago.

G....

Gandy Dancer—track laborer, also "Guinea."
Gangway—space between rear cab post of a locomotive and the tender, also the "apron."
Gate—a switch.
Goat—a yard engine.
God and His Disciples—the General Manager and his coterie of "yes-men" out on an inspection trip.
Go High—getting on top of cars for purpose of signalling or to set old-type handbrakes, also "decorating."
Greasy Spoon—restaurant, also "ulcer mill."
Gum Shoe—railroad policeman, cinder dick. So called because wore shoes with gum soles that made no noise while slipping up on someone violating Rule "G" or collecting cumshaw from a hobo.
Guns—torpedoes, a warning device set on the ball of the rail to give an audible warning of some obstruction or danger ahead—they were part of a Rule 99 flagging kit.

H....

Hay Burner—prior to electric battery lanterns, an oil burning lantern used to give hand signals at night.
Head Man—the brakeman who rode the engine of a freight train and did all the switching work, always the youngest man by seniority on a train crew.
Highball—a hand or lantern signal, depending on visibility, given in a high to low sweep and says, "Dammit, get her out of town."
Highballer—an engineer noted for fast running—fired frequently for exceeding track speed restrictions.
High Iron—the main track.
High Wheeler—a fast, passenger locomotive; also a highball artist.
Hitting the Grit—falling off a car.
Hog—a locomotive.
Hogger—a locomotive engineer, also "hoghead."
Hog Law—the Hours-of-Service Act which provided that train and enginemen could not work more than 16 consecutive hours. Later reduced to 12 hours. (Also applied to train order operators—9 hours at 24-hour offices; 12-hours at 1-man offices.)
Hole—term applied to a track where one train gets in the clear for another to pass or meet it. For many years called a "passing" track; later rules designated such a track as a "siding."
Home Guard—the opposite of a boomer.
Hook—a wrecker derrick or crane.
Hot Box—overheated journal or bearing, also a "stinker," "squealer," or "blazer". Trackside employees who saw a hot box in a passing train gave signal to rear end crew members by holding nose and pointing down the train.
Hot Shot—a fast train of high priority, also "Redball."

I....

In the Hole—train in the clear on a siding.

J....

Jack—a locomotive.
Jewel—a journal brass.
Johnson Bar—reverse lever on a locomotive.

K....

Kangaroo Court—an investigation (hearing) held to develop facts and place responsibility in a case involving rules infractions or accident.

D&RGW #60 40-ft-long refrigerator car sits at Alamosa in January of 1950. Stencil on side of car reads, "New roof Ala. (for Alamosa) 6-26." ***Colorado RR Museum/R.W. Richardson***

Engine No. 481 is on the Monarch Branch at the switchbacks, pulling gondolas back and forth between the mines at Monarch.
John Krause/Dr. Richard Severance collection

It's been a busy day already on the Narrow Gauge as the fireman makes an inspection of the locomotive in the Durango yards. D&RGW locomotive #493, a 2-8-2 Class K-37, was one of the engines rebuilt at the Rio Grande Burnham Shops from Class C-41 standard gauge 2-8-0's. Originally built by Baldwin in 1902, this locomotive was numbered 1005. ***Photo by Chris Burritt, September, 1965.***

It's a bright, clear day at Durango in September of 1965 as #50, a Davenport-Besler 0-4-0 with 30″ wheels, sits quietly awaiting her next assignment. The 200 hp locomotive sported a Caterpiller D-1700 engine. The Rio Grande purchased it from the Edward Hines Lumber Co. in 1963 after having been built originally for the Sumpter Valley Railroad. It now resides at the Colorado Railroad Museum in Golden, Colorado. *Chris Burritt photo*

A Class K-36 2-8-2 suns itself near the roundhouse before its next trip on the Narrow Gauge. This Baldwin-built locomotive was constructed in 1925 and went to the Cumbres & Toltec Scenic Railroad in 1970. Note snowplow bracket to the left of the builder's plate. ***Chris Burritt photo***

#493 pulls a string of empty gondolas and flats over the line in 1965. Note the weeds growing up between the rails on the sidetrack—the end is coming. ***Chris Burritt photo***

Chama, the town at the foot of the westward Cumbres grade, has a history, a culture and an atmosphere of the Old West. The tall, black coaling tower stands even today as a symbol of the once-strong narrow gauge system operated by the Rio Grande. Engine #493, complete with a doghouse on the tender, goes about its chores at Chama in 1965. ***Chris Burritt photo***

She's a comin'...

First you hear a slight hissing and clanking sound, almost inaudible. Then you see the black smoke, and you know a train is coming. With a cattle guard to frame it, D&RGW K-37 #493 pours it on west of Chama, New Mexico, on August 20, 1965. ***Photo by Charles H. Zeiler***

Through the countryside...

With 36,200 pounds of tractive effort, #484, a K-36 built in 1925, lifts its load over the line east of Chama in August of 1965. The beautiful countryside presents refreshing views to the crew at every turn. ***Charles H. Zeiler photo***

#487 and train take a break from work on a hot summer day in August, 1965. #487 eventually went to the Cumbres & Toltec Scenic Railroad. *Photo by Chris Burritt*

BELOW. The Poncha Junction to Maysville portion of the Monarch Branch, a distance of 7 miles, was built in 1881, the year the most Rio Grande trackage was constructed system wide. The branch followed the South Arkansas River. The 9-mile Maysville to Monarch portion was completed two years later. The branch extended to the gold mines at Monarch; a double hairpin curve at Maysville and a double switchback at Garfield were included. Engine #480 does the honors in this photo taken in 1955. *John Krause/Dr. Richard Severance collection*

Keeley (Can)—a metal container devised to hold a quantity of water that can be hung on the side of a car above a hot box and having a hose that will carry water into the box and over the journal to cool it enroute.

Kick—a switching movement. A switchman lifts a pinlifter to free the pin gives a "kick" sign. The engine is accelerated and stopped suddenly—the car(s) break away and roll away from engine or other coupled cars.

Kicker—a malfunctioning triple valve that causes the same trouble a dynamiter does.

King Snipe—foreman of a track gang.

L....

Ladder (or Lead)—the track down through a yard that has a number of other tracks diverging from it for the purpose of classifying freight cars in switching.

Lap-Order—a train order issued by a train dispatcher in error that gives two trains a "lap" of authority that permits both to occupy a main track at the same time and location. A head-on collision most often results.

Lightning Slinger—a Morse telegrapher.

Longhorn—on the narrow gauge in early days, a dump bottom coal car with high racks attached above solid part of car, used to haul coke Durango to Alamosa Transfer.

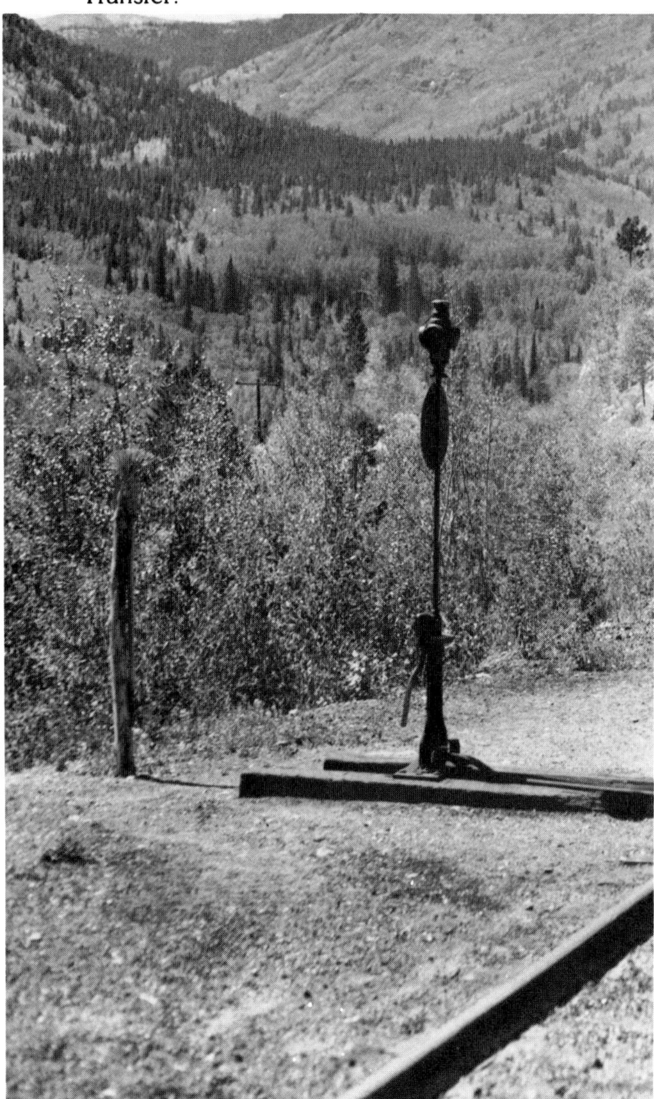

Monarch Branch, September, 1955. ***John Krause/Dr. Richard Severance collection***

Louse Cage—caboose.

Lung—see Drawbar.

M....

Main Iron—main track, also main stem.

Markers—two lights burning red to the rear attached at roof line of caboose to indicate rear of train.

Master Maniac—Master Mechanic.

Master Mind—trainmasters, train dispatchers, yardmasters, conductors, or anyone else capable of screwing up the operations.

Mill—a typewriter, or, sometimes, a steam engine.

Mud Hop—an overworked, thoughtless, kid sent out in the rain and cold to check car numbers, etc., on yard tracks or in trains made up to be moved. When checking tracks he always overlooks checking the one the yardmaster needs to know about the most.

Murphy's Dick—a specially designed air hose to be used in an emergency when the regular hose and fittings break off at the threads of the trainline and a new one cannot be screwed on. At the car end the hose has a semi-hard tapered rubber fitting that is the male fitting that is shoved into the female, the trainline. Control of train air is restored. Cripple was supposed to be set out at first side track. Train crews often carried the car through to a terminal.

N....

Number Dummy—or Number Grabber—see "Mudhop."

Nut Splitter—machinist.

O....

Old Man—Superintendent.

O.R.C.—conductor.

Order Board—a fixed signal to indicate to a train that operator has orders for delivery to the train. There were three types: semaphore, Swift and lights.

OSing—reporting the arrival, departure or passage of a train to the train dispatcher.

Outlawed—see Hog Law.

P....

Paddle—blade of a sempahore signal.

Pie Wagon—passenger train dining car.

Pig—a locomotive.

Pin—the pin that dropped and locked the knuckle stationary in the coupler. (A carryover from link-and-pin coupling days when cars were coupled together by a "link," each end of which was secured in a pocket on the drawbar by a pin that was manually placed. Survivors of this era could be identified by the fact they had one or more fingers missing.)

Pin-Puller—the employee who makes cuts while switching.

Pounding the cinders—hobos who could not catch a ride or track workers laid off and looking for another job.

Pull the Pin—disgusted with the entire operations, resigns, quits, or just walks off.

R....

Rail—a railroad employee, more especially those in transportation service.

Rat—a device secreted in cars to check whether or not cars (loads) are being handled in a manner that will not cause damage due to overspeed impacts in switching or train operations. Yard clerks cooperated by telling switchmen what cars had a "rat" and switchmen posted notice for everyone likely to handle the car by chalking a clock face on each side of the car.

Rawhider—anyone especially hard on men or equipment. Usually a trainmaster or roadmaster earned this title. Or an engineman who punished locomotives to the limit, including widening on the throttle in a manner that sucked the fireman's fire out the smokestack.

Red Board—fixed signal to stop. A train to go past a red train order board had to receive a clearance card.

Rule G—Thou shalt not drink, use drugs or narcotics.

Rule K—Thou shalt not fight, nor hold intercourse other than courteously.

S....

Scissor-Bill—an uncomplimentary term, a student in train service.

Shack—a brakeman. He could be recognized because he carried his brake club wherever he went, and maybe a lantern—walked cockily and leered at women.

Shanty—sometimes a caboose, usually "switch shanty" or "car shanty" where switchmen or car toads hid out to get warm, play penny ante, or to sneak a drink.

Shoo-fly—a temporary track built around a wreck, obstruction, or other distruption of the main track.

Sidedoor Pullman—a boxcar.

Slave Driver—yardmaster.

Smoke Signals—sometimes called "smoking it," going into a work train's limits trying to locate it by watching for smoke—this won't work in the era of diesel engines.

Snake—a switchman.

Snipe—track laborer, also gandy dancer or guinea.

Spotter—an undercover operative snooping around to check up on employees'activities (including what houses of pleasures or saloons frequented). Hated and despised by all, including the official he reported to.

Sprag—a block or wedge, usually of hardwood, carried in the pocket and placed under a car's wheel as an extra precaution after brakes set to keep car from rolling out. It took only a small block to do this if it was of hardwood. Rocks and pieces of slag did not work as they shattered or crushed.

Staff System—a system of controlling use of a block of track. A "staff" or "key" was carried from block station to block station by the engineer just like drivers on highways now carry a flag on a detour or one-way restricted section.

String—a cut of cars.

Stub-Pencil—another term for a boomer operator. They universally carried a stub of indelible pencil in their vest pocket.

Student—a pain in the neck and barely tolerated.

Super—a superintendent—an abbreviation—not to mean he was a "super" person.

T....

Tallowpot—a fireman. Goes back to the days when to illuminate his work the fireman used a special pot that had a spout into which a wad of tow was stuck that drew melted tallow from the container. When lit it gave a smoky, flickering light.

Three-hour break—see Hog Law. Provisions of the Act were that to break continuity so that time could be aggregated, there had to be an unbroken period of three hours during which there must be no service or responsibility (one hour in the case of telegraphers). Strictly according to the Act the break had to be taken at a location where there was feed, water and rest—just like animals had to have to break continuity of their confinement.

36-hour Law—by law livestock was to be confined no more than 28 hours without being unloaded for feed, water and rest. If the shipper (owner) chose he could extend this an additional eight hours by signing a "36-hour release."

Thousand Miler—had three meanings. 1. A durable shirt of a dark blue color and with celluloid collar and cuffs that could be freshened by wiping with a damp cloth. 2. A horde of food (lunch) that would last you for a thousand mile tour of duty, or a week's time in a snow blockade. 3. The heavy reusable envelope furnished to transmit company mail deadhead before Mail Service made the use of postage necessary.

Tie 'Em Down—wrap up them staff brakes tight.

Train Detainer—Train dispatcher. Also "home wrecker" because he sometimes gave errant wives a wrong E.T.A. that caused the wife and visitor to be caught in flagrante delicato.

Train Line—the pipe that carries the compressed air used to operate the air brakes—connections car to car was done by the use of flexible air hoses and their specialized fittings.

Traveling Grunt—a road foreman of equipment. He smoked big, cheap cigars that made almost as much smoke and smelled as bad as the coal smoke he gave firemen hell for making. While showing engineers how to handle a train or the air brakes caused a lot of break-in-twos.

Trick—a tour of duty or a shift.

Trip—the course of a tour of duty from a terminal to another and return.

V....

Varnish—a passenger train. Varnished wagons, for varnished passenger cars.

W....

Washout—a violently waved stop signal to halt all movement of a train or cut of cars immediately.

Way-Car—a caboose.

Wing Her—set the brakes on a moving train or cut.

Wipe the Clock—an urgent command to go to emergency.

Y....

Yard—a system of tracks within specified limits provided for the making up of trains, storing of cars and other purposes which Yardmasters try to keep more cars out of.

Early Emblems

Colonel Shadrach K. Hooper! Now there's a name long to be remembered for publicizing the early day Rio Grande. Within six months after this gentleman entered service as general passenger and ticket agent in June, 1884 his vivid imagination, active mind and facile pen had coined slogans and devised emblems to make his railroad well-known throughout the nation.

In December, 1884, Rio Grande train schedules published in the *Official Guide of Railways* proclaimed the Rio Grande "The Scenic Route Across the Continent" on the first page, and on the next, "The Transcontinental Route." All this, embellished in Victorian script, and the narrow gauge line between Denver and Ogden at the time was barely 18 months old!

By June of 1887, the emblem which would identify Rio Grande for many years became a familiar sight.

(Data and illustrations furnished by Jackson C. Thode.)

The first emblem, shown here below a Marshall Pass scene, was used as early as 1887. The early emblem pictured the Curecanti Needle against the rising sun in the Black Canyon of the Gunnison River, just as the scene would appear from the window of an eastbound train on the original narrow gauge main line. *Scenic Line of the World,* on panel at bottom of the badge, had already become the slogan of the railroad.

The original emblem enjoyed popularity, with the variation shown here. (The letters "R.R." were omitted in the company name.)

Silverton Railroad: To celebrate completion in 1889 of his little narrow gauge ore hauler north out of Silverton over Red Mountain (Sheridan) Pass, Otto Mears designed and issued a silver watch fob pass. The roadbed of Mear's toll highway between Silverton and Ouray, built in 1882-1883 and christened the "Rainbow Route," was used for right-of-way for the railroad, and the colorful designation was adapted to the Silverton's silver pass and emblem.

Rio Grande Southern: The famous R.G.S., built by Otto Mears in 1890-1892 between Durango and Ridgway, north of Ouray, also was a part of "Around the Circle" trips. Emblem used for this road closely resembled that of Denver and Rio Grande, utilizing, however, a view of Lizard Head peak and the legend "Silver San Juan." This herald was famous from 1895 until about the time of World War I, although railroad continued in operation until 1951.

The emblem most generally used by the Rio Grande Western was the "Great Salt Lake Route" diamond, which was in use from 1896 until 1901 when control of the Utah company was acquired by the Denver and Rio Grande Railroad in Colorado.

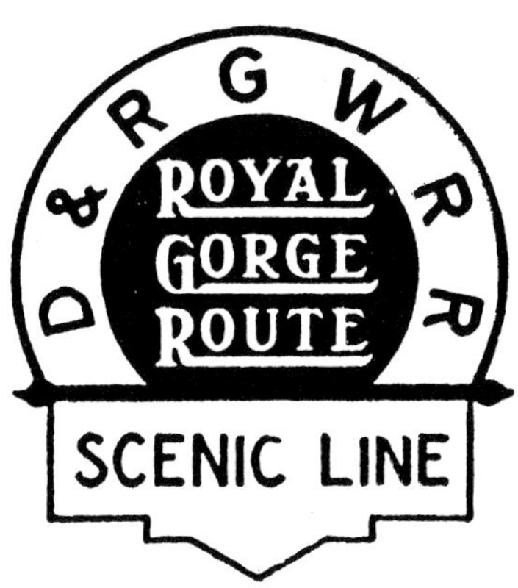

Emphasis was shifted to the standard gauge main line via the Royal Gorge and Tennessee Pass in the mid-twenties. While the original outline of the insignia was retained, new wording and colors (white lettering, red border, blue center), were approved by the Board of Directors on July 1, 1926.

Inauguration of Rio Grande service via the Moffat Tunnel on June 15, 1934 voided use of the Royal Gorge herald. While new design was being prepared, timetables carried additional slogan, "The James Peak Route." In 1936 the revised emblem incorporating the Moffat Tunnel identification came into use.

Change in company name required an alteration in wording in 1922.

Rio Grande

Modernization of the property under the guidance of Trustees Wilson McCarthy and Henry Swan encouraged a contest in *Green Light* for a streamlined adaptation of Rio Grande name. The design submitted by Miss Laura Bramkamp, now retired from the Purchasing department, was accepted and is still in use, having first appeared on company publicity in Fall of 1939.

Last insignia used by the Rio Grande Western, from 1900 until 1908, when the two companies merged, is a Utah adaptation of the original D.&R.G. Herald.

Independence of the Utah company was strikingly illustrated in September of 1889. While not an emblem in the true sense, "The Little Giant" holding the world in his hands, supplemented by Colonel Hooper's Denver & Rio Grande slogan "Scenic Line of the World" that appeared on public timetables of that date, indicates announced importance of the busy little railroad.

The top of this cover forms a straight edge for detaching mileage

SCENIC LINE OF THE WORLD
RIO GRANDE WESTERN RAILWAY

No. 1346
Rio Grande Western
RAILWAY.

REGULAR
1000 MILE TICKET
(Regulation amount of baggage allowed free.)
ISSUED FOR THE EXCLUSIVE USE OF
Mr. M. H. Coffin
G. R. Cooper

NOT TRANSFERABLE.
GOOD ONLY
When officially stamped and presented with coupons (mileage strip) attached, subject to the conditions named hereon.
Void for passage after date canceled in margin.

General Passenger Agent.

NOTICE—IMPORTANT.
The person in whose favor this ticket is issued MUST SIGN THE CONTRACT IN INK. It will NOT BE HONORED unless so signed, nor will any portion of the mileage strip be accepted unless signed for each ... terms of the contract (see Section 2).
Care should be taken to keep the mileage strip in its original fold within the cover, that it may be more easily handled by Conductors, and will not be liable to mutilation.

Read all the Conditions and Notices hereon.

24 23 22 21 20 19 18 17 16 15 14 13 12 11 10 9 8 7 6 5 3 2 1

25 26 27 28 29 30 31 Jan. Feb. Apr. May June July Aug Sep. Oct. Nov. Dec. 1891 1892 1893 1896

Patented June 1st, 1886.

Subsequent to 1890, when the Utah lines were built on their present location through Ruby Canyon west of Grand Junction, tracks standard gauged and the name of the company changed to Rio Grande Western, there began to evolve a diamond-shaped insignia, first publicized in 1893. Although still independent, the railroad continued use of the familiar Colorado lines' slogan. Note emblem in upper-left corner.

With emergence in 1947 of the heavy-duty, high-speed railroad we know today, a striking new herald in keeping with Rio Grande's position in the transcontinental picture became a necessity. The colorful emblem, now so familiar on freight and passenger equipment and in advertising, is indeed appropriate. Designed by Publicity Manager Carlton Sills and his staff, it was adopted in 1948.

Courtesy of Green Light, 1959, Denver and Rio Grande Western.

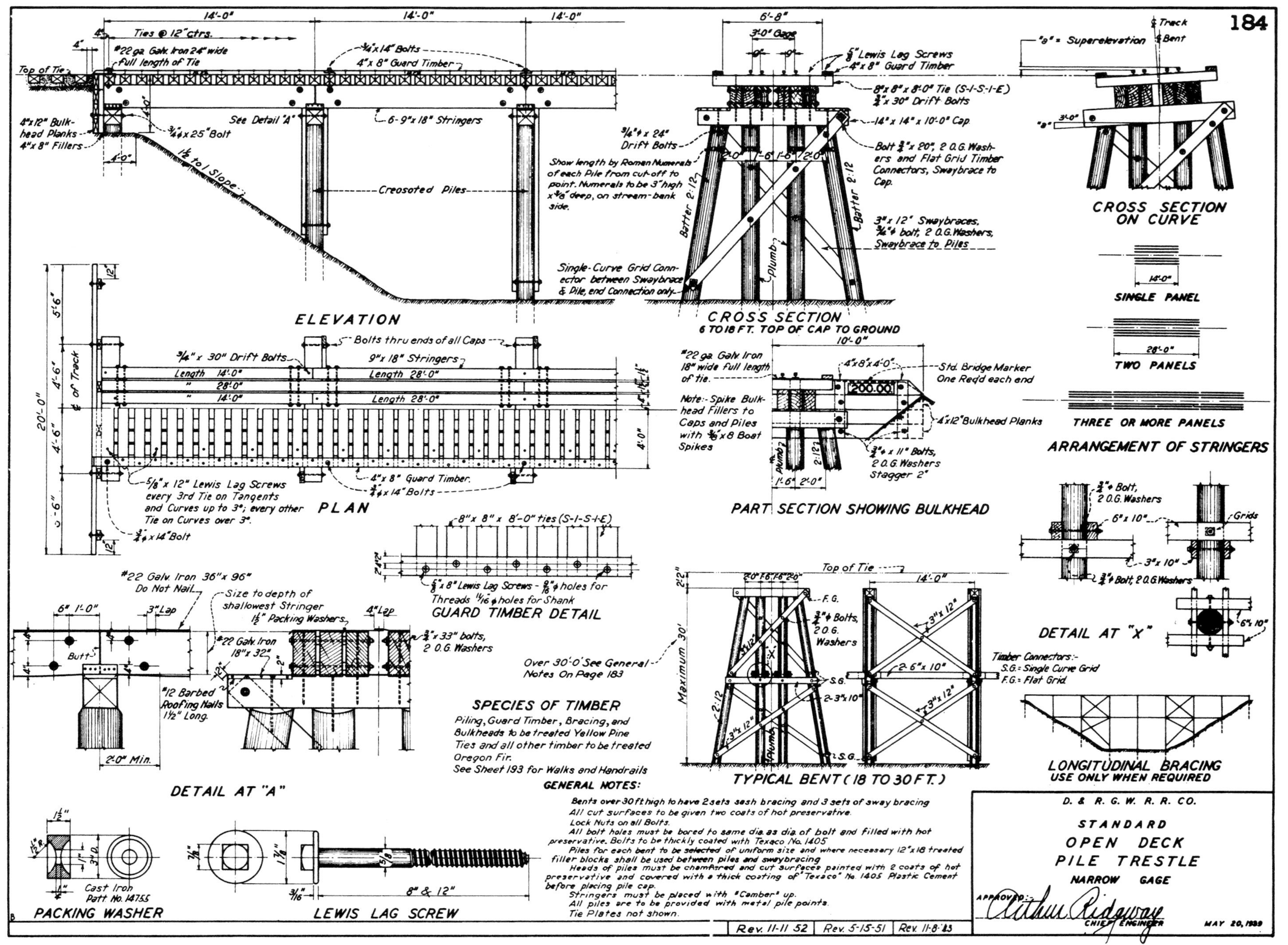
184
ELEVATION
PLAN
CROSS SECTION
6 TO 18 FT. TOP OF CAP TO GROUND
CROSS SECTION ON CURVE
SINGLE PANEL
TWO PANELS
THREE OR MORE PANELS
ARRANGEMENT OF STRINGERS
PART SECTION SHOWING BULKHEAD
DETAIL AT "X"
TYPICAL BENT (18 TO 30 FT.)
LONGITUDINAL BRACING
USE ONLY WHEN REQUIRED
GUARD TIMBER DETAIL
DETAIL AT "A"
PACKING WASHER
LEWIS LAG SCREW
Ties @ 12" ctrs.
#22 ga. Galv. Iron 24" wide full length of Tie
¾"x 14" Bolts
4"x 8" Guard Timber
See Detail "A"
6-9"x 18" Stringers
4"x 12" Bulkhead Planks
4"x 8" Fillers
¾"φx 25" Bolt
1½ to 1 Slope
Creosoted Piles
Show length by Roman Numerals of each Pile from cut-off to point. Numerals to be 3" high x ⅛" deep, on stream-bank side.
Single-Curve Grid Connector between Swaybrace & Pile, end Connection only.
⅝" Lewis Lag Screws
4"x 8" Guard Timber
8"x 8"x 8'-0" Tie (S-1-S-1-E)
¾"x 30" Drift Bolts
14"x 14"x 10'-0" Cap
¾"φ x 24" Drift Bolts
Bolt ¾"x 20", 2 O.G. Washers and Flat Grid Timber Connectors, Swaybrace to Cap.
3"x 12" Swaybraces, ¾"φ bolt, 2 O.G. Washers, Swaybrace to Piles
"e" = Superelevation
℄ Track
℄ Bent
Bolts thru ends of all Caps
¾" x 30" Drift Bolts
9"x 18" Stringers
⅝"x 12" Lewis Lag Screws every 3rd Tie on Tangents and Curves up to 3°; every other Tie on Curves over 3°.
¾"φ x 14" Bolt
4"x 8" Guard Timber.
¾"φx 14" Bolts
#22 ga. Galv. Iron 18" wide full length of tie.
Note:- Spike Bulkhead Fillers to Caps and Piles with ⅜"x 8 Boat Spikes
4"x 8"x 4'-0"
Std. Bridge Marker One Req'd each end
4"x 12" Bulkhead Planks
¾"φ x 11" Bolts, 2 O.G. Washers Stagger 2"
8"x 8" x 8'-0" ties (S-1-S-1-E)
⅝"x 8" Lewis Lag Screws - 9/16"φ holes for Threads 11/16φ holes for Shank
#22 Galv. Iron 36"x 96" Do Not Nail.
Size to depth of shallowest Stringer
1½" Packing Washers
¾"x 33" bolts, 2 O.G. Washers
#22 Galv. Iron 18"x 32"
#12 Barbed Roofing Nails 1½" Long.
Over 30'-0" See General Notes On Page 183
Top of Tie
Maximum 30'
¾"φ Bolts, 2 O.G. Washers
Timber Connectors:-
S.G. = Single Curve Grid
F.G. = Flat Grid
¾"φ Bolt, 2 O.G. Washers
Grids
Cast Iron Patt. No. 14755
SPECIES OF TIMBER
Piling, Guard Timber, Bracing, and Bulkheads to be treated Yellow Pine
Ties and all other timber to be treated Oregon Fir.
See Sheet 193 for Walks and Handrails
GENERAL NOTES:
Bents over 30 ft high to have 2 sets sash bracing and 3 sets of sway bracing
All cut surfaces to be given two coats of hot preservative.
Lock Nuts on all Bolts.
All bolt holes must be bored to same dia. as dia. of bolt and filled with hot preservative. Bolts to be thickly coated with Texaco No. 1405
Piles for each bent to be selected of uniform size and where necessary 12"x 18 treated filler blocks shall be used between piles and swaybracing
Heads of piles must be chamfered and cut surfaces painted with 2 coats of hot preservative and covered with a thick coating of "Texaco" No. 1405 Plastic Cement before placing pile cap.
Stringers must be placed with "Camber" up.
All piles are to be provided with metal pile points.
Tie Plates not shown.
D. & R. G. W. R. R. CO.
STANDARD
OPEN DECK
PILE TRESTLE
NARROW GAGE
APPROVED: Arthur Ridgway
CHIEF ENGINEER
MAY 20, 1939
Rev. 11-11 52
Rev. 5-15-51
Rev. 11-8-43

Chapter 18

One Hand For The Ship

One of the inviolable rules of safety practiced by sailors in the days of the windjammer was one hand for the ship and one hand for a safe handhold.

This was a good rule to follow when riding the rear end of a Narrow Gauge freight train. There were no hydraulic shock absorbers on the crackerbox crummies, the track left a lot to be desired for smoothness, and slack adjustment was often times rapid and unannounced.

Couple these facts with the interior dimensions of the waycar on top of the wheels set three feet apart, and you have not only an impractical set-up for installing Chic Sales, but an ideal condition for ludicrous and embarassing accidents. The Rio Grande was not about to install toilets in the narrow gauge cabooses, and the train crew members preferred to use the available space for bachelor quarters. So they used whatever was convenient as safely as possible.

On each end of a narrow gauge crew car was a steel ladder twelve inches wide located near the center and rear edge of the platforms to provide access to the roof should it become necessary to go high for brakes or retainers.

Though spindly and narrow, these ladders were sturdy. When the intake of strong black caboose coffee exceeded the

Locomotive #489 helps a train over the Monarch branch in September of 1954. ***John Krause/Dr. Richard Severance collection***

tank capacity of the drinker, the time-proven safe method for relief was to go to the back platform and belly up tightly to the ladder.

This first move was followed by wrapping both arms around the steel beams, carefully unbuttoning your fly and proceeding with what was at hand, being sure, of course, that the wind was favorable. But above all, looking out for any sounds or other warnings foretelling slack adjustment.

All of these precautions were taken only when disposal of surplus coffee was entirely safe. Forget any one of them or become careless, and you were in trouble.

One conductor who epitomized all a trainman on the old Narrow Gauge was expected to be *did* get careless. He was long, lank and surefooted, and a veteran of many miles of narrow gauge freight train operation.

But even a man such as this could get involved in an embarrassing situation he would prefer not to have raked up to be laughed about. So, without naming names, this model of a Narrow Gauge brakeclub wielder found himself one fine summer morning flying through the air toward a sandy spot just west of the first bridge over the Animas River on the Farmington Branch with his fly unbuttoned and his coffee discharge tool in hand.

The callboy had misread his clock and woke up the Skipper a half hour earlier than he should have. To kill time, the too-early-awakened conductor polished off a large pot of coffee. Reporting for work, the crew found their engine still on the cinder pit, so they returned to the beanery for a few more cups of mud.

FEELING PRESSURE

By the time the train left Carbon Junction, the Skipper was feeling the pressure of too much coffee, but the track was too rough and curvy to make an immediate trip to the rear platform. He just sat and squirmed until he reached the smoother track beyond Posta. Then he made a rapid descent from the cupola and hurried to the back platform.

He bellied up to the ladder in approved fashion, carefully wrapped both arms around it, and prepared for action. But with the anticipation of relief and the beauty of a perfect morning to appreciate, he plain forgot where he was. Fully relieved, he stepped back from the ladder and started to use both hands to make himself presentable.

At the same instant, on a left-hand curve just beyond the bridge, a doe and her fawn broke out of roadside brush and started across the track. The engineer put a shot of air under the cars, causing the rear end to run in without the usual clatter of couplers to warn the Skipper. He found himself being tumbled rear end over appetite toward a patch of sand just beyond the west abutment of the bridge.

The rear brakie saw him go and pulled the air to stop the train and went back to pick up the remains. But that Skipper was a tough man, with the reflexes of a cat. The brakie found him sitting in the sand just finishing putting away his discharge tool and buttoning up. He was cussing the hoghead in three or four languages, swearing that the first s-o-b that told what had happened would be licked.

You can't keep a good man, or a good story, down. After a couple of days, the word was out, and the bosses at Division headquarters were sending wires asking why rules were not being complied with and reports, giving full details, of the accident made and transmitted.

#268 handles a clean-up train and makes smoke signals in the clear Colorado sky. *John Krause/Dr. Richard Severance collection*

A couple years later the rear brakie on an eastward extra forgot for a few precious seconds as the caboose came off the east end of the Willow Creek bridge five miles west of Chama. The conductor was busy preparing his reports and waybills and not watching his working partner closely. Needing him for some information, he looked for him but unsuccessfully; there was only himself on the rear car nor did he see anyone going over the top. Concerned, he pulled the air and stopped his train about two miles beyond the bridge. To be sure the train stayed anchored, he opened the rear anglecock and started walking back at full speed.

This time there was no soft, warm bed of sand to cushion the landing of the flying trainman. He landed in a thicket of scrub oak. Needless to say, the conductor found a mighty sick and badly lacerated trainman, fortunately with no broken bones.

These were not the only two men "throwed" by a narrow gauge caboose or car. It happened every once in awhile, but the crews were close-mouthed about the incidents. A man was not considered fit to belong to the clan until he could go high and over the top from one end of a train to the other through wind, rain, hail or snow. A few falls were the way of learning, so to ridicule a brother for taking a spill just was not ethical. But when the incident was caused by getting careless and using both hands to button up, the story had a habit of being made public.

D. & R.G. W. R.R.

SYSTEM

Chapter 19

An' Some of 'Em Was Brave An' Some Was Not

Bravery in a man is proven by the doing, not by the noise he makes, and the truly courageous man is fuller of bravery in the midst, than in the beginning of danger.

When Monero coal mines were producing coal most actively, the miners constituted a hodgepodge of races. There were New Mexicans, Italians, Scots, Welsh, English and other nationalities. Among these was Big George from Alabama. Big George was bigger than big and twice as strong. He was a kindly man with a mouthful of white teeth that showed often as his shiny black face split to smile. And Big George smiled a lot, for he was a happy, go lucky man, and every man's friend—until he started drinking.

Then he was mean, big and mean, and murderous. Whisky

Santa Fe, New Mexico's joint D&RGW and New Mexico Central RR yard and depot circa 1928. Note three-rail tracks in yard account of the interchange with the Santa Fe; but not all tracks in yard were standard gauge, and crews had to be careful. It seems D&RGW engine #174 was in NMC RR use with a postal car, combine and coach. The D&RGW and NMC also had an interchange near Gallinas, New Mexico involving the Rio Grande and Southwestern RR which joined the main D&RGW narrow gauge line at Lumberton, New Mexico. By 1928 the RG&SW had been pulled up, but the NMC RR was still operating. ***Santa Fe Railway Co. collection/Museum of New Mexico***

spelled trouble to Big George, and if it did not come to him, he went looking for it. His search meant trouble for the people he mixed with when he was looking for it. The giant Black, ordinarily kindly, was doubly dangerous because, living alone, nobody knew at what point he started drinking. His demeanor, talk, and actions changed but little until that monment when among a group of people he went amok.

When the little voices started talking to him, Big George carried a heavy folding Case knife with a long sharp blade and two Colt's 44's in the pockets of an old army overcoat. The Colt's were not well cared for, but they were workable. George wasn't very proficient with them. And that is a most deadly combination—two heavy pistols and a man who does not know how to use them. Innocent bystanders often are the victims.

It was during a Chinook period one February when George started a drinking bout. He climbed on the Durango-bound passenger train looking sober and smiling at idlers on the station platform. The next Monero heard of him was a few days later when Peg Leg Steve, the station agent, copied a message for the deputy sheriff to arrest Big George when he arrived on that day's train. George had gone berserk at a dance in Webtown at Durango. Two or three men were badly, but not fatally cut up; a woman bystander had been wounded by a pistol shot and the dance hall was a shambles.

Big George had walked away in the darkness and boarded No. 116 east of Durango. The conductor had reported from Ignacio that George was on board and had bought a ticket for Monero.

Now, for political reasons, and to cater to the vanity of his constituents, county sheriffs very often appointed several deputy sheriffs in each community. About all that went with the appointments were a star and an engraved certificate. Few people took the deputies seriously, least of all the deputies themselves.

When Peg Leg Steve delivered the message of George's coming to the senior deputy, he acted as he thought a defender of the public should and armed himself, pinning on his badge first, of course. Then he searched out the other pseudo law officers, and they pinned on their badges, and belted on their pistols. At the mine commissary about a dozen other guys wanted to play posse men. So they were deputized and armed.

There were enough Matt Dillons and firearms assembled at the depot to have stood off Clay Allison, the James Boys, and the Dalton Gang all at the same time. And what each posse man said they were going to do to poor old Big George was a crime to the jay birds. George was unanimously considered as the monster of the year and open season was declared on him. The only man not talking loud was Peg Leg Steve—he just went on methodically selling tickets and preparing for the train's arrival.

HEROES LINED UP

A few minutes before the engine appeared around the curve, the bloodthirsty army of self-proclaimed heroes divided and lined up on each side of the tracks. Weapons were given.a final inspection and readied for firing.

The engineer pulled the string of varnish to the usual smooth stop at the platform, and all the passengers, forewarned by the train crew, unloaded from the car Big George was in and scuttled for safety.

George was on the train all right, and he had no intentions of coming off peaceably. There he sat in a seat at the rear of the coach, garbed in his old army coat and holding a Colt's in either big black fist rested on the back of the seat ahead.

The brave possemen were not saying a word. They stared through the windows at Big George, then self-consciously at each other. A lot of clicks were heard as gun hammers were raised then lowered, raised and lowered. But not a man made

Passenger train enroute to Lake City on high trestle five miles below Lake City circa 1890. *Colorado RR Museum/R.W. Richardson*

a move to point a gun toward George nor started toward the coach steps to go after the waiting man. All of a sudden all the brave defenders of the community were all very unbrave, and wished they had not accepted the pretty badges.

Peg Leg and the conductor stood in the waiting room door watching. A few words passed between them and Steve turned into his office, laid his Agent's cap on the top of the safe and picked up a three pound single-jacking hammer from the same place. The wooden peg tapped a rhythm on the waiting room floor that was muted as Steve reached the cinder platform and walked leisurely toward the step box at the vestibule of George's fort-up. A foot was raised to the step box, and the peg leg drawn up. This was repeated until the handicapped station agent stood on the vestibule platform of the coach.

Then Steve transferred the hammer to his left hand, rubbed his right dry on his pants leg and returned the hammer to it. With his left he opened the door and stepped through.

"George, lay down your guns and come out, or I'll have to come for you."

"I ain't goin' to lay 'em down, Mr. Steve, and I ain't coming out." The two big bored pistols came up a little higher and the hammer of one clicked as it came to full cock.

"Then I'm coming for you, Big George." And the peg leg started a steady tapping toward the rear of the coach. One seat, two seats, then three, were passed.

"God Almighty, Mr. Steve. Don't make me blast you. Please stop. I ain't comin' out. Man, don't make me shoot you."

"Either shoot or come, George." The slow, even tapping continued and sweat broke out on the black face as the second Colt was cocked.

When Steve was midway of the coach, the right pistol came up to firing position and George's hand started tightening, but the wooden leg just kept tapping by one seat after another.

GUN HAMMERS CLICK

All of a sudden, tears joined the sweat on George's face. Two gun hammers clicked as they were carefully lowered and there were two thuds as the pistols were dropped to the seat in front of George. The two big arms folded on the seat back and a black head fell on them. Great muffled sobs came from the sagging body.

Steve laid down the hammer and walked to the crying man and laid a comforting hand on his shoulder, "Come on now, George. You're all right and ain't anybody going to touch you."

George wiped his eyes and blew his nose, and the two walked out together with George ahead and down the steps. George turned to help Steve down. The posse men, again brave, started toward them.

Steve took George's arm and said, "Come on into the office with me, George."

Then he swept the line of armed men with his mild eyes and snapped out, "Don't a one of you yellow-bellies try to lay a hand on George."

Diesel #3000 was tested on the D&RGW by the United States Army Transportation Corps. ***Photo courtesy Douglas Harley***

Chapter 20

Justifiable Mayhem

Rule "K" in the General Rules of the Operating Department of the Rio Grande Railroad reads in part: "Boisterous, profane or vulgar language is forbidden. Employees are required to be considerate and courteous in their intercourse with each other, and must not enter into altercation with any person."

It was a rule that was almost impossible to enforce. Not everyone was boisterous and not everyone was vulgar, but profanity was universal. Officials were as guilty of it as the men they supervised, and the brass pounders had a vocabulary of usswords reduced to Phillip's Code that let a man do a heap of swearing over the wires with a minimum of dots and dashes. On the Narrow Gauge, profanity reached heights of expression unknown anywhere else because it drew upon American, Mexican, Apache, Ute, Navajo, and some Japanese, with a little Greek for good measure.

Respect for the injunction requiring them to be considerate and courteous in their intercourse depended on who they were holding intercourse with.

Then, that part about being forbidden to enter into altercation with any person was just wishful thinking. Men working under the conditions that existed, confined as closely as they were at times, were going to have questions or confrontations arise that only swinging fists could settle.

The one unbreakable rule in the code of ethics convering these fistic engagements was that neither witnesses or combatants went to the officials of the railroad with information. At least, not until the matter had cooled to the point where disciplinary action was improbable. Of course, the officers always knew about any fights within a short time, but they waited until they heard it direct at a date late enough to avoid a formal investigation that would make it necessary to fire the participants.

HE WAS DETOURED

If one of the battlers broke the code and came to the Superintendent, Trainmaster, or other officer with a charge and complaint, he was detoured with a standard answer. He was reminded that a complaint made by one employee

Form Local 2-4 R. T 18

THE DENVER & RIO GRANDE R. R. CO.

"DREWRY TICKET"

AGENT'S STUB,—NOT GOOD FOR PASSAGE.

When sold on order for any special individual case, the order with number of Ticket noted thereon, must be returned to Auditor's Office with Monthly Ticket Report. Where any considerable number of tickets are sold, and authorized by P. D. Circular, as for instance for a Convention, County Fair, Exposition, or anything of the kind, the number of the P. D. Circular authorizing the sale of tickets should be noted opposite the number of the tickets on Monthly Ticket Report to Auditor Passenger Receipts.

FARMINGTON, N. M., to Station Named in Margin Below and Return.

ISSUED DATE STAMPED ON BACK. VIA DIRECT ROUTE ONLY.

Expires .... 19...... Fare, $..................

CLASS ★ CLASS ★

133

If Clergy Put No. of Certificate Here.

THE DENVER & RIO GRANDE R.R. CO.

"DREWRY TICKET"

Form Local 1-F-C

AGENT'S STUB.—Not Good for Passage.

FARMINGTON, N. M. to Station Named in Margin Below.

ISSUED DATE STAMPED ON BACK. VIA DIRECT ROUTE ONLY.

Expires ________ 19____ Fare, $________

CLASS ★

Collection of Doug Harley

489
489

against another had to be written with the original to the company and copies for the appropriate union's General Chairman and one for the man complained against. This invariably squelched the complaint, for none of these men wanted to be on written record as being a fink.

One historic slugfest was staged on the platform at Cumbres one cool autumn morning. Its features caused real misery for the officers who could not let it be known they knew about it.

The Turn was called out of Chama about daybreak to move a train of lumber to the top of the hill. The wind was blowing hard, and all conditions were just right to bring the black frost out of the rails and make a slippery journey up the 4-percent. It was sand, sand, sand all the way, and constant attention to the firebox and throttle.

The engineer of the second helper had been running in the Valley and over La Veta Pass, but had just bumped back so he had to place on the Chama end of the operation. Upon his arrival at Chama on his first trip, he was careless, and drank Chama water before he had built up immunity to its impurities. The results were predictable: Montezuma visited his revenge upon him, and by the time he was called for the Turn, he had a severe case of dysentery.

The rear trainman, killing time around Chama and with money in his pocket, found a most beautiful pair of gloves, Indian handicrafted of buckskin. They were the color of sand and as soft as a young Indian girl's skin. On payday, cost was of no consequence. The proud possessor of the beautiful gloves reported for work on the Turn wearing them.

By the time the Turn stopped at Cresco for water, the hoghead was in misery, but he had time to leave the engine and relieve himself at roadside. He hoped he could hold off the next go around until the Turn reached Cumbres. But with the tonnage drag and slippery rail, time ran out on him. About halfway up Windy Point, he just had to go, and this put him in a fix. The fireboy could not leave his fire to handle the throttle and sanders, and the engineer could not leave them unattended. If he did not keep his power up against the train, a stall or break-in-two would result. Montezuma's victim did not want to be responsible for either of these.

Finally, he had only two choices. One was to foul himself, and he ruled that out. The other he resorted to: dropping his pants, he crawled up on the seat and stuck his bare rear end out of the cab window and let fly, literally. The strong wind picked up the watery discharge and plastered the side of the engine and the handrail at the steps. The biggest deposit was on this rail that was used to mount or leave the engine cab.

FEELING FINE

Pulling into the top of the hill, he was feeling fine, and greeted the rear brakie as he came over the top to cut out the helper and lead it around the wye with a cheery and profane greeting.

The proud possessor of the fine buckskin gloves answered in the same vein as he backed to the edge of the cab floor to grab the rail for descent to the ground. He was young and exuberant and instead of dismounting step by step he held the rail and slid to the ground.

First load of scrap rail from the Baldwin branch leaves Gunnison for Salida behind #489 in May, 1955. *Colorado RR Museum/R.W. Richardson*

1504. MARSHALL PASS AND MT. OURAY N

His well lubricated descent was fast and his landing hard. He sprawled and got up with a puzzled look on his face. Then he saw the mess on his gloves and got the first whiff of the stuff he had squeegeed off the iron railing. The puzzled look was replaced by a most wrathful one, and he started to breaking Rule "K" with a vengeance. He was using profanity, vulgar words, being inconsiderate, and not a bit courteous in the remarks he directed at the engineer.

Now, the hogger was not easily aroused, and he was sorry as he could be over the brakie's fouled gloves and tried to placate the mad, swearing man as he wielded the squirt hose to clean off the side of engine, the rail and steps. And all the time his ears were being bombarded with the choicest of impolite language, some leading to the question of the engineer's ancestry and mother's origin. That was going a bit too far. The hoghead shut off the squirt hose, took off his cap and jacket and climbed down to the ground.

Then the two went at it, and neither pulled any punches. Two days later when they got back to Alamosa, the marks on both their faces did not leave any doubt that it had been an epic violation of Rule "K", although the confrontation *had* cleared the air. The brakie was satisfied with the action and the engineer felt better because the brakie got it out of his system and withdrew his doubts about the origin of the engineer's mother. He had gone so far as to buy another pair of gloves to replace the trainman's soiled pair.

I was trainmaster at Alamosa at the time, and had noted the evidence displayed on the two men's visages that there had been an altercation, but did not ask any questions that would lead to me having to take disciplinary action. However, under the circumstances that started the battle, it was one that would be talked about. I had a difficult time evading receiving reports in a way I would not have to call for an investigation and hearing.

After a while with me procrastinating long enough, the story died, and I let the matter rest. To have done otherwise would have made it necessary to discharge a couple of good employees quilty of nothing more than a little justifiable mayhem.

Aerial view of Marshall Pass, east side. Buildings in the foreground are probably old Mears Jct. ***Colorado RR Museum/R.W. Richardson***

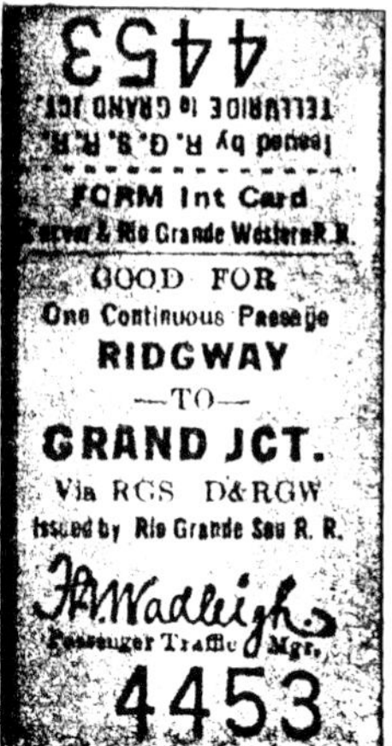
4453
TELLURIDE to GRAND JCT.
Issued by R. G. S. R. R.
FORM Int Card
Denver & Rio Grande Western R. R.
GOOD FOR
One Continuous Passage
RIDGWAY
—TO—
GRAND JCT.
Via RGS D&RGW
Issued by Rio Grande Sou R. R.
Passenger Traffic Mgr.
4453

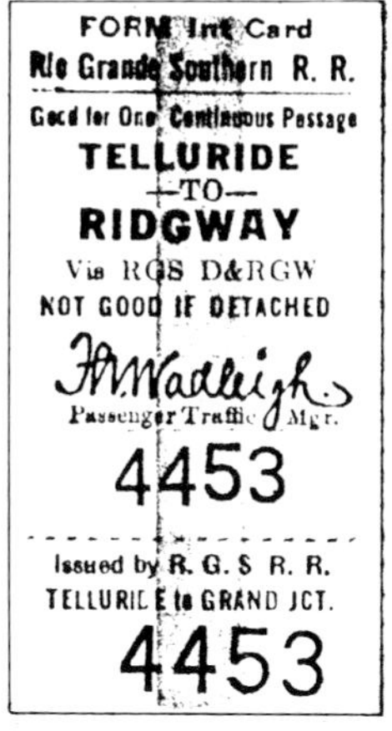
FORM Int Card
Rio Grande Southern R. R.
Good for One Continuous Passage
TELLURIDE
—TO—
RIDGWAY
Via RGS D&RGW
NOT GOOD IF DETACHED
Passenger Traffic Mgr.
4453
Issued by R. G. S. R. R.
TELLURIDE to GRAND JCT.
4453

Chapter 21

Narrow Gauge Hemorrhoid Cure - Without Surgery

Walter ("Walt") Ashbrook was a conductor on the narrow gauge, and he was a mighty big man. Usually he worked out of Alamosa on local San Luis Valley runs, east to La Veta or west to Chama. Wherever he worked, he was the biggest man on the district, for he weighed at least 250 pounds and most of it was muscle.

Walt had a few other unique characteristics. He never raised his voice, and he did not know what "hurry" meant. His handwriting was undecipherable, and he was the bane of life to any poor telegrapher trying to translate what his delay reports meant.

On one occasion his illegible scrawl caused two carloads of sheep to be set out at a blind siding named Darlington. The sheep were destined to Burlington, Colorado, off on another railroad. Those sheep violated the Hours of Confinement law before the mistake was discovered.

When Walt was called on the carpet for causing the mix-up, all he had to say to the Superintendent was, "Boss, I ain't responsible for that other man's education."

Now, Walt was, above all, a hard worker, always ready to do more than his share, and he was not a complainer. Far as anyone knew he had never known a pain or ailment.

That is, up until the big snow in late 1929 when Walt was stuck at Chama. Cumbres Pass was snowed in, and Walt's crew was called to man a plow and flanger train from Chama to Lumberton and return. The westward trip was without incident, but on the eastward leg the Ray flanger on the engine packed some ice in the switch point at the west end of Willow Creek siding, so the car flanger following the engine ended up on the ground with wheels on an angle and away from the rails. It was a four frog job.

MAKE TWO TRIPS

There were two frogs on the engine. Walt told the rest of the crew to start setting them while he got the two from the crummy. Ordinarily, two men would buddy up to carry each frog, but the gang with Walt had seen him handle one by himself many times so they just supposed he intended to make two trips. But that was not what the big man did.

He toted the two frogs out to the rear end of the caboose and lined them on the platform so he could walk between them. One under each arm, he came wallowing through the snow to the derailed flanger. He was blowing a bit hard, but

No. 50 diesel at Durango, Colorado, in June of 1966. ***Photo by Douglas L. Jones, courtesy Swede Norlin***

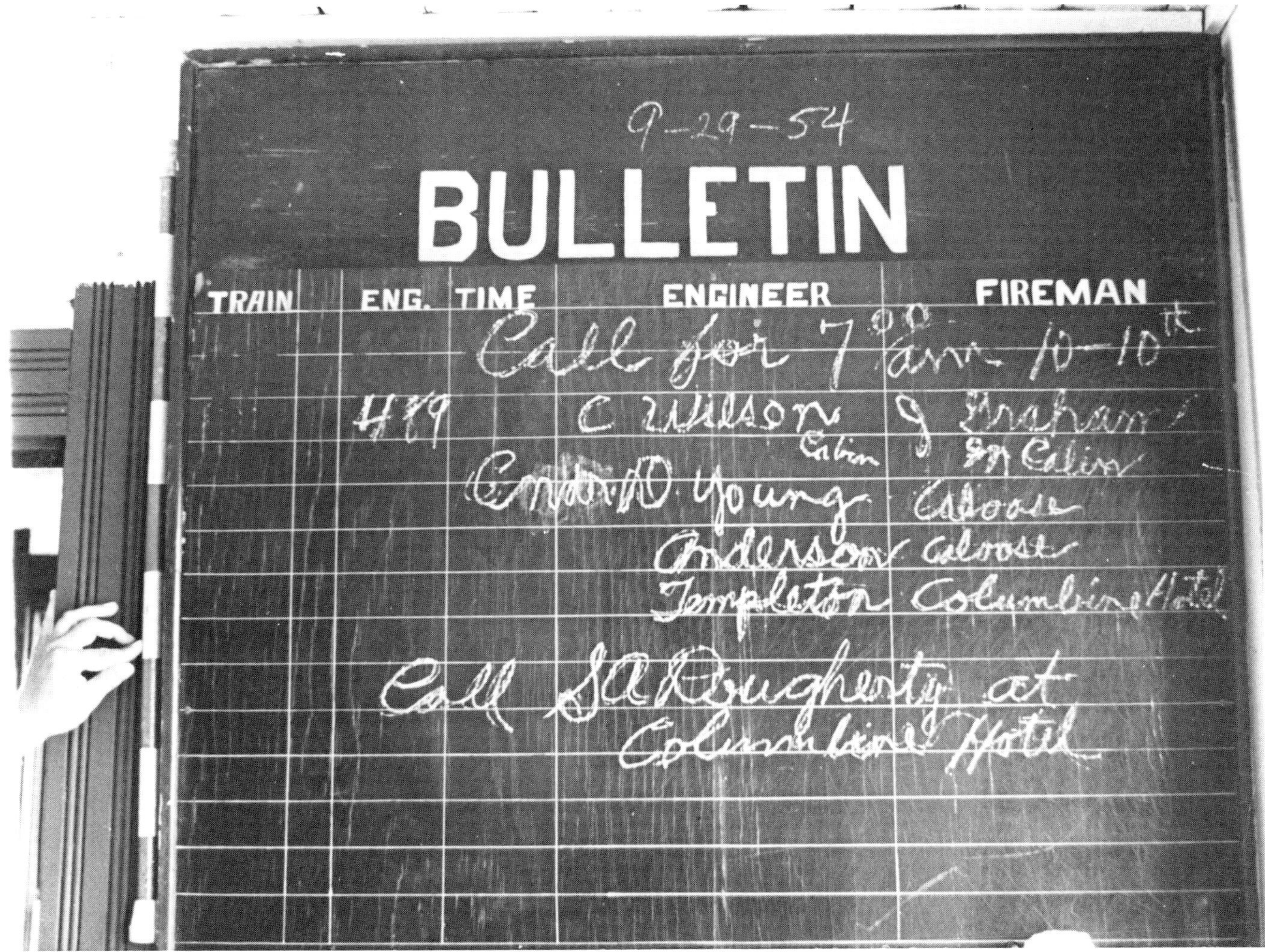

9-29-54
BULLETIN
TRAIN
ENG.
TIME
ENGINEER
FIREMAN
Call for 7 am
C Wilson
Anderson
Templeton
Columbine Hotel

Sargent Depot call board for September 29, 1954. ***Photo by Bill Wilson, courtesy Robert Sloan***

otherwise did not make any show of having done anything unusual as he dropped the two rerailing frogs at the derailment.

A couple of weeks later he was saying plenty—about his "affliction." Walter had developed a painful and pronounced case of piles. He quit being a willing worker, sharing in all activities, and became the narrow gauge world's worst complainer. He griped continually about his hemorrhoids and how a man just couldn't work when it hurt every step he took. The company doctor offered to work him over and relieve him of his discomfort, but too many of his co-workers talked about the godawful misery of being strung up by his legs like a beef being butchered while the doctor operated.

Walt wanted no part of this kind of butchery, so he went on griping, shirking his work and trying all the homemade and quack remedies he heard of. To hear him tell it—and he never let up—his affliction just kept getting worse. Later he even blamed the rest of the crew members and section men who had been with him at Willow Creek for letting him carry the two frogs all by himself.

At first his complaints were funny, but then they became a plain nuisance, and Walt's friends started evading him. Something had to give. Either the sufferer had to be talked into surgery or more drastic means had to be taken. The narrow gauge bunch, and Walt's wife, could not take much more. The campaign to lead him to surgery came to an absolute impasse. Walt would not agree to any knife work.

Finally, one evening in the cardroom of the old Chama Reading Room, a popular gathering place for railroaders, when Walt was going great guns about his woes, one of those present spoke up.

"Walt, there is one cure that never fails. It is mighty drastic, and hurts a little, but you can do it yourself."

The sufferer is all ears and bites. "You just name it. I'll try anything but cutting."

A lot of others were listening and kept straight faces when the amateur doctor said to Walt, "You just go down to the drug store and get you a bottle of Sloan's liniment. Tonight before you go to bed you take a palm of that liniment and you slap it on your piles."

"It will really do the job, will it?"

"Yes, sir, I'll guarantee you will never think about the pain of your piles again, no sirree."

BOUGHT LINIMENT

So the big sucker walked out the door, went to the drugstore, and bought his bottle of Sloan's liniment.

Now, two things the uninformed must know. One is that Sloan's liniment was mighty powerful as a cure for muscular aches of either man or beast, but must not be rubbed or come in contact with sensitive areas of the body. The other was

D&RGW eastbound freight just passing tank at Los Pinos. ***Museum of New Mexico***

that train crews batched and slept on their cabooses. When not on a train, these were spotted on a spur west of the depot. The night the boys advised Walt to try the liniment cure, his crummy was parked at the end of the spur against three feet of cold snow.

A lookout at the Reading Room watched Walt come out of the drugstore and head down the hill to his caboose. When sparks started coming from the smoke pipe to show the big man was preparing to retire, and to apply the cure, the gang put on coats and walked to a vantage point just above the caboose. A few allowed the joke had been carried far enough and should be stopped. Others said nothing doing, they were tired of Walt's moaning and groaning.

In the middle of the debate, a bloodcurdling scream of anguish came from inside the little red caboose. The next sound was the crash of the rear door coming off its hinges. Then a big ball of man dressed in red wool underwear dived head first through the door and over the railing into the snow.

The red ball straightened out, turned on its back and spread its legs, then started dragging big handfuls of snow up through the seat opening of the underwear to the liniment-pained area. Little moans of pain were coming from the heaving chest, but they turned to a deep sigh of relief as the cold snow became effective.

The spectators sort of slunk back to the Reading Room without saying much. They knew they had gone a little too far, and the usual evening of camaraderie fell flat so, one by one, individuals slipped away to feel ashamed of their actions in private.

In the long run, however, the results were good. For they became convinced, although Walt had suffered, they had done him a favor. For Walt never again spoke of his affliction. In the spring he let the company doctor arrange an appointment for him at the Salida company hospital where he had his piles taken care of properly.

Walt continued working for quite a few years on the narrow gauge, but nobody ever had the nerve to ask him about his affliction, or how he had got rid of it.

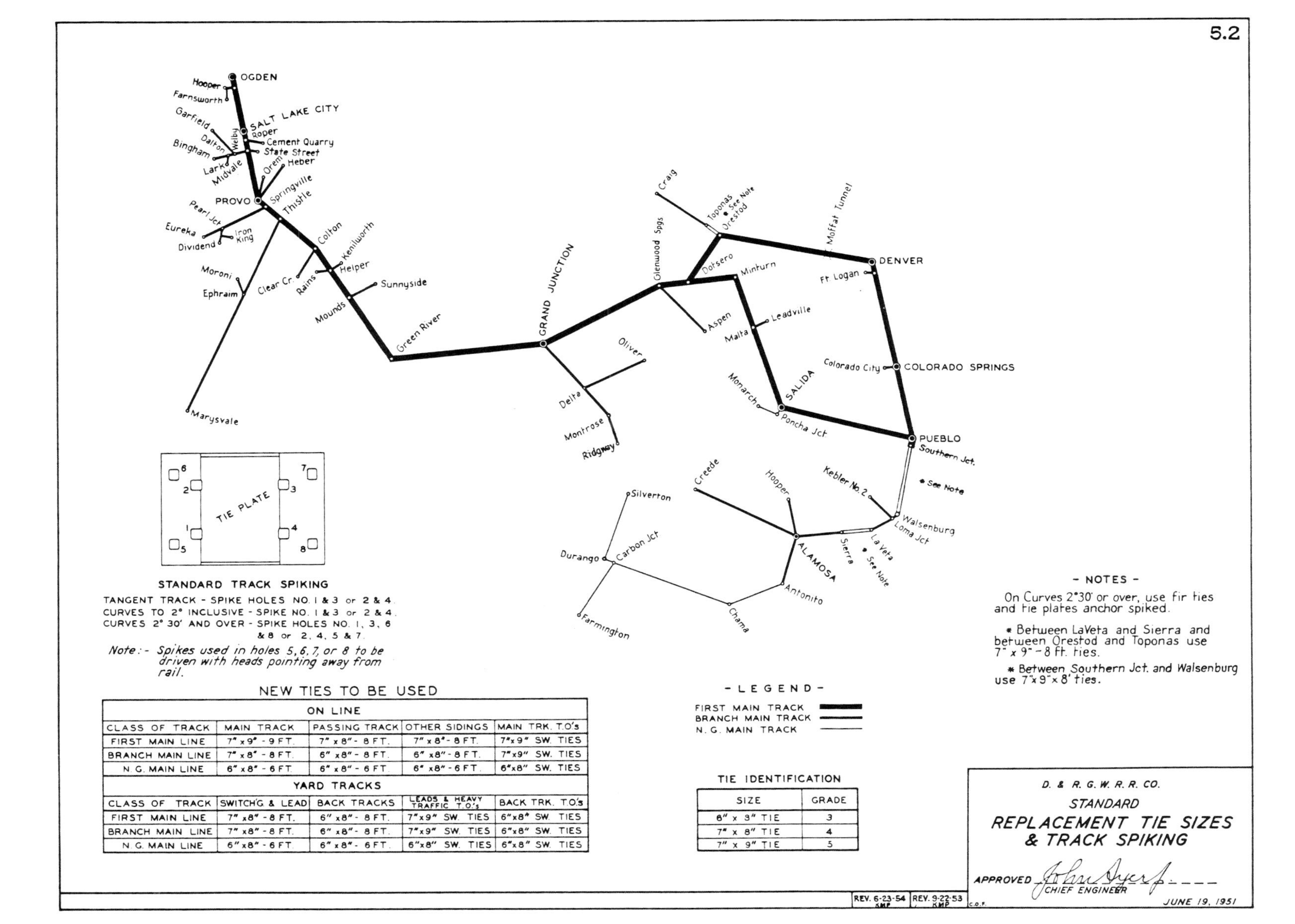

STANDARD TRACK SPIKING

TANGENT TRACK - SPIKE HOLES NO. 1 & 3 or 2 & 4.
CURVES TO 2° INCLUSIVE - SPIKE NO. 1 & 3 or 2 & 4.
CURVES 2° 30' AND OVER - SPIKE HOLES NO. 1, 3, 6 & 8 or 2, 4, 5 & 7.

Note:- Spikes used in holes 5, 6, 7, or 8 to be driven with heads pointing away from rail.

NEW TIES TO BE USED

ON LINE				
CLASS OF TRACK	MAIN TRACK	PASSING TRACK	OTHER SIDINGS	MAIN TRK. T.O.'s
FIRST MAIN LINE	7" x 9" - 9 FT.	7" x 8" - 8 FT.	7" x 8" - 8 FT.	7"x9" SW. TIES
BRANCH MAIN LINE	7" x 8" - 8 FT.	6" x 8" - 8 FT.	6" x 8" - 8 FT.	7"x9" SW. TIES
N. G. MAIN LINE	6" x 8" - 6 FT.	6" x 8" - 6 FT.	6" x 8" - 6 FT.	6"x8" SW. TIES
YARD TRACKS				
CLASS OF TRACK	SWITCH'G & LEAD	BACK TRACKS	LEADS & HEAVY TRAFFIC T.O.'s	BACK TRK. T.O.'s
FIRST MAIN LINE	7" x 8" - 8 FT.	6" x 8" - 8 FT.	7"x9" SW. TIES	6"x8" SW. TIES
BRANCH MAIN LINE	7" x 8" - 8 FT.	6" x 8" - 8 FT.	7"x9" SW. TIES	6"x8" SW. TIES
N. G. MAIN LINE	6" x 8" - 6 FT.	6" x 8" - 6 FT.	6"x8" SW. TIES	6"x8" SW. TIES

- LEGEND -

FIRST MAIN TRACK
BRANCH MAIN TRACK
N. G. MAIN TRACK

TIE IDENTIFICATION

SIZE	GRADE
6" x 8" TIE	3
7" x 8" TIE	4
7" x 9" TIE	5

- NOTES -

On Curves 2°30' or over, use fir ties and tie plates anchor spiked.

* Between LaVeta and Sierra and between Orestod and Toponas use 7" x 9" - 8 Ft. ties.

* Between Southern Jct. and Walsenburg use 7" x 9" x 8' ties.

D. & R. G. W. R. R. CO.

STANDARD

REPLACEMENT TIE SIZES & TRACK SPIKING

APPROVED John Ayer Jr. ----
CHIEF ENGINEER

JUNE 19, 1951

REV. 6-23-54 KMP | REV. 9-22-53 KMP | C.O.F.

Chapter 22
Gertrude

One day while the *San Juan* waited for a Cumbres Turn out of Chama, I saw a face at the lounge car window, went aboard and took this picture. Homesick? You bet.

Chama was the away-from-home terminal for crews working out of Alamosa and Durango, and the layover time was dreaded by all.

There were no kind of amusements, if you except the Chama Reading-Room, and nothing to do after sleeping and eating. The term "Reading Room" was a euphimism—the only "reading" done there was that of black or red pips on a piece of cardboard illustrated by some stylistic kings, queens and lesser nobility. It cost money to spend layover time in the Reading Room, even if the time being killed was spent at the pool tables instead of the card tables.

There was only one hotel (after the Star, owned by Mrs. Brown, burned in 1930). The one hotel was owned and operated by "Ma" and Bert Foster. In addition to rooms, it also had the only restaurant in Chama in the thirties and a large room for loafing and talking. After Prohibition was repealed, this room became a bar. Foster's Hotel was not a luxury hotel, but it was all there was; it was comfortable and homey and the food was tasty and appetizing (if you could overlook an occasional few strands of cow's tail or barnyard debris in the milk).

Railroads who did not shoot pool or gamble spent a lot of hours in the Foster "rec" room. At its best Chama was no place to try to kill time. It was boring, monontous and socially lonesome. So much so that some school teachers and other single females working in Chama and boarding with Ma Foster or living in some small nearby apartments she owned and rented, spent frequent evenings in the "rec" room with the railroaders and other male sojourners. In 1930 when I was working for Ma doing chores to pay for my eats while attending the Chama High School, I was too young to be permitted to spend my evenings with them. Maybe it was because I was young and naive, but it always appeared to me the people present were just spending social evenings together. Although occasionally as I cleaned the dining room, or swept the halls, I would see a couple climbing the stairs with the man assisting the girl with a fatherly arm supporting her buttocks or waist. I thought this was right gentlemanly of the man, for the stairs were steep and the runner worn. Once in awhile the girl would be loosening the man's tie or unbuttoning his shirt as they climbed to let him breathe easier.

2M Bks.-9-17 Form 3508

THE DENVER AND RIO GRANDE RAILROAD COMPANY

Engine No. 276 *Date* 5-6 *1918*

Train	FROM	TO	MILES Regular	Helper	Light	Time Departed	Time Arrived	Hrs. on Road	Hrs. on Duty
X	Durango	Glencoe				930			
	Glencoe	Durango	101				1055	1325	1340

Time Claimed—Mileage 101 *Overtime* 5 *Hrs.* 35 *Min.*

Called to report for duty at 915 *A.M.* *To leave at* 930 *A.M.* *Tied up at* 1055 *P.M.*

White *Conductor* Fred Nims *Engineer*

Explain Delays on Back F. W. Seybold *Fireman*

Collection of Doug Harley

FORM 3249
SECTION B

THE DENVER AND RIO GRANDE WESTERN RAILROAD COMPANY

CLEARANCE CARD

Station Durango Date March 12, 1960

Conductor and Engineman Extra USA 3000 East

Clearance Card No. ______ Authority to run extra from ______ to ______

I have 1 Orders for your train

ORDERS No. 219 No. No. No. No.
No. No. No. No. No.
No. No. No. No. No.

have been delivered and there are no further orders for your train.

Block Restrictions None

OK at 841 A M ______ Chief Dispatcher ______ Weaver Operator

This Clearance Card does not affect any orders you may have received.

Chief Dispatcher's initials are not required when orders are to be delivered and executed in ABS territory except as required by Rule 210-B.

______ Conductor ______ Engineman

To be signed by Conductor and Engineman when required by Rules 217 and 219

Collection of Doug Harley

WOODEN STRUCTURES

At this time, the indoor toilet facilities had not been installed. At the end of the hall toward the back of the hotel was a two-story wooden structure. The lower story was the toilet for the first floor of the hotel; the upper story, offset behind the first toilet above a metal lined chute, was the toilet for the second floor. Both of these dumped into a deep pit, and some twenty feet away was the well from which domestic water was taken by an electric pump. Back of all this was the barn and yard for three or four milk cows.

Each room, strung along the carpeted hallway, was equipped with a white enameled "thunder-mug" for nighttime use by the occupant who had to empty its contents each morning, as the hotel did not provide chamber pot service. Individual rooms had doors secured by old-style flat, cast-iron, locks that gave only token security, for any of them could be unlocked with a key common to all. If the occupant did not want to be distrubed while sleeping, or engaged in other activities, it was the practice to brace a straight-backed chair between the doorknob and the floor. Bare, low-wattage bulbs lighted the rooms.

One of the boarders, as I remember her, was tall, blonde, about 25 years old and with a good figure, a bit heavy in the upper structure. Her dress was subdued and her manner the same. She almost gave the impression of being an old maid Sunday school teacher, although she did spend time in the "rec" room and liked to talk and mingle with all present. She quietly but firmly resisted anyone's efforts to get close or familiar, and displayed a tendency to be aloof, almost a manner of hauteur. Her name was Gertrude. She would not stand for the men calling her "Gertie".

The consensus was that if Gertrude, with all her blonde hair, attractive face and fine fingers, was not such a cold potato, she would be a grand old girl. Then came speculation about what might bring about such a conversion. Take a bunch of railroaders with time on their hands, and an interesting subject to pursue, and pretty soon they are going to come up with an answer. If the object is to test a fellow employee for worthiness to belong to the fraternity, the answer will almost always be a practical joke, usually a rough one.

PROJECT GERTRUDE

Project Gertrude was put into effect one evening while Gertrude was occupied in the "rec" room talking. One of the jokesters slipped up to her room and checked her "thunder-mug" to be sure it was dry, then dumped in a large bottle of Bromo-Seltzer and a handful of soap flakes, recovered the pot and returned to the crowd.

After while, Gertrude retired to her room, slipped off her clothes and, before donning her nightgown, made use of the chamber pot. When her water hit the effervescent salts and soap flakes there came an explosion of foam that quickly boiled up around her lower abdomen and upper thighs. Gertrude was immobilized by shock and the foam kept on coming.

Breaking out of her shock, she screamed, and ran out of her room and down the stairs loosing one bawl after another. Wild-eyed and hysterical, she ran into the "rec" room and moaned, "Please! Someone get a doctor. I've got hydrophobia."

She stood there shaking and staring down at her foam—covered midsection, then looked up and saw all the laughing faces and realized she had been took.

Gertrude, "Gertie", became a member in good standing in the railroaders' fraternity when she let a tremulous grin split her face and said, "Oh! You *bastards.*"

Chapter 23

Ayer, Hoy, Manana, Y Para Siempre

(Yesterday, Today, Tomorrow and for Always)

Occasionally, when I was Trainmaster at Alamosa, I would get fed up with routine, especially during the summer season. For a break on a Saturday and Sunday, when there would be no motorcar activity on the line, I would take a light inspection car and leave Alamosa behind No. 215, the *San Juan,* and leisurely ride the iron to Chama to spend Saturday night, then go on west Sunday morning.

To justify the trip, I reported them as inspections, and made notes of any out-of-line conditions found, took pictures and observed the operations of any freight trains running. I scheduled my arrival at Chama to have time enough to look the yard, roundhouse and station over. The evening was given to consuming a big T-bone at Annie's Cafe, followed by a few hours in the bar at Foster's Hotel swapping tales and lies with anyone present, including off duty railroaders. My reputation with Rio Grande people was that, except when they were on duty, I did not see or make records for future reference of what employees did during their leisure time. Management was not always happy with my attitudes and actions, but employees understood and accepted the fact I might take a drink with them tonight and the next day if a man was drunk on duty, fire him. They did not see this as hypocrisy but as confirmation of their code. They believed each had a job to do, must do it fairly and impartially, but when it was play time, you played. They knew, from years of close association, I adhered to this code.

On one of these outings, along in late July, I left Chama a bit later than usual and spent some time at Monero sort of visiting around and talking to the few people left there. It was about noon when I reached Lumberton, and seeing that Max Read's General Store was open to accommodate the Mexican ranchers who had come to town to attend Mass at Father Myer's church, I set off the pop-car and went to buy some lunch material.

Unidentified Mexican home near Embudo. Autumn harvesting of chilis colorados (red chili peppers) was under way. Every house from Embudo to Santa Fe was festooned with strings of these chilis, hence the reason the Santa Fe branch was called "The Chili Line." Circa 1895. ***Museum of New Mexico***

Espanola Mercantile, Espanola, New Mexico, owned by Bond and Nohl. This was the single biggest trader and operator between Santa Fe and Antonito, Colorado, dealing in sheep, wool, beans, fruit, you name it. This was about the best customer of the Rio Grande on the Chili Line. ***Museum of New Mexico***

The large whitewashed adobe store had a shaded board porch and a number of natives were there enjoying a treat of cold bottled drinks, cheese, crackers, bologna and their favorite snack, sardines in cottonseed oil. I bought about the same and joined them.

Among the group, sitting a little apart, I recognized Antonio (Tony) Manzanarez, an old retired section man I had known well while living at Monero and his wife, Eulalia. 'Lalia was a few years younger than Tony and, after finishing their pop, took a book of wheatstraw cigarette papers and a sack of Bull Durham from her bag and rolled neat, thin cigarettes for both. Each smoke only lasted three or four puffs and she rolled more steadily as they talked together.

I did not pay much attention to their conversation until I heard Tony say, "Lalia, do you remember how it was when we left Velarde one fine morning after our wedding baile?"

Lalia's wrinkled old face looked almost young again as she turned to Tony and said, "Si, Tony, mi esposo, tengo muchos recuerdos—seguramente." (Yes, Tony, my husband, I have many memories—surely.)

MEMORIES ALSO

The old man laid a brown, work-scarred hand on Lalia's knee and tenderly said, "Si, cara de por vida, yo tengo muchos recuerdos, tambien." (Yes, my lifelong beloved, I also have memories.)

"I remember, so early in the morning, and looking back at Velarde from the hilltop and the smell of cedarwood smoke of the cooking fires, the dew on the grass and chamisa brush, the spider webs on them all strung with drops like the pearls on the Padre's robe. And your teeth as you smiled looked the same, you so small and straight in the saddle, the crows in the cottonwoods, your hair with its high silver comb was as black and shiny in the early morning sun. We turned our horses to go, and you began to sing. Your voice was like the bells on our pack burro. The long, slow miles, and our talking and laughing, the lunch on the bank of the stream, the love-making in the cool grass while our animals grazed.

"And, in the night with the moon so bright and the stars so close—in the blankets you were so soft and loving. Lalia, do you remember it thus?"

"Yes, Tony, I remember, it was like that. And you said to me as we lay close together, 'Ayer, hoy, manana y para siempre'. Yes, Tony I remember well."

A lot of people have wondered why I respected and loved the Mexican people of the Narrow Gauge so much. It was the little unexpected insights such as this that made it so with me.

481

Chapter 24

Long Jim McIvor

On one of my motorcar jaunts between Alamosa and Durango, I set off at Pagosa Junction and spent a couple hours talking with Felix Gomez.

In the course of the conversation, he told me of an old man named Jim McIvor, Long Jim, who had worked on the line when it was being built. Felix said Long Jim was approaching 90 years of age, living out his life in a sort of nursing home in Pagosa Springs, but was still a talker with a sharp memory. If the visitor brought a gift of a bottle of bourbon, he could be sure Long Jim would talk his ear off.

You can be assured I soon found an excuse to be in Pagosa Springs, accompanied by not one but two bottles of Kentucky dew. Jim was not hard to locate, and I was soon with him in a sunlit room, presented the gift and told him who I was, and explained I was Trainmaster on the Rio Grande between Alamosa and Durango.

It was easy to see why he was called Long Jim. Allowing for shrinkage due to age, he must have been at least six foot four or five inches in his prime. His shoulders still were as wide as the easy chair he sat in and the hand I shook, still strong, swallowed mine. Gloves and shoes must have been a problem for him when he was working—his shoe size must have been at least a fifteen. His eyes were clear and alive, a faded blue, and his voice had not a quiver of advanced age. What a man he must have been a half century or so earlier.

Long Jim shook hands, took the two bottles and sat one on the floor beside him. The other he broke the seal on, and taking a water glass from a table close to his chair, poured it half full. All this without having said hello or anything else.

DOWNED IT QUICK

He took a big mouthful and let it caressingly slide down his throat, smacked his lips and said, "Sonny, that is good stuff. Went two years once without tasting a drop. I'll tell you why after while if it don't slip my mind. Rio Grande you say. Boy, I built that railroad over Cumbres Pass and down the old San Juan. Well, got to be honest, I had a little help. Great old days then for a thirteen-or fourteen-year-old boy, guess I was about that age. 'Course there were a few a year or so younger but, Sonny, we was men."

While Jim was sipping his drink, savoring it and remembering, I asked him how he came to be working on the construction of the railroad. He oiled his tonsils again and started talking with me listening and afraid to interrupt.

"My old man was a rough cob. Went to church Sundays and let the preacher man beat it out of his conscience for his sins, real or otherwise. Rest of the week he whipped it out of us boys to make him feel better. I was the oldest, and he figured I should be out behind the team of mules plowing up rocks on that hardscrabble farm when the sun came up, and not come in 'til dark. One day for some reason, don't remember why, he come for me swinging a hame strap. I picked up a chunk of wood and hit him 'longside his head.

LEFT. A Class K-36 #481, a product of Baldwin in 1925, walks a string of gondolas over the Monarch branch in May of 1953. ***John Krause/Dr. Richard Severance collection***

Form 3530—300M.

The Denver and Rio Grande Railroad Co.

OIL TICKET

Date 1/29 1921

Station

Engine No. 272

From to

Valve Oil 1 pts.

Car Oil 1½ pts.

Rod Cup Grease lbs.

Driving Box Grease lbs.

Wool Packing lbs.

Headlight Oil pts.

Signal Oil pts.

Cotton Waste lbs.

Wool Waste lbs.

Roundhouse Foreman

THE DENVER & RIO GRANDE RAILROAD CO.

AGENT'S STUB.

COUPON PREPAID TICKET ORDER.

Drawn on Agent R.R.

At Denver Col

In favor of

For 1 ( ) 1st Class

Ticket.

From Denver

To Farmington

and

Via

Amount received, $22.15

Order Expires Sep 15 1906

The value of this Order to be included in report to Auditor Passenger Traffic for current month.

9303 FORM P.O.2

All items, collection of Doug Harley

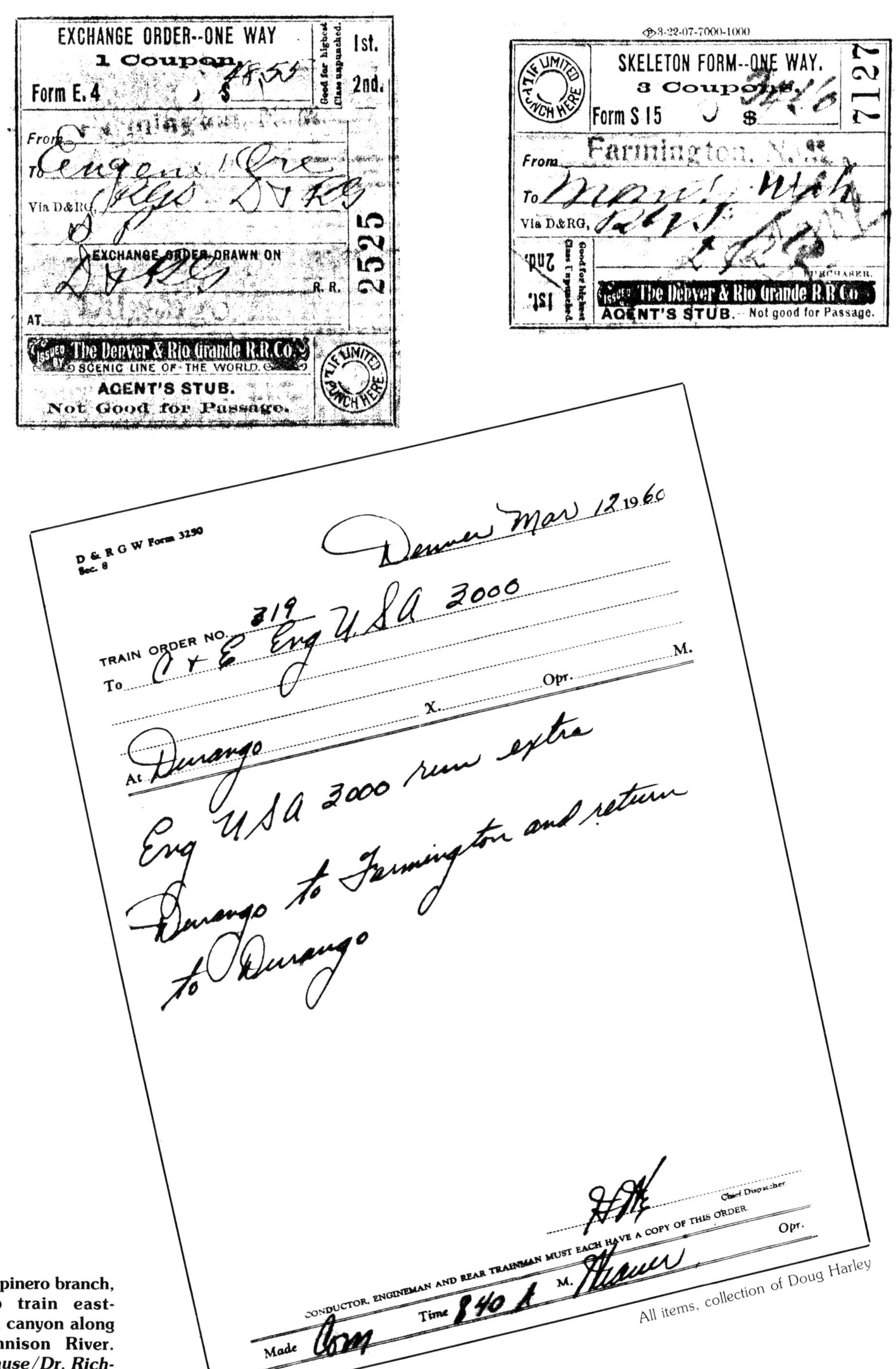

EXCHANGE ORDER--ONE WAY
1 Coupon.
Form E. 4 $
Good for highest Class unpunched. 1st. 2nd.
From
To Engine Ore
Via D&RG,
EXCHANGE ORDER DRAWN ON
D&RG R. R.
AT
2525
Issued by The Denver & Rio Grande R.R.Co.
SCENIC LINE OF THE WORLD.
AGENT'S STUB.
Not Good for Passage.
"LIF" LIMITED PUNCH HERE

3-22-07-7000-1000
"LIF" LIMITED PUNCH HERE
SKELETON FORM--ONE WAY.
3 Coupons.
Form S 15 $
7127
From Farmington, N. M.
To
Via D&RG,
Good for highest Class Unpunched. 1st. 2nd.
PURCHASER.
Issued by The Denver & Rio Grande R.R.Co.
AGENT'S STUB. Not good for Passage.

D & R G W Form 3290
Sec. 8
Denver Mar 12 1960
TRAIN ORDER NO. 319
To C & E Eng USA 3000 M.
Opr.
X.
At Durango
Eng USA 3000 run extra
Durango to Farmington and return
to Durango
Chief Dispatcher
CONDUCTOR, ENGINEMAN AND REAR TRAINMAN MUST EACH HAVE A COPY OF THIS ORDER
Opr.
Made Com Time 840 A M.

All items, collection of Doug Harley

LEFT. Sapinero branch, clean-up train eastbound in canyon along the Gunnison River. ***John Krause/Dr. Richard Severance collection***

He dropped, and I high-tailed it for the house, grabbed me a coat and a slab of cornbread, told Maw goodbye and headed down the road.

"Ended up in Kansas City, hungry and no money, but for sure wasn't going back to that farm. Met a man said he was going out to Colorado where there was a railroad building a new line, if you wanted to work they'd give you a ticket and feed you on the way there, then put you to work. I didn't know where Colorado was, and not much more what a railroad was, but figured would be far enough from Missouri my old man could not send the sheriff after me. And any work was better than walking behind a team of mules gouging out rocks and roots.

"Went with the man, lied about my age and when the hiring boss had about 20 of us lined up, fed us and took us down to the railroad yards. Loaded us in a boxcar that had straw on the floor, gave each of us a tarp and couple of blankets for sleeping. There was a stove in one end, a stack of firewood and a barrel of water with a dipper and another barrel to relieve ourselves in. Told us we would be fed once in awhile along the way and to stay with the car 'til we got told we had reached a place called Alamosa.

"About three or four days later we did. A man gave each of us a few dollars and told us to buy some heavy gloves, shirts, pants and socks and come back to him and he would feed us. We did and he did, then loaded us into a little car that had beds built up the walls. Car started moving about midnight and stopped about sunup, 'way up on a mountain, ground covered with snow and the wind blowing. Led us to a cookcar and fed us fatback, beans and cornbread. Coffee tasted like the potash likker Maw used to make hominy. Then he lined us up to tell us where to work.

DRIVE MULES

"Man asked me what I could do, told him could drive mules. And that is what I done that winter until the rails were laid over Cumbres and down into a place called Chama. Wished I was back in Missouri a lot of times, days when the wind blew the snow into my face, and my feet and hands were numb and white with cold. Then at night the bunk cars were warm, and our guts were full of lots of heavy greasy grub that was better cooked than Maw could. And we were promised we would be paid when we got to Chama.

"We were paid at Chama, and I had pockets full of big silver dollars, and after buying a new outfit of clothes, I decided to see what was so great about whiskey and women. Nobody, man or woman, asked me how old I was. Overdone it the first time with whisky, couple of drinks just made me feel good so I kept drinking, got real sick and heaved it all. Waste of money but didn't learn: turned into a real man-size drinker later. Was so sick it was a couple of days before I felt like learning about women. That sure did not make me sick, found out I loved them females and up 'til we left Chama building west, spent most of my money on trying to be with them a lot. Never got married but sure had a lot of good times with the gals. It's been a lot of years now I ain't even craved one.

"Well, we kept laying rail west, over the Divide and into Monero Canyon. Held up awhile at a place named Amargo waiting for more rail and ties. Bunch of drunk 'Pache Indians rode around and around our camp, shooting and yelling, what guns they was in camp was fired back and we all yelled, no blood spilt.

"Come to the Navajo River, us grading crew boys swum our teams across and rafted over our scrapers and kept on grading while a bridge was being built. Had to do the same thing at the San Juan and couple smaller rivers before we got to Durango. Think we laid into Durango about the 4th of July, anyway remember there was a couple of days of big celebration. Don't recollect much about it, paycar had not got to us, but them Durango people were so happy they was giving away a lot of drinks, women didn't give away nothing so had to just settle for a lot of free drinking and eating.

"Celebrating wasn't but just over when we started grading toward Silverton. Laid rail to Rockwood and then had to shut down for winter while rock gang blew a shelf around a bluff just beyond Rockwood. Same time, bridge gang was building a high bridge beyond the rock wall. Most of teamsters laid off temporary, I stayed on and hauled timbers and stuff over the hill to the bridge gang.

"Bitter cold, working and sleeping. Some toughed it out in the bunk cars, others dug some dugouts in the hillside. Paycar got to us a couple of times and, funny thing, when the paycar came, right with them came some wagons with some women from Durango. Couple biggest dugouts turned over to them for a warm place to operate. Them women was satisfying, but they must of been tough ones and wanting money, none of us had had a bath since cold weather set in, and it was too cold, even in the dugouts, to take off our shoes or pants. The gals only stayed three or four days when they came, but we enjoyed it while they was in camp. Some men even heated water and shaved. Me, I didn't have much beard yet."

EMPTY BOTTLE

Jim was lubricating his tongue and tonsils occasionally, and by this point had emptied the bottle below the half mark, although you could not tell it from his speech. His eyes did

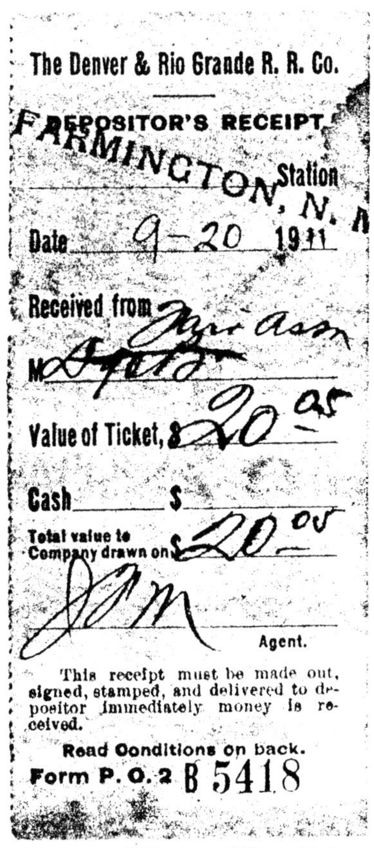
The Denver & Rio Grande R. R. Co.

DEPOSITOR'S RECEIPT

FARMINGTON Station, N. M.

Date 9-20 1911

Received from Mr. Asa ...

Value of Ticket, $20.05

Cash ______ $

Total value to Company drawn on $20.05

J.M. Agent.

This receipt must be made out, signed, stamped, and delivered to depositor immediately money is received.

Read Conditions on back.

Form P. O. 2 B 5418

Collection of Doug Harley

get brighter, and he was sitting up straighter. He did not have to be prodded to keep his story going.

"Got the railroad into Silverton middle of the summer and was out of work. Lined up with an outfit hauling with mules over the Pass to Del Norte, sometimes to Alamosa or far as Pueblo, but the railroad was cutting into our business. Worse, coming down the Pass toward Silverton was one man and animal killing bitch. Served notice on my next trip to Del Notre someone else would have to drive back. Boss asked me to go on to Alamosa to leave the wagon. So I did.

"Had a good stake, had been on the road so much couldn't spend any, and I heard a man named Sullenberger was cutting timber west of Chama and needed drivers. Rode the cars from Alamosa to Chama and hired out to Sullenberger. He sent me to his No. 3 mill at the head of Monero Canyon and east of the Spring Creek Divide. Got bulls instead of mules, but lots of ways easier to handle than mules.

"About a week before Christmas, boys in my bunkhouse made up a pot and laid in a supply of cheer from Chama for Christmas. Lot of 100-proof stuff. Christmas Eve the other dozen or so men of our bunkhouse went to a big shindig being held in the mill's hay and stock barn. I had a bad foot and stayed to home. Along about midnight it got to hurting terrible, and I thought a drink would ease the pain. One drink led to another, and I made a big hole in the stored likker supply, sometime during the night must have passed out.

"Along in the morning came to, as four of the boys, one each leg and arm, was carrying me out the door. I was pretty sick, wanted a jug of water the worst way, but all I got was cussing out for drinking more than my share of the booze. Carried me to a cross they had built alaying on the ground, laid me on it and tied my arms and feet to it solid. Then they drug me and the cross to a hole dug in the ground, stuck the bottom of the cross with me on it in the hole.

"Crucified on Christmas morning, and all I had on was my red underwear. Seemed like the whole camp showed up to see me punished for being a hog, and I got sicker and sicker and pretty soon all that whiskey had to come out. Spewed from my mouth, and I wet my underwear, no sympathy, just laughs and more telling me I deserved it. Women and most kids stayed away, but wasn't many men or big boys absent.

"When I started crying whiskey tears and begging for water, what I got was some more whiskey poured down my throat. Got sick again. Then the cars whistled for town and all the men took off to meet it to see if any pretty girls riding at the windows or getting off.

"When the men left, several of their wives came and cut me down and doused a lot of water over me to wash off most of the sick. Fixed me a big tub of hot water so I could bath and clean up and brought me a pot of coffee and another of hot, thick soup. Finished both off and held them down, then rolled in my bunk and plain died. Woke up next morning and got ready to go to work, so did my bunkmates and they didn't say anything to me. During the day, one by one, they came to me to tell me they was sorry about crucifying me.

"Some ways they did me a favor. I couldn't stand the smell of booze and for two years never touched a drop but then, one thing and another, gradually got back into the habit, drank whenever I could get it, have ever since, but have never took enough to get drunk again, course I got a big capacity."

A couple of long pulls direct from the bottle and he must have reached his capacity, brightness went out of his eyes and he sort of slumped in the chair, but had a little more to say while a couple of tears squeezed out.

"Mighty fine whiskey, son, glad you came by, come again soon, got a lot more to tell you. Wish some of my old pards could be here to drink with me. Just wish there was some of them left around to dig my hole and put me in it. Then shovel the dirt over me, and when the last shovel was thrown that they could line up around the mound, and piss on it. That's what we used to do for them we figured was the kind to ride the river with."

I lost track of Long Jim, but I'm sure he is up there driving a team of mules ahead of a Fresno scraper and helping Saint Peter build a narrow gauge railroad in the sky, still liking his likker and loving the girls.

D&RGW #453 leads a northbound freight with 13 Civilian Conservation Corp cars near Placerville on June 30, 1940. ***Otto Perry/Denver Public Library, Western History Dept.***

Chapter 25

Telling My Beads — My Narrow Gauge Rosary

Down along the San Juan I enjoyed the friendship once of a fine and gracious old Mexican lady. With her husband gone, and the children and grandchildren widely scattered, she spent many hours in her rocking chair before the family altar with a candle burning and her rosary, polished from much counting of the beads, in her delicately boned hands. Her still abundant hair was of a silvery sheen and as bright as the heavy cross of silver I had made for her to append to the string of rosary beads.

I do not know while running the beads through her fingers if she was going through the standard Catholic routine or if she was using them to stimulate memories of the past precious to her. I do know that occasionally while the beads slipped through her fingers she would smile to herself and start talking—not always directly to anyone in her presence. Her talk was usually of some remembered tender moment with her husband or some incident out of her childrens' past, either joyous, painful or ludicrous.

I wish I had her rosary and that it could talk.

I am neither a Catholic nor a devout person; I am not a fine, gentle old person rocking in a chair before an altar. Above all I do not have a well-worn rosary with beads to be used to recall memories, at least none such as Elena had.

My rosary is in my head, a string of beads composed of recollections of people, places, incidents (some ludicrous, some joyful, some tragic) of the Narrow Gauge.

My rosary is a string of beads that cannot be considered as a perfect circle, for there are pendant loops that are still part of the whole. Neither is there a starting point nor an ending point. Depending upon the circumstances and who or what brings a memory to mind, I can start telling my beads at any point of the string. If I were to affix a silver cross to my rosary to remind me of all the best, the worst, the most joyous, the most painful, I would place it at the bead that represented Cumbres Pass.

MAP OF NARROW GAUGE

The string of beads would fall into place, if laid down, to look like a map of the Narrow Gauge from Alamosa to Salida; a loop to Monarch, than over Marshall Pass to Montrose, through Gunnison, with loops to Pitkin, Baldwin, Crested Butte and Lake City. From Montrose the circle would continue unbroken to Ridgway, with a loop to Ouray. Thence from Ridgway to Dolores and onward to Durango over the Rio Grande Southern. Back to Rio Grande iron at Durango the circle would loop to Farmington and Silverton; to Pagosa Springs on a loop then to Chama to ascend Cumbres Pass and the downhill coast to Antonito for a side trip to Santa Fe before returning to Antonito to continue to a closure of the rosary at Alamosa.

During the 45 years I spent on Narrow Gauge territory, 39 of them actually employed by the Rio Grande in some capacity, I came to know intimately all of the circle, including the RGS where, for a period, I was assigned by the Rio Grande on a loaner basis to work during a time of crisis brought on by a water problem involving many washouts, washins along the Dolores River and westward to Ridgway.

Although Alamosa was Division Headquarters of the Narrow Gauge, and I lived there while working as Train Dispatcher, Chief Dispatcher, Trainmaster and Acting Superintendent, the longest time spent at any location on the Rio Grande, excepting Denver, for personal reasons I always start telling my beads at Cumbres and on Cumbres Pass. Marshall Pass and the Silverton Branch share a position in the string awfully close to Cumbres.

There was something about these three segments of the Narrow Gauge that built memories and produced pictures better than any others of what railroading was in the early days. And, even today, in recollection to me and thousands of railfans say to us, "This was railroading as it was in the beginning and it took MEN to build and operate this 3-foot wide Empire Builder."

Cumbres to me is a hodgepodge of memories of drifted snow waiting for the rotary to remove it; of being alone except for the clatter of Morse; of nights so cold it was necessary to stay awake to keep the cannon heater stoked to keep from freezing; of wondering if you and the section men down in the section house trying to keep warm had enough food to last until the plow finally broke through; of walking on a summer's eve out to Windy Point to look down the valley of Wolf Creek to Chama; in the Fall, from the same point, to be mesmerized by the panoply of autumn colors; in winter, on snowshoes, to view the same scene under an unbroken blanket of wind-driven snow and to see away down toward Cresco the black plumes of coal smoke of an eastbound rotary plow.

C.R. LIVELY DAYS

Then you could sit and wonder how C.R. Lively, the dean of Cumbres telegraphers, in his crippled state was able to abide spending all the years he did at Cumbres with only his wife, the sectionmen and car inspector for company, with the only break in the day's monotony the arrival and departure of the eastbound and westbound passenger trains to be depended on or the irregular pattern of freight train operations.

Then, there is a bead on the string represented by the high trestle over Wolf Creek at Lobato that recalls the many times I walked up from Chama when my father was operator there; early in the morning while grasshoppers along the creek bank were still sluggish from the night dew; of catching enough of these to fill a Prince Albert can to use for bait and catching foot-long Cutthroat native trout. And, cleaning those beauties while No. 115 rolled across the trestle and the fireman waved at me.

At Chama, remembering earning some spending money helping the agent unload the L.C.L. cars across the worn wooden deck at the freight room; of once earning a whole $5 bill painting the baggage/express trucks for him because he did not want to work out in the sun to do it himself. Much later when I was telegrapher at Chama to find there was still a feeling of excitement each day when No. 115 arrived going west and No. 116 later in the day arrived and departed toward Cumbres Pass. Even later, as Trainmaster, the deep feeling of satisfaction of a cold hazardous job accomplished when I rode the snow covered, iced-up rotary plows into town.

In memory, on westward, counting a bead at the old Azotea sectionhouse site and remembering Rosa, the Rose of Azotea, and the overwhelming, adolescent crush I had on her. Through Monero and hundreds of memories of the Big Depression and all that entailed, and my father trying to beat Morse and the provisions of the D&RGW Rulebook into my resistant head.

Lumberton, and the home with the Catholic altar in a corner of the guest bedroom, sleeping one night in the folding bed below the altar and having a nightmare of the blood of Christ's wounds dripping on me. To Dulce and a bead that brought back Emmet Wirt's store front and stopping to pay four times the regular prices for a Coca-Cola, cheese and crackers. The Apaches and the depot windows that for a long time when Tim Looney was agent there were painted black because Tim's brother, John, was serving a term in a Federal prison (his, John's, daughter in another) after being sentenced as one of St. Louis's most prominent racketeers. The daughter was there for reasons connected with the sales of bootleg liquor and the services of some ladies of pleasure.

Pagosa Junction (Gato), pulling our infant son out of the flooding San Juan River, holding him up by the heels while his mother squeezed his rib cage, and both saying a prayer of thanks when enough water had drained out so he could start yelling. And, a bit east of Gato in the season when the purple asters were blooming in profusion, walking home from fishing I saw a cluster of purple down in the willows and decided to pick a bouquet for my wife. I walked up to the willows and discovered why the purple color was so prominent. Our section foreman had a broad bottomed local Mejicana on her side with her dress up around her midrift but he had not yet fully overcome her reluctance and her bright purple bloomers were showing.

DURANGO MEMORIES

Durango, if there was a bead in my rosary for every memory of Durango, the Silverton and Farmington branches the string of beads would reach to Timbuctoo. There is the still-rankling memory of being hated for being one of the officers involved in discontinuing the *San Juans* and passenger service, and much later during the hearings aimed at final abandonment of the last of the Narrow Gauge.

Working in the upstairs of Durango's depot as the entire operating staff of the RGS, excluding Graebing, the superindendent and Boucher, the secretary-treasurer. And, the secretary-steno, a very bashful young lady who blushed scarlet every time I spoke to her, and was reputedly a man hater. (A number of years later as Trainmaster at Alamosa I was part of a raiding party serving a warrant of search and arrest on one of our dispatchers charged with mailing obscene material through the mail. In his files we found hundreds of nudes [his photography was explicit and excellent]. One group of transparencies was of my one-time steno taken in the Silverton area with mountains and waterfalls in the background. Lordy, that gal must have got awfully cold for she sure did not have any protective clothing on.)

One of my beads at Durango would be called L.K. Rust. He was a cantankerous operator about 5 feet two inches and a scant one hundred pounds, every inch and pound unadulterated meanness. He often said, "No big S.O.B. is going to maul me." To guarantee this away from the office he carried an old SA Colt pistol of .45 caliber tucked in his belt.

I was with him one evening going to supper when the pistol slipped from its berth and slid down his pant leg to the sidewalk. Unfortunately there was a city policeman near. He picked up the gun, unloaded it, returned it to LKR and warned him to never be found in public with it again.

On the RGS the agent at Placerville was a woman. She had taught her son to telegraph. Now, all movements on the RGS, including motorcars, were made by train order. One day the lady agent was uptown when Roadmaster Murphy showed up and wanted a running order to go west of Placerville. I let the son copy one and he repeated it back and got a "Com." About a half hour later I called Placerville and asked the boy if he did not think it was about time he asked for a clearance card for the order and asked where Murphy was. The boy answered that Murphy left some time ago. I asked, "What about his running order?" The reply I got was, "Murphy read the order over my shoulder and said OK and left." In reply to my next question he said, "I just filed the order for Murphy knew what it said." (My nerves held up because the only opposing movement was the eastbound "Goose" and it was scheduled.)

A number of years later as Assistant Chief Transportation Officer this same boy, now grown and working for us as a telegrapher, was promoted to train dispatcher. While examining him I reminded him of the filed train order. He looked at me a few seconds, dumbfounded, then said, "Migawd, don't you ever forget anything?"

RGS TENURE

My tenure on the RGS lasted only while the crisis was on, and until I insisted on Rio Grande pay scale, *plus* expenses. Graebing got rid of me quick as being too expensive for the RGS. But the short time I was there let me add a number of beads to my Narrow Gauge rosary.

While telegraphing I worked Montrose and Gunnison only on a temporary basis from the operators' extra board. These assignments were of long enough duration to give me more on-the-ground memories to cherish and make additional beads.

As regular agent at Crested Butte for about two years, I added several more pleasant ones. Like rushing to finish billing the day's coal production from the Big Mine (C.F.&I.), pushing Bill Purcell, Ernie Dean or Andy Anderson to get their train moving so I could "OS" them, then beat it across the hay meadows to Slate Creek for an evening bout with the hungry Brown Trout that came from under the grassy banks to feed each evening about an hour before dark.

On the Chili Line, a spot to remember was the depot at Embudo where, over the years while agent there, Mr. Wallace had covered the entire original structure with semi-precious stones collected in the area. The safe, except for the door, was covered with beautifully cut and polished slabs of agate, petrified wood and lavendar lepidolite. Wallace, using agate he cut and polished, made train order stylus points he sold all over the 48 states. He made the handles from cured pinon (pinyon) wood from the area and made the ferrules from native gold. (One of the few honest-to-God bawling-outs my father ever gave me was for breaking the point on his Wallace stylus while I was practicing copying train orders at Monero, when I was first learning Morse.)

Elena, the gracious old Mexican lady needed her rosary to recall the past—all I need is the sight of a picture, a few words from an old-timer, or a railfan, and the beads of my rosary start racing through my mind.

Southbound #461 emerges from the snowshed at Lizard Head, Colorado, on the Rio Grande Southern. Date is October 4, 1947. ***Otto Perry/Denver Public Library, Western History Dept.***

Rio Grande #454 at Placerville, Colorado with a 16-car freight train over Rio Grande Southern tracks in 1944.
Otto Perry/Denver Public Library, Western History Dept.

RIO GRANDE SOUTHERN

Rio Grande Southern

The Rio Grande Southern Railroad was incorporated in 1889 with Otto Mears as its first president. In 1893, the D&RG was appointed receiver, and the next year the RGS became a subsidiary of the D&RG. In the early years of the 1900s, the RGS was virtually left abandoned by the D&RG. The D&RG gave up control of the RGS in 1921, and the RGS was dismantled in 1952 and 1953.

Roundhouse and yards, with #375 switching, at Durango on October 2, 1947. *Otto Perry/Denver Public Library, Western History Dept.*

LEFT, TOP. Train #426, a mixed, was the last Santa Fe branch train at Antonito, Colorado, with eight cars in 1941.

LEFT, BOTTOM. This is Embudo, New Mexico, in 1940. Note all the rocks at right of station.

ABOVE. #484 sits at Dulce, New Mexico, in March of 1951 with a combine. *All three photos, Otto Perry/Denver Public Library, Western History Dept.*

Northbound freight crosses trestle near Leonard, Colorado, on the Rio Grande Southern with 16 cars and #461 helping.
Otto Perry/Denver Public Library, Western History Dept.

Rio Grande
Rio Grande

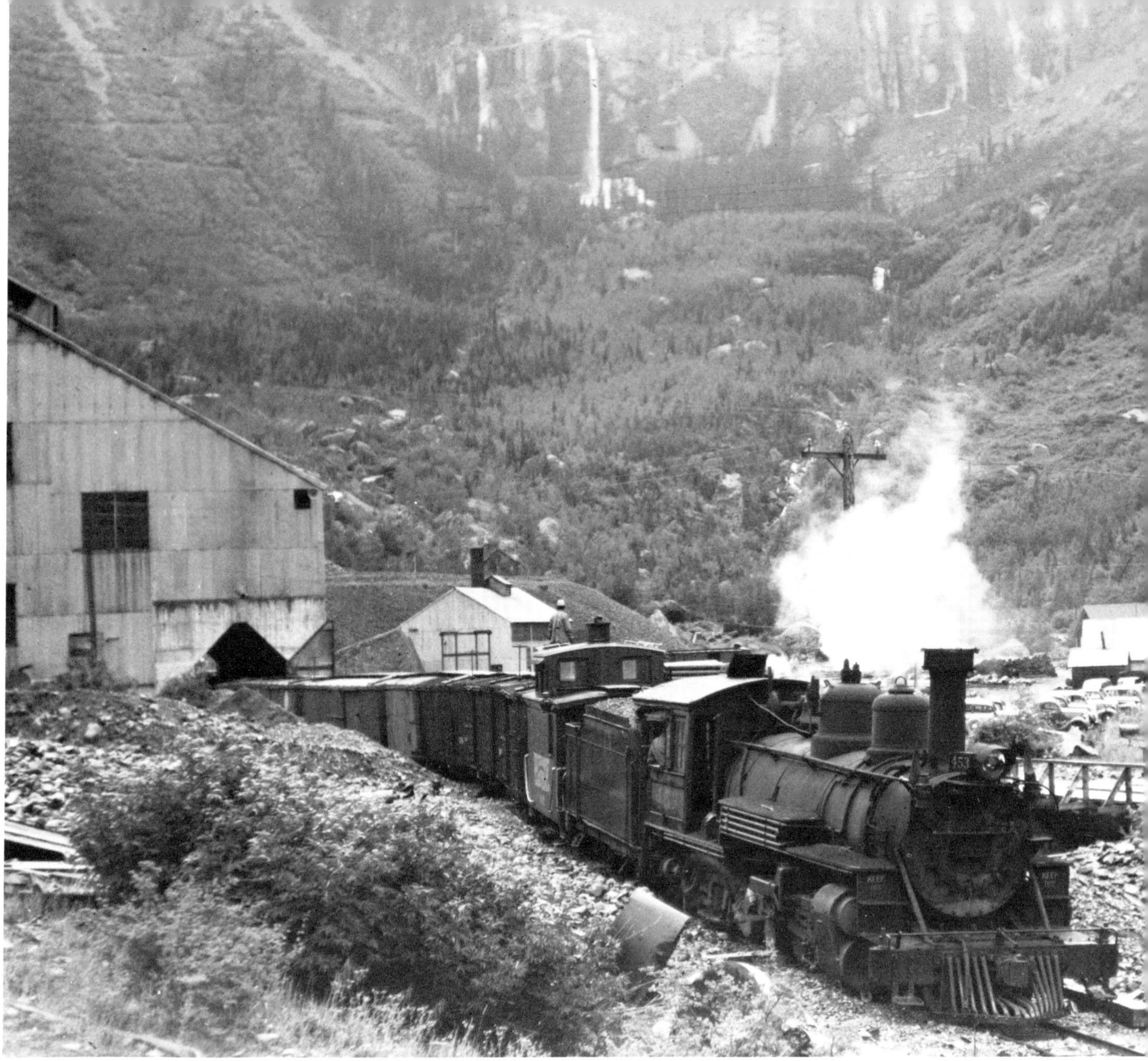

We're at Pandora, Colorado, on the Rio Grande Southern with Bridal Veil Falls in the background. Date is June 29, 1940. *Otto Perry/Denver Public Library, Western History Dept.*

The Denver and Rio Grande Western Railroad Company

Train 115, the *San Juan,* at Cumbres, with five cars. Date is July 31, 1938. *Otto Perry/Denver Public Library, Western History Dept.*

The *San Juan* at the Durango depot with five cars on September 6, 1941. Note the old cars outside the depot and the milk cans on the railroad wagon near the second car back. The good old days...*Otto Perry/Denver Public Library, Western History Dept.*

DURANGO
CARS & TRUCKS
DO NOT CROSS
YELLOW LINE

ABOVE. It's September 3, 1939 at Chama, and the conductor and another employee discuss business with the engineer of #477 during a stop. Note old vehicles at left of station.

NEXT PAGE, TOP. Roundhouse at Gunnison, Colorado, in the fall of 1947.

RIGHT. Train time at Embudo, New Mexico on January 12, 1940. *All three photos, Otto Perry/Denver Public Library, Western History Dept.*

319

Overview of Salida, Colorado, with both standard and narrow gauge trains in the foreground. Note *Silver Vista* on the narrow gauge line that crosses bridge and Rio Grande semi trailers in bottom center of photo. Date is May 21, 1950. *Otto Perry/Denver Public Library, Western History Dept.*

PALACE
HOTEL

A mixed train leaves Durango with five cars on June 12, 1945. Krille-Nichols Wool & Hide Co. at right is an interesting structure. ***Otto Perry/Denver Public Library, Western History Dept.***

WOOL & HIDES
WOOL

The *San Juan* crosses Lobato Trestle with three passenger cars, an RPO and a baggage car. Engine #473 is a Class K-28 Schenectady-built 2-8-2. *Otto Perry/Denver Public Library, Western History Dept.*

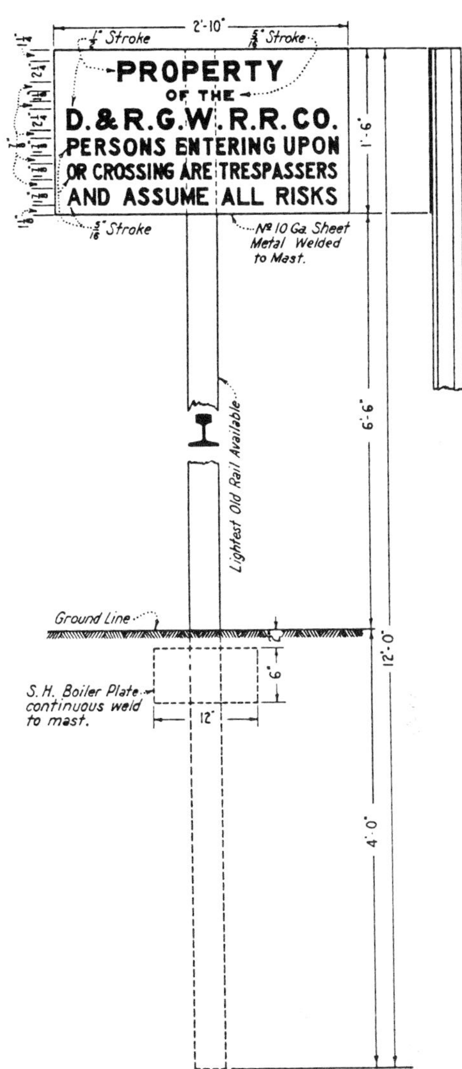

Train #425 is at Antonito in 1949 with three cars. ***Otto Perry/Denver Public Library, Western History Dept.***

Mixed train #426 is near Santa Fe on September 5, 1938. The fireman appears to be surveying the rather desolate countryside. ***Otto Perry/Denver Public Library, Western History Dept.***

471

Train #426 is on her last run on September 1, 1941 with five passenger revenue cars and one freight car. Fireman takes a peek at rear of train making sure it crosses safely. ***Otto Perry/Denver Public Library, Western History Dept.***

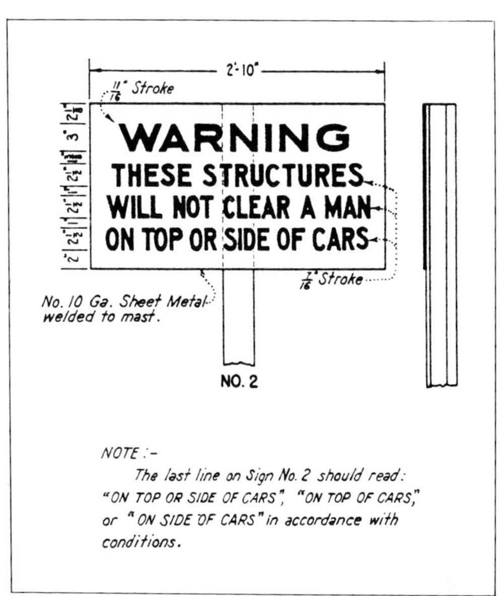

BELOW. Same spot on March 22, 1941, with a mixed freight train. ***Otto Perry, Denver Public Library, Western History Dept.***

Here we are at Los Pinos again, this time with Train #215 on December 3, 1949. ***Otto Perry/Denver Public Library, Western History Dept.***

Chapter 26

Severe Storm Enroute From Artic Circle

The Rio Grande had a Vice President-General Manager one time who had reached that level via the "old buddy" route. In his own sphere, clerical-financial, he was competent, but he knew from nothing about operations.

He came to us with the Pyatt-Shields hierarchy the Missouri Pacific burdened us with during the period it had control of the Rio Grande. To make matters worse, this VP-GM did not trust the hoi polloi in matters of policy, or worrying about possible catastrophes, whether they ever happened or not.

To keep the lower ranks, the working stiffs, fully aware of the fact troubles should be anticipated, whether they ever happened or not, he kept a poor, overworked secretary busy all day taking dictation and typing up messages of possible dire things that might happen to be rushed to our "DC" relay offices to be transmitted to outlying Superintendents. (This was before our net of teleprinters were installed and it made extra work for telegraphers. His output was tremendous.) Once in awhile he anticipated correctly, then woe betide the culprit who had glanced at his warning and threw it in the waste basket without taking action.

I was on the relief (swing) dispatcher assignment at Alamosa in November, 1946, and just recovering from wounds to my posterior received during a near fatal attack on it by our Superintendent. To make the pain worse, the chewing out I got was justified. A train of cattle came to us at Durango from the RGS that had been delayed enroute, and the cattle had just enough time on the 36-hour release to make Alamosa if given the railroad. It left Chama on the ragged edge and the conductor came on the phone while the engines were taking water at Cumbres. I was working as Night Chief at the time and assured him he had a clear track. Also, I instructed him to line up his engineman to run the water stop at Sublette. He demurred, in no uncertain terms. Well, I was young and proud of the clout my position carried, I yelled, "Walter, do what you're told" and hung up on him.

Unfortunately, he did what he was told. The engineman stopped the train at Big Horn, whistled the conductor to the head end and told him he had just enough water left to run light to Lava for a refill, but not enough to take the train with him. So the engine was cut off, went to Lava, got a drink and returned to the train. This extra move resulted in the cattle violating the maximum confinement time, and we had to make a report of the incident.

Live and learn (a sore rear end makes the learning more permanent). But there will still be lapses of memory.

CHIEF DISPATCHER

On November 2, 1946, my swing schedule made me the Chief Dispatcher. I was in the process of putting out our program for the next 24-hour operation of trains when the Superintendent came in, laughed and threw a message on my desk: "Severe storm reported left Artic Circle yesterday. Due our area tomorrow. Take all precautions necessary." I joined the Super in his sarcastic reception of the VP-GM's warning and threw it back to him.

Alamosa territory at the time included responsibility for movements over La Veta Pass. When first built, the line was narrow gauge and remained so until it was standard gauged and the location of the line changed. In the years after the changeover, several decades, there had never been a snow heavy enough to stall a train on the new route. In fact, none had been more than minimally delayed. But taking a leaf from the VP-GM's modus operandi, I included a note in the program that "if snowstorm develops, reduce tonnages for trains 10% and increase adjustment factor 4 tons per car."

November 3rd was my day off. I left home early and went hunting, returning very late in the evening. My wife met me with a message that I was to immediately contact the office. This I did, and received the news that we had a stock and perishable train stuck in the snow at the top of La Veta Pass (Fir) with engines out of water, a blizzard still piling snow on the five feet already on the ground, and a gale force wind blowing. The Superintendent was on the job and told me everything that could be done was being done, so it was not necessary for me to come to the office.

The account that follows comes from a transcript of the formal investigation held to place responsibility (to appease the VP-GM) and from information I gathered later. For a couple of weeks, both the Super and I thought we would be fired, but sanity finally prevailed, and the VP-GM conceded it was not only the train stuck at Fir that was caught by the snowstorm of a century. The train, when it was rescued, reached Pueblo and the stock, way overdue for feed, water, and rest, could not be moved to the stockyards because of snow. At Denver, bulldozers had to be used to get the stock to the stockyards.

Scenario of the story: At 6:20 a.m., November 3, 1946, 1/68/B - engines 3408-1501 departed Alamosa with 61 cars of stock and seven cars potatoes, 2943 tons adjusted factor 7. It picked up 2 spuds at Blanca and 1 spud at Ft. Garland to bring the train to 71 cars, 3117 tons adjusted factor 7, which was 81.3% of the power's rating. The train arrived Sierra where it was to get an additional helper, engine 3401, at 9:55 a.m. Engine 3401 did not arrive until 12:10 p.m. off an Extra West that had been delayed getting out of La

Christmas is a couple of weeks past in this January, 1940 snow scene. Engine #475 appears to need a brushing off! ***Otto Perry/Denver Public Library, Western History Dept.***

Veta by a snowstorm moving in. Engines 3408 and 1501 took water on arrival at Sierra, but engine 3401 could not replenish water supply due to snow blowing into and stopping tank supply. Helper coupled in, train air pumped off and departed 1:03 p.m. Stalled at MP 211, doubled head 28 cars to Fir and left on the main line; second cut of 44 cars, including caboose, arrived Fir at 4:40 p.m. Engine 3408, a small tank engine, out of water, killed. Unable to get train together account snow, wind, engine 3401 also running out of water. 1/68's engines and 5 cars of stock and 1 caboose departed Fir 9:00 p.m. towed by engine 1000, from flanger train, and to La Veta without other delays.

Plow and flanger, engine 1000, departed Alamosa 2:20 p.m. Passed 2/68/B, engine 3563, at Sierra. (2/68 had departed Alamosa at 10:50 a.m., arrived Sierra 3:00 p.m. finally took its train back to Ft. Garland and left it. Cab and engine ran to Alamosa, arriving at 9:35 p.m.) P&F 1000 arrived Fir at 5:20 p.m. performed some plowing and assisted in trying to get 1/68 back together—unsuccessful and towed engines from 1/68 plus 5 cars to stock to La Veta.

3/68/B was called at Alamosa to follow 2/68; train and crews tied up when situation at Fir became impossible to clear.

The VP-GM, when he put out the notice of a possible storm from the Artic Circle, was only indulging in his usual practice of crying wolf. Only this time there was a wolf. Carman H. C. Johnson was the U.S. Weather observer at Fir. His report, summarized, for November 2nd and 3rd: Nov. 2: Clear and calm, no snow, an automobile came to Fir from Blanca (from Russell to Fir this was a dirt road) without difficulty. Nov. 3: No. 15, passenger, late off Pueblo Division, by Fir OK, no storm or indication of any (No. 15 received 5′07″ late at 6:35 a.m., departed 6:52 a.m.; arrived Alamosa 9:50 a.m., made running time.)

An Extra West departed Fir 3:25 a.m., Nov. 3, arrived Alamosa 5:10 a.m., no snow, no troubles.

No. 16, Nov. 2, departed Alamosa 9:40 p.m., arrived La Veta 12:25 a.m., no snow, no troubles.

Two freight trains east operated out of Alamosa to La Veta the afternoon of Nov. 2nd. Both made normal runs with no snow problems.

An Extra West followed No. 15 out of La Veta Nov. 3rd and made an excellent run to Alamosa, 5′05″ (No. 1/68/B had departed Alamosa at time this Extra West left La Veta, and there were still no indications of a snowstorm on La Veta Pass.) This Extra West got out of La Veta at 8:55 a.m., delayed conditioning one of the engines. Arrived Sierra 12:10 p.m., helper engine 3401 off this train to 1/68/B at Sierra.

Shortly after, Extra West left Fir, snow began to fall lightly and kept increasing in intensity and was driven by a wind of gale force. By the time the second cut of 1/68/B arrived Fir, there was about 3 feet on the ground; when the P&F 1000 left with engines and 5 cars, there was 5 feet of snow on the ground.

OTHER FACTORS

In addition to the snow and wind conditions, numerous other factors were involved, even granting that the weather conditions were almost beyond human endurance. The snow being driven by the strong wind made it impossible to pass signals by lamps or hands. It was so deep trainmen could not carry oral instructions except with the greatest of difficulty, and they could not travel along the cars but had to go high and walk the tops of the cars while the wind buffeted them.

Mountain sheep come down to feed during the winter months at Ouray, Colorado depot. Early day photo from the collection of Ruth Gregory.

290.2

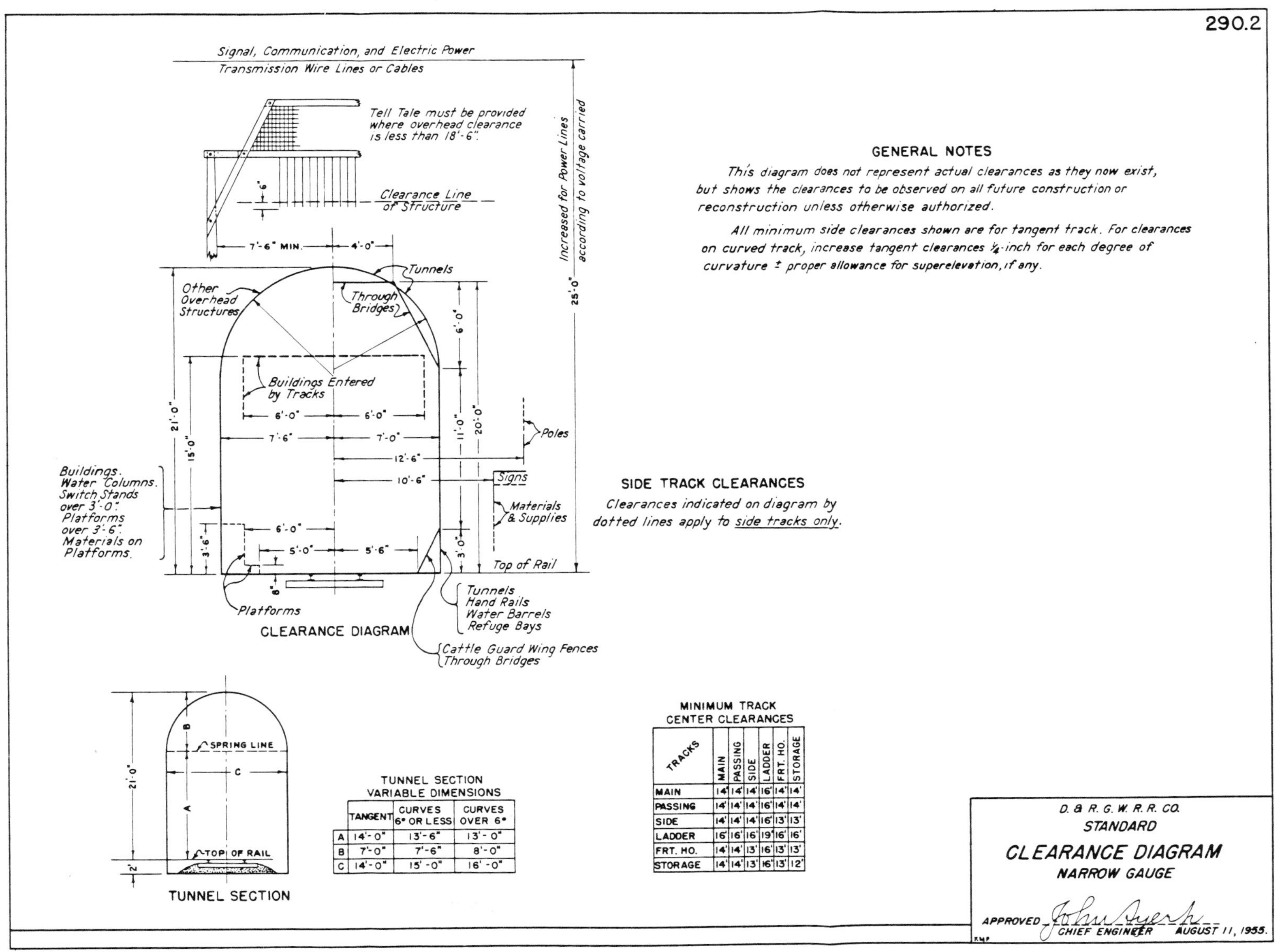

GENERAL NOTES

This diagram does not represent actual clearances as they now exist, but shows the clearances to be observed on all future construction or reconstruction unless otherwise authorized.

All minimum side clearances shown are for tangent track. For clearances on curved track, increase tangent clearances ¼-inch for each degree of curvature ± proper allowance for superelevation, if any.

SIDE TRACK CLEARANCES

Clearances indicated on diagram by dotted lines apply to side tracks only.

TUNNEL SECTION
VARIABLE DIMENSIONS

	TANGENT	CURVES 6° OR LESS	CURVES OVER 6°
A	14'-0"	13'-6"	13'-0"
B	7'-0"	7'-6"	8'-0"
C	14'-0"	15'-0"	16'-0"

MINIMUM TRACK
CENTER CLEARANCES

TRACKS	MAIN	PASSING	SIDE	LADDER	FRT. HO.	STORAGE
MAIN	14'	14'	14'	16'	14'	14'
PASSING	14'	14'	14'	16'	14'	14'
SIDE	14'	14'	14'	16'	13'	13'
LADDER	16'	16'	16'	19'	16'	16'
FRT. HO.	14'	14'	13'	16'	13'	13'
STORAGE	14'	14'	13'	16'	13'	12'

D. & R. G. W. R. R. CO.
STANDARD

CLEARANCE DIAGRAM

NARROW GAUGE

APPROVED John Ayer Jr.
CHIEF ENGINEER AUGUST 11, 1955.

KMP

D&RGW Rotary OY in 1923. It appears from this photo that it is fairly new, or recently outshopped. OY weighed 140,500 pounds. ***Otto Perry/Denver Public Library, Western History Dept.***

This is Rotary OM on January 19, 1946 at Chama. Weight was 101,500 pounds. Length is 38′8″ and 14′4½″ high. *Otto Perry/Denver Public Library, Western History Dept.*

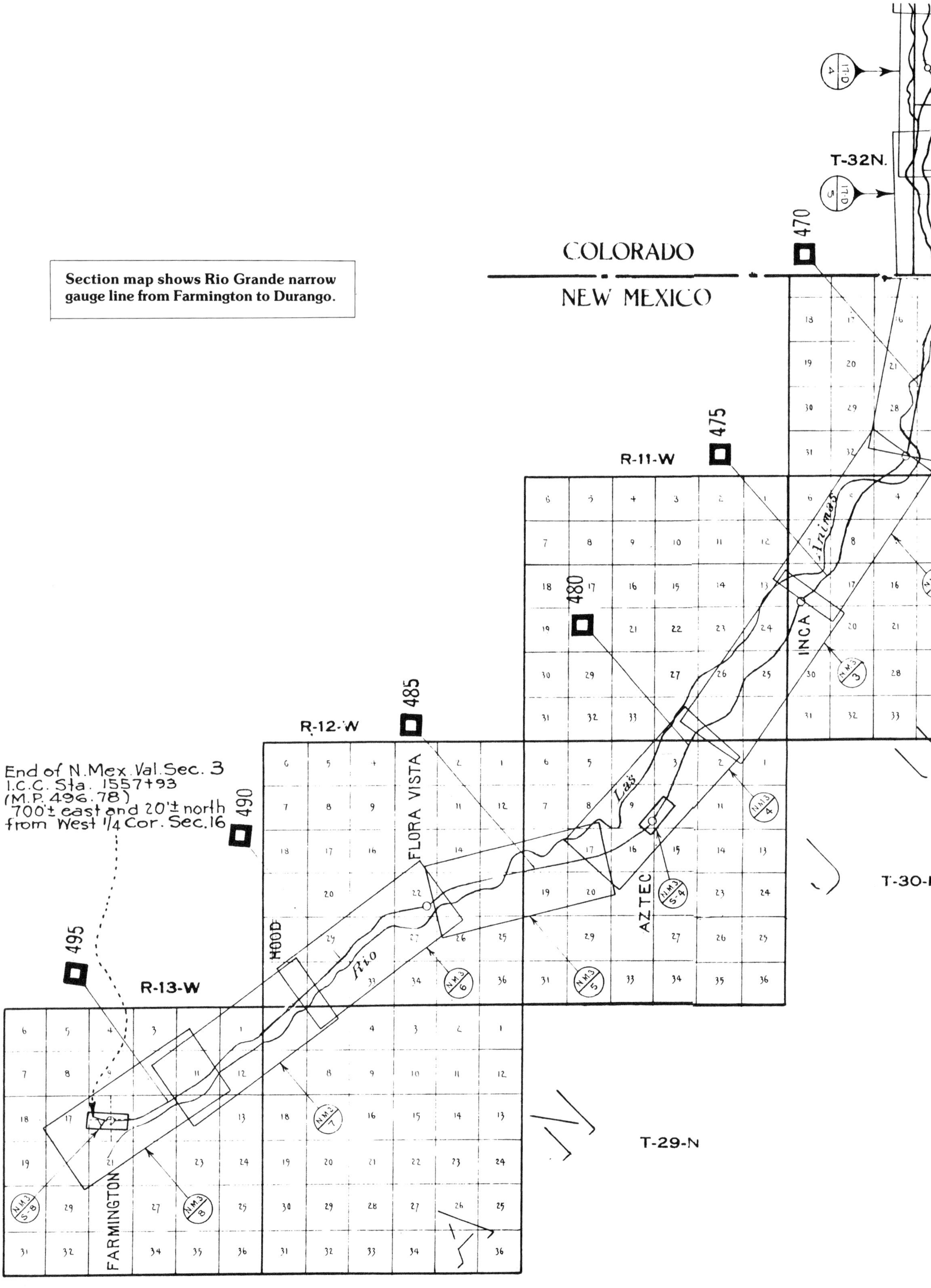

Section map shows Rio Grande narrow gauge line from Farmington to Durango.

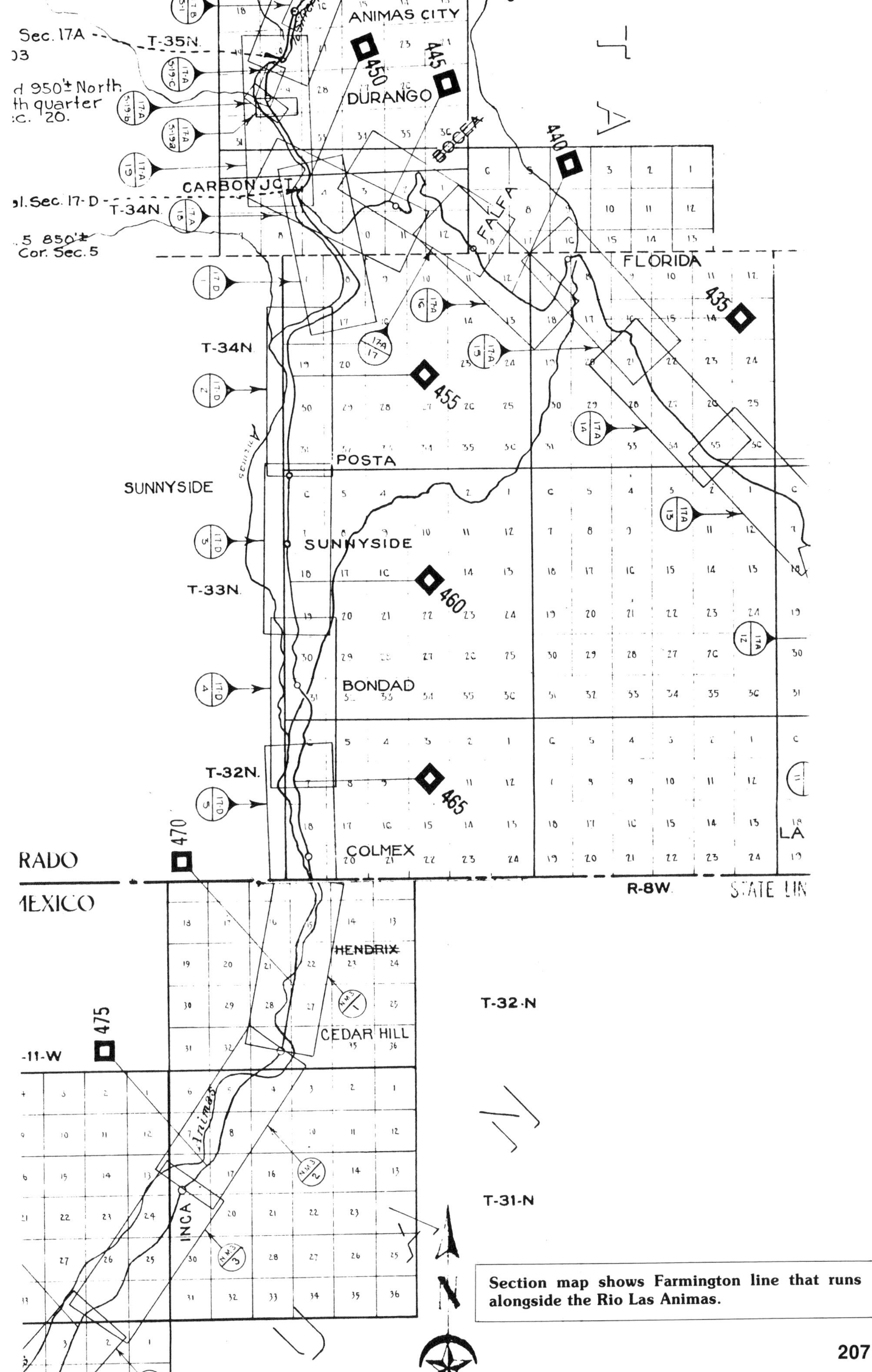

Section map shows Farmington line that runs alongside the Rio Las Animas.

Section map shows Rio Grande from Antonito to Lobato Trestle.

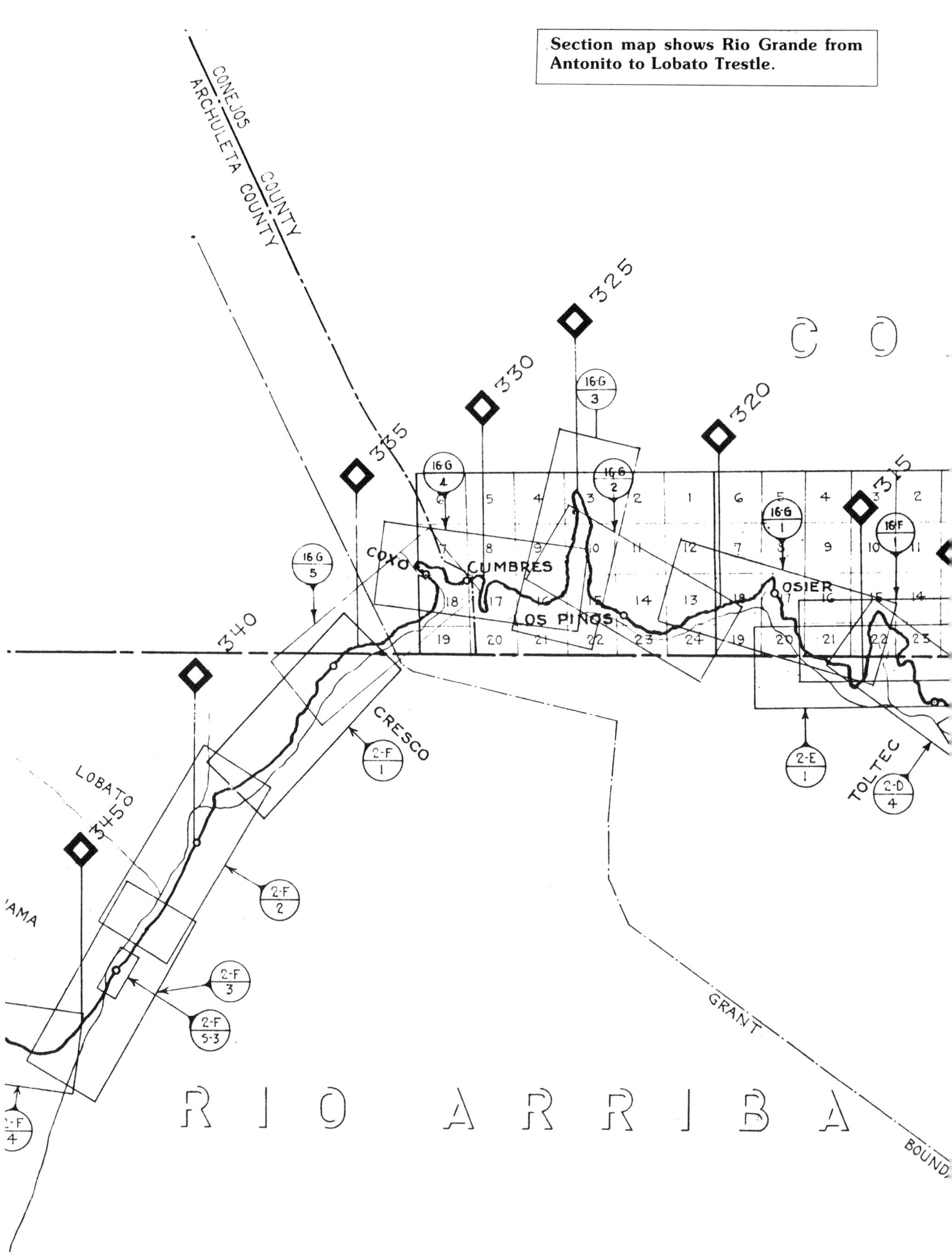

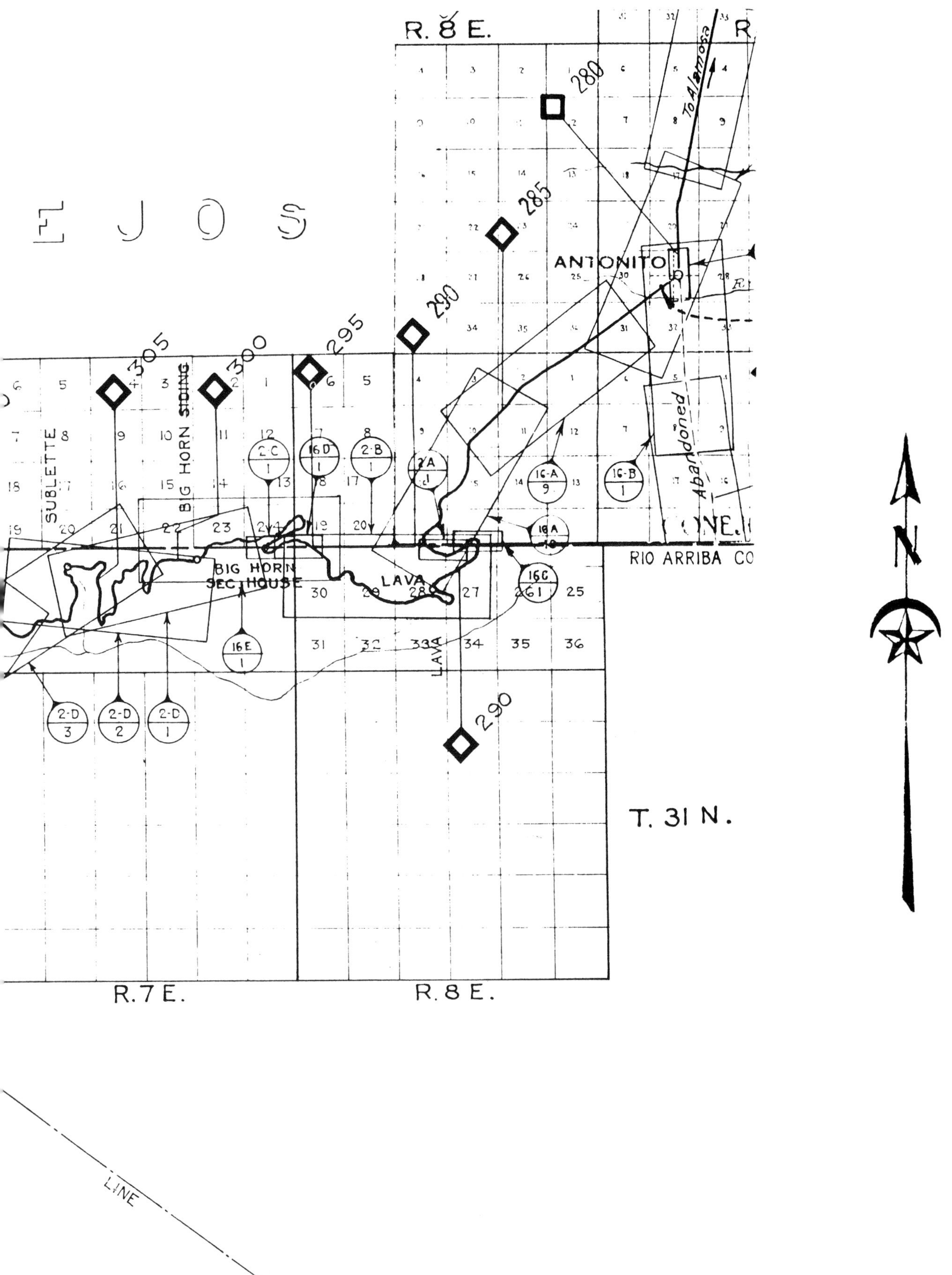

R. 8 E.

E J O S

To Alamosa

280

285

ANTONITO

290

305

300

295

SUBLETTE

BIG HORN SIDING

BIG HORN SEC. HOUSE

LAVA

CONE.

RIO ARRIBA CO

Abandoned

290

T. 31 N.

R. 7 E.

R. 8 E.

LINE

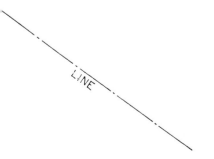

The *San Juan* pulls away from Cumbres with a five-car train in June of 1942. Note snowshed at left of locomotive. Snow still lingers at Cumbres' 10,015 feet. *Otto Perry/Denver Public Library, Western History Dept.*

The first example of this occurred when the second cut, upon arriving at Fir, stopped short of the location it should have, either because it was impossible to see "markers" used as guides, or a signal from the tank of one of the engines was misconstrued, if even given. The cut stopped on the main line considerably short of where it should and still on ascending grade.

The Roadmaster, who arrived Fir with the plow and flanger, was young, had no experience in snow problems, and failed to assume authority under the mistaken idea that he, as a roadway man, had no responsibility or authority where train operation was involved.

The conductor in charge of and responsible for 1/68/B was old and worn out, just waiting out his retirement which was due within a few months. He was first employed in 1904. To increase his shortcomings, for some time he had been carrying a chip on his shoulder for the railroad and his fellow employees. He was guilty of rascality, at times irrational, and at all times such a character, that it was only with difficulty we could keep trainmen on his crew.

To demonstrate, when questioned during the investigation as to why he had not taken prompter action, or communicated with his other train and engine crew members, and to explain why he tarried in the telegraph office, he made this answer to the interogating officer: "I did not figure I should make suggestions. I would just try to do what they told us. (Question) You made no attempt to make any suggestions as to what you could do to save the stock from violating the 36-hour law? (Answer) I did not at any time.

He excused his inaction by explaining he was just waiting for instructions, but could not explain why, having arrived at 4:40 p.m. with the final cut, and being given his orders and clearance card at 4:59 p.m., he stayed in the office almost an hour before going to his train to start putting it together. He readily admitted that during this period he had no idea what was going on, where his engines were, or that the 3408 was out of water and being killed and that the 3401 was rapidly running out of water. Later, after the P&F 1000 with the engines and 5 stock in tow departed Fir, he was left behind. His time under the Hours of Service was up at 9:30 p.m. which he had the operator tell the dispatcher. To get him off the law, at 9:28 p.m. the dispatcher cleared him with an order annulling all the orders previously issued to him plus an order that authorized him to leave his train on the main line without flag protection.

There were no section men at Fir. Nov. 3rd was a Sunday and at the close of work Nov. 1st they had gone to Alamosa in their automobiles. Train crew members had no assistance in cleaning switches to make moves and the switches drifted full as fast as they were cleaned.

Due to the storm, communications between crew members, including those on the plow and flanger train, were nonexistent. Confusion and disorganization ruled the day.

The two trainmen of 1/68/B were almost as old as the

Marshall Pass with snowshed in September of 1955 as abandonment of the narrow gauge was taking place. *Museum of New Mexico*

Map of line from Durango to Silverton showing points of interest, elevations and roads.

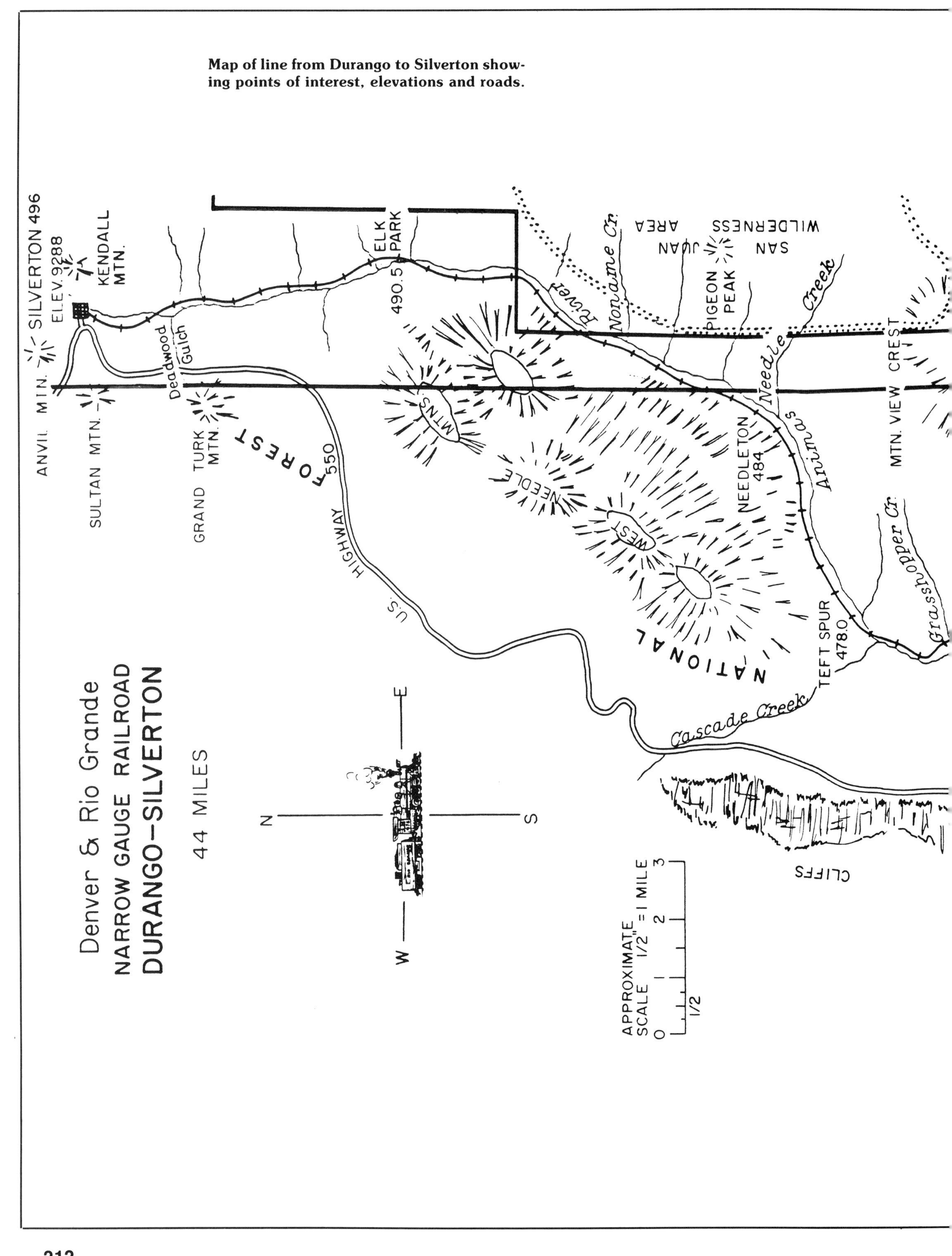

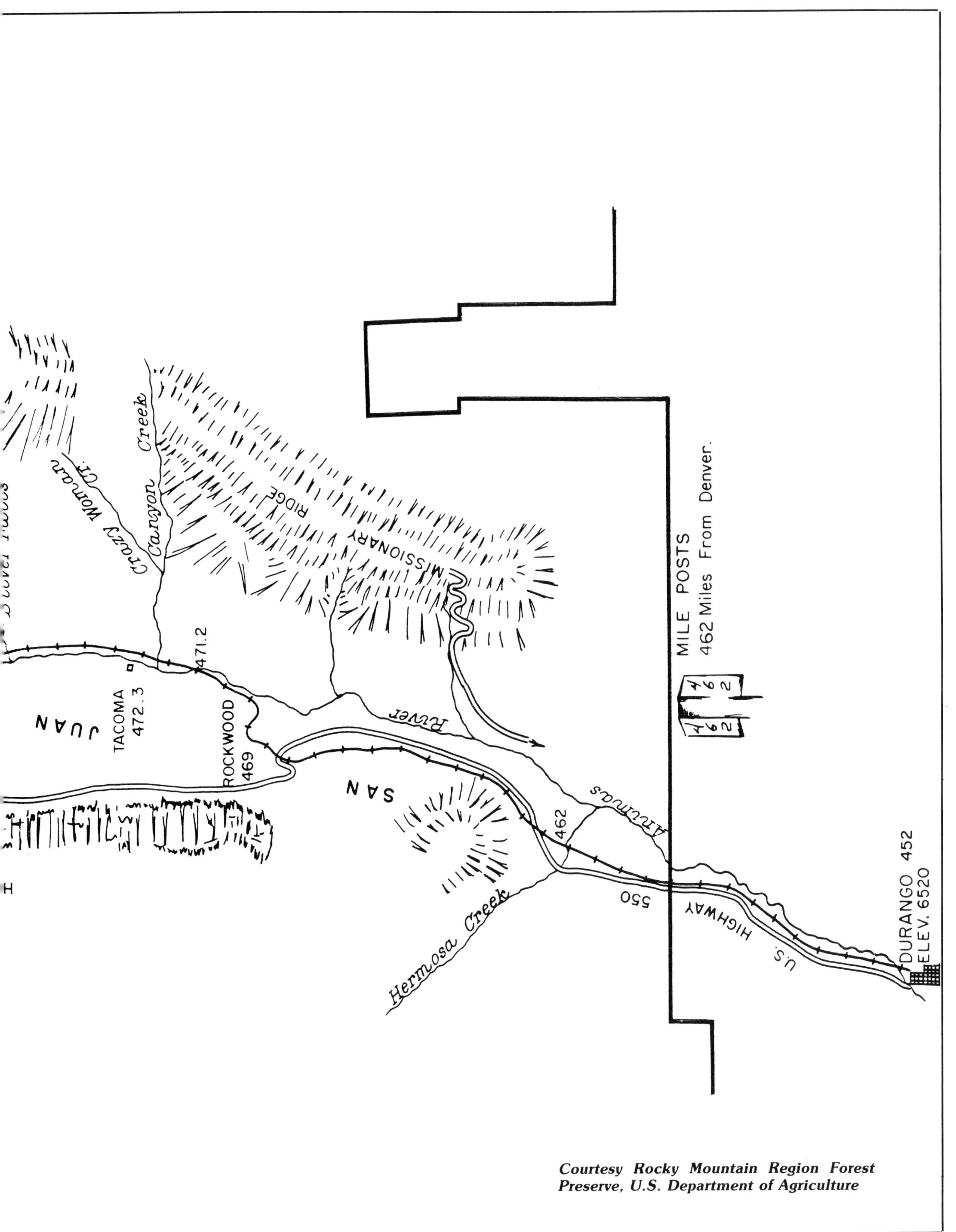

Courtesy Rocky Mountain Region Forest Preserve, U.S. Department of Agriculture

Los Pino water tank is steeped in powder snow. Snowshoe tracks by author Norwood indicate that he has inspected tank since the snowfall.

conductor, and they too were nearing retirement. Both of them and the enginemen, backed up by the conductor of the plow and flanger, agreed that had prompt action been taken, the train, while still warm, most likely could have got together and advanced. Without exception they attributed this delay to the conductor of 1/68/B being lost and out of contact with them.

ONLY THREE COWS

No one suffered pneumonia or other illness. The stock which was dug out and forwarded Nov. 4th was not too much harmed. Only 3 cows died: the Claim Department paid for them without argument. Other claims for shrinkage and damage presented by other owners were denied on the basis the storm was an Act of God and could not be anticipated. (The VP-GM's message was destroyed, including any copies.) A judge and jury agreed with our defense, and we swept the whole thing under the carpet. The conductor was permitted to resign to accept his retirement pension and the Roadmaster resigned a short time later to go into business away from the railroad.

About a year later the Superintendent was elevated to the position of Chief Transportation Officer and eventually took over the VP-GM's job. In the years that followed this Superintendent kept pushing me along at various jobs to Trainmaster, Superintendent, Chief Transportation Officer and eventually to a newly established title, Assistant VP of Operations with the same duties and responsibilities the "Artic Circle" VP-GM once held.

Maybe sometime in the next 50 years another "storm of a century" will tie up a train on La Veta Pass, but I won't be worrying about it.

AGENT'S STUB.

Denver & Rio Grande

RAILROAD.

COMMERCIAL TICKET

1000 MILES.

No. H 5285

ISSUED TO

This Stub to be kept on file by the Agent.

DETACH HERE.

Collection of Doug Harley

Chapter 27

Bits and Pieces and Legends

No matter how carefully my wife controlled our budget, we were barely keeping our heads above water at Chama on an operator's salary. (I was even having to curtail my expenditues for hunting and fishing.)

Each fall during the stock season and increased winter coal movements from the Gunnison area, and the Monarch quarry working overtime stockpiling limestone at the CF&I steel mill at Minnequa, the Rio Grande put on a temporary train order office at Poncha Junction. It paid heavy overtime, so I bid it in, and we left Chama.

It proved to be a wise move. Safeway was moving into Salida, and to drive out competition, was practically giving away groceries. We lived high on the hog for about $10 per week, with the living quarters, fuel and coal oil for lighting costing us nothing. Before the job was closed, we were again on a cash basis, our automobile was paid for, and I bought a new rifle. The disadvantage that we endured was that the living rooms in the old station house were too well ventilated and the wind blew constantly at Poncha. It was cold enough all the time to emasculate a brass monkey, but we were young, tough and wanted money, so we stuck it out until the end of the job at which time I bid in the agency at Crested Butte.

My good frau does not talk much about the hardships there,

Locomotives Nos. 474-492-493 take 23 cars under their wings eastbound out of Sargent, Colorado on October 16, 1941.
Otto Perry/Denver Public Library, Western History Dept.

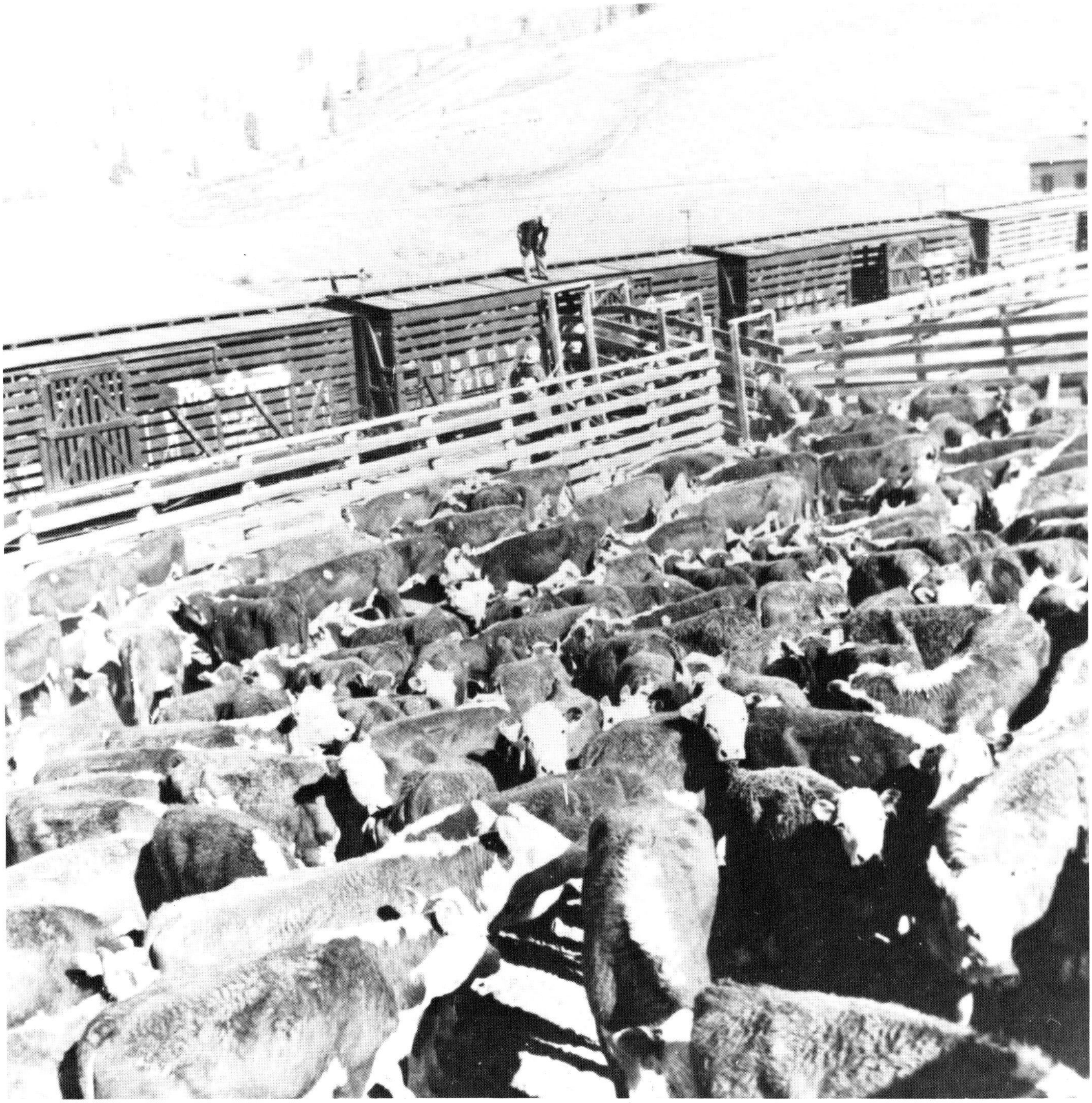

Unloading the spring range cows at Osier. In the fall, they'll be loaded up for movement to market.

LEFT AND BELOW. The long, dusty drive is nearly over! With the last steer in the pens, the air on the cars is set and loading can begin. It is the end of another year's work and worries for the Powderhorn Pool ranchers. Wives, children and girlfriends usually looked on as the loading took place; then it was into Gunnison to celebrate. *Photos by Mason M. Light, M.D.*

Denver & Rio Grande depot in spring of 1912, Montrose, Colorado. Note huge headlight on front of locomotive and three-rail tracks. Looks like they're ready to pour concrete for depot walkways. ***Photo from collection of Cameo Restaurant, Montrose, Colorado***

but occasionally she rakes up the subject of how one evening after consuming a great quantity of Joe Ventura's, the section foreman, homemade dago red, along with his good wife's Italian superbly cooked meal, I required her assistance to get home. The path between the houses was cut up by automobile tracks made during the heat of the day, and the ruts froze hard as quick as the sun went down. I swear every one of them was a microcosm of the Grand Canyon, and I fell all the way to the bottom of several such hazards.

AT ONLY HOTEL

...We arrived at Crested Butte late in the day and put up at the only public hotel. Below our room was the bar, and it was noisy. Our supper was eaten in it and consisted of heavy, greasy, miners' fare. To add insult to injury, heat for the room was provided by steam radiators that could not be shut off and the windows were nailed shut. There was no lock on the door and after a bad night, upon awakening my wife swore some thief had come in and stole her nylon hose. (Nylon hose then were scarce and expensive, but I had bought her some for Christmas.) I knew no thief had been in, for I did not sleep that much, so I asked her where she had left the hose when she undressed. She said she had laid them on top the radiator. Yeah, they had melted from the heat. (Over the years I have ruined several good nylon-shell jackets when I stood too close to a fire at a derailment.)

Snow fell often, piled up and did not thaw during the winters at Crested Butte. This *did* make for good hunting of coyotes as we hunted them on skiis or snowshoes. But it was tough on the women on wash days. A normal type clothes line was impossible to keep dug out, so each backyard had a tall pole solidly set in the ground. A rope doubled in a loop traveled through a pulley at the top of the pole. Piece by piece clothes were attached to the rope and pulled high to dry.

Nothing much of note happened while I was at Crested Butte. Living was cheap as we had no expenses for living quarters or utilities. I made a little extra money preparing income tax reports for people. The CF&I doctor had a real messy set of books, and after paying me, he gave me a quart of bonded medicinal whiskey. I had been using it carefully until it was down about half way, then made a mistake one day when Bill Purcell, the branch conductor, came to the office with the granddaddy of all colds. I felt sorry for him and went up to the living quarters and got the medicine and a glass. Bill took the bottle and glass, placed the glass on a desk and tipped up the bottle. When his Adam's apple quit bobbing, the bottle had only one small drink left in it. It was a bitter lesson, never hand a bottle to a sick man, instead, pour him a drink and lock up the bottle.

...The Irish mine telegrapher for the Colorado Fuel and Iron died, and one of the CF&I officers and I were appointed executors. The deceased was named Mike Gavin, and that was about all that was known about him. He had been at the mine a couple of decades; unmarried, he lived in one room at the company boarding house and never mixed with people except for casual conversations. Bill Gilbert, the man working with me, and I, inventoried Mike's belongings and found only a few clothes, fewer records or letters and over $20,000 uncashed salary checks. The CF&I agreed to honor them and we put them in a bank while trying to find heirs. At last we found one living relative, a sister living in Ireland, and had the money transmitted to her through the Catholic Church. She was almost as old as Mike when he died, and I always (maybe unjustly) surmised that her church ended up with most of the money.

The *San Juan* at Cumbres with five cars on May 26, 1939. *Otto Perry/Denver Public Library, Western History Dept.*

DENVER
AND
RIO GRANDE
WESTERN

Northbound freight starts up Dallas Divide near Peak, Colorado, with a D&RGW loco at the headend over Rio Grande Southern tracks. The train consists of 16 cars and #461 pushing and pulling in the middle of the train. ***Otto Perry/Denver Public Library, Western History Dept.***

Maybe this did not happen, for if it had of been done, there would have been an explosion at Mike's grave. A subject he would expound on was his hatred for any church and the insanity of people believing there was a God or Hereafter.

SECOND CHILD

...At Crested Butte, our second child, a daughter, was conceived. The high altitude affected my wife unfavorably, so she moved to Chama to stay with a couple of her cousins and was there for Doc Dunham to make the delivery. I laid off to be there and not long after, our Superintendent, C. B. Carpenter, and the O.R.T. chairman worked out a deal for my father (working night operator at Antonito) and I to trade jobs.

The night operator's job at Antonito was a sinecure. The Rio Grande was looking for train dispatchers, so arrangements were made to permit me to close the office when No. 116 came through, ride it to Alamosa, set in with the dispatcher on duty all night, then ride No. 115 back to Antonito. I never did draw any of the usual trainee dispatcher break-in pay. This went on several weeks until the Chili Line was officially closed and the night operator position at Antonito was abolished.

I was assigned to close out the records and overdue bills at stations on the Chili Line. The job took about two weeks and was the only agency work I ever did on the Santa Fe Branch.

...Before I made a dispatcher's date on the Rio Grande, I was loaned to the Rio Grande Southern as dispatcher, car distributor and general supervisor while the RGS was being rebuilt after a seasonal period of high water had washed out many miles of track. Finally, after several weeks as a relief telegrapher working the extra board, I made my dispatcher's date at Salida.

Eventually, after the usual round of retirements, deaths and discharges, Leonard Hale, then Alamosa Division Superintendent, called me into his office to review my record and inform me that neither he or any other higher officers thought I had what it took to be a competent train dispatcher. Sitting in solemn conclave, he said, they had decided there was only one logical thing to do to stop me delaying trains and otherwise keeping the Division in turmoil and that was to make me the Chief Dispatcher of the narrow gauge. After a period of fooling around making believe I was a Chief Dispatcher, I was promoted to Trainmaster to get me out of their hair again.

Speaking broadly, the position of trainmaster on a railroad is the most interesting, but at the same time, most challenging one you can be assigned to. In a literal sense you are the on-line Superintendent, his representative, his stand-in authority, buffer and, at times, his whipping boy. During the first year as trainmaster you are frequently tempted to say,

"To hell with it." For it is the period when you must learn to assume authority, use it wisely and only as a last resort. It is a period when you must start building a wall around yourself, yet leave an open door through which you may be approached. The most difficult trial comes when it is necessary to discipline, even discharge, someone who you came up through the ranks with and called friend. Fairness and impartiality in judging must be developed to the point that the imposing of discipline does not leave a bitter taste in the mouth of the recipient.

Then you must learn to forget there is such a thing as a home, a bed, good meals, a relaxing drink or soothing bath. Learn also when to turn your back, shut your eyes and ears. ...About a year after becoming Trainmaster, I was placed in a position, along with my working partner, where we had to put all our pre-conceived ideas away and turn our eyes away from, and forget what was without doubt a killing.

It was during a big strike by S.U.N.A. (Switchmen), and the Rio Grande had shut down. We still had the mail contract, but no trains were running on the narrow gauge, plus there were no means in the territory for setting up substitute service. Payday came a couple days after the shutdown and management wanted to deliver checks on schedule. The Roadmaster and a Special Agent worked by automobile out of Salida; myself and a Special Agent were given the chore out of Alamosa. Locating some of those we had checks for required a lot of searching, driving over goat trails and sleeping and eating in some less then desirable places.

HARD TO FIND

At Pagosa Jct. (Gato) there was one section laborer the foreman informed us was going to be extremely difficult to get to. He had gone to his family ranchito at the head of a broad canyon some five miles from Arboles. A portion of a road existed only as the bed of an arroya, when it was dry. Three or four families of the same name had adobe homes there where they raised corn, squash and beans and tended some goats and sheep. The foreman told us they were really isolated and wanted to remain so because they were at outs with some others in the area. The old Mexicans still left in some portions along the narrow gauge had several things in common with Kentucky-Tennessee hillbillies. They were people of honor, tight-mouthed and volatile. Feuds between families existed and were settled at times like among hill people—settled and details kept secret from the outsiders, even from other uninvolved Mexicans.

The foreman gave us directions and drew a crude map to guide us. We found the canyon and the so-called road, and eventually came in sight of the collection of houses. They were built in a sort of a loosely defined plaza arrangement. Near one of the houses a group of 6 or 8 men was standing, and a few yards from them was a battered pickup truck with its tailgate open. The access led by it. As we drew closer, we saw the form of a man on the truck bed. His clothing was disheveled, there was considerable blood, and he was cut all to pieces where bare flesh showed.

The waiting men were neither excited nor threatening, so we kept our eyes front and drove on up to them. From a rolled down window, we inquired for the party we wanted. He stepped from the group, accepted his check and signed the receipt book. We then turned our car around carefully and hit the back trail. Passing the pickup, we maintained an even speed, and our eyes still front.

Back in civilization, we kept our mouths shut. Had we driven to Pagosa Springs and reported to the sheriff, he would have been unable to do anything. By the time he could reach the scene, the body would have been buried off somewhere, the truck concealed, and, for sure, he could have questioned every Mexican for miles around and met only blank stares and the assurance that, "No, senor, there has been no fighting, no killing and there is no one missing."

Then, we could sort of salve our consciences with the thought that maybe the man was not dead; maybe he still lived, but bore some ugly scars. We were sure of one thing: it was no time to play hero and try to make citizen arrests. ...By the time I was working for the Rio Grande, the "good old days" on the Chili Line were long gone, and the branch was already facing abandonment, but it was not too late to have been privileged to listen to tales told by those who had worked on it as trainmen or enginemen—or other categories and there were tales of derring-do and high jenks.

Engine #491 heads up a very long string of box cars and a water car directly behind the locomotive. ***Collection of Don Heimburger***

Engine #471, a 2-8-2 built in 1923, chugs along slowly with a mixed freight north of Skarda, New Mexico, on June 14, 1941.
Otto Perry/Denver Public Library, Western History Dept.

One of the high jenks I always enjoyed hearing of was told by men who, at the time of the party, were in their early twenties, and apparently as wild as railroaders were reputed to be.

Business was rushing on the Branch at the time, and there were a number of crews at Santa Fe being delayed while a washout was cleared up around White Rock. Must have been about 25-30 train and enginemen in town with nothing to do, and enough ready money to do more than lay around in their rooming houses. The party got into full, or more than full, swing toward the end of the first 24 hours, many of which had been spent in cantinas around the plaza or in the burdellas (cat-houses) up Goat Alley. The longer they were held awaiting call, the wilder they became.

Late on the second evening they commandered a carriage used for sightseeing tours and since there was no horse with it at the time, they lined up along the tongue and, with some riding, took off at a lope for one of the bigger burdellas. They loaded on the madame and some of her boarders to take them for a ride. At the top of a high street the "horses" got tired, cocked the tongue of the carriage in the air, and sat down to rest. Gravity took over and the carriage, full of squealing "girls" and the madame went rolling down the street.

It stopped rolling when it crashed into a tienda de comestibles or bodega (grocery store). Not much damage was done, but there were a lot of females screaming and a local keeper of the law showed up. The madame invited everyone, including the officer, to her place for a drink. Following several drinks and a bit of pleasure on the house by one of the girls, the officer decided he must have been mistaken—no accident or disturbance of the peace had occurred.

Along about midnight, an absent railroader showed up with

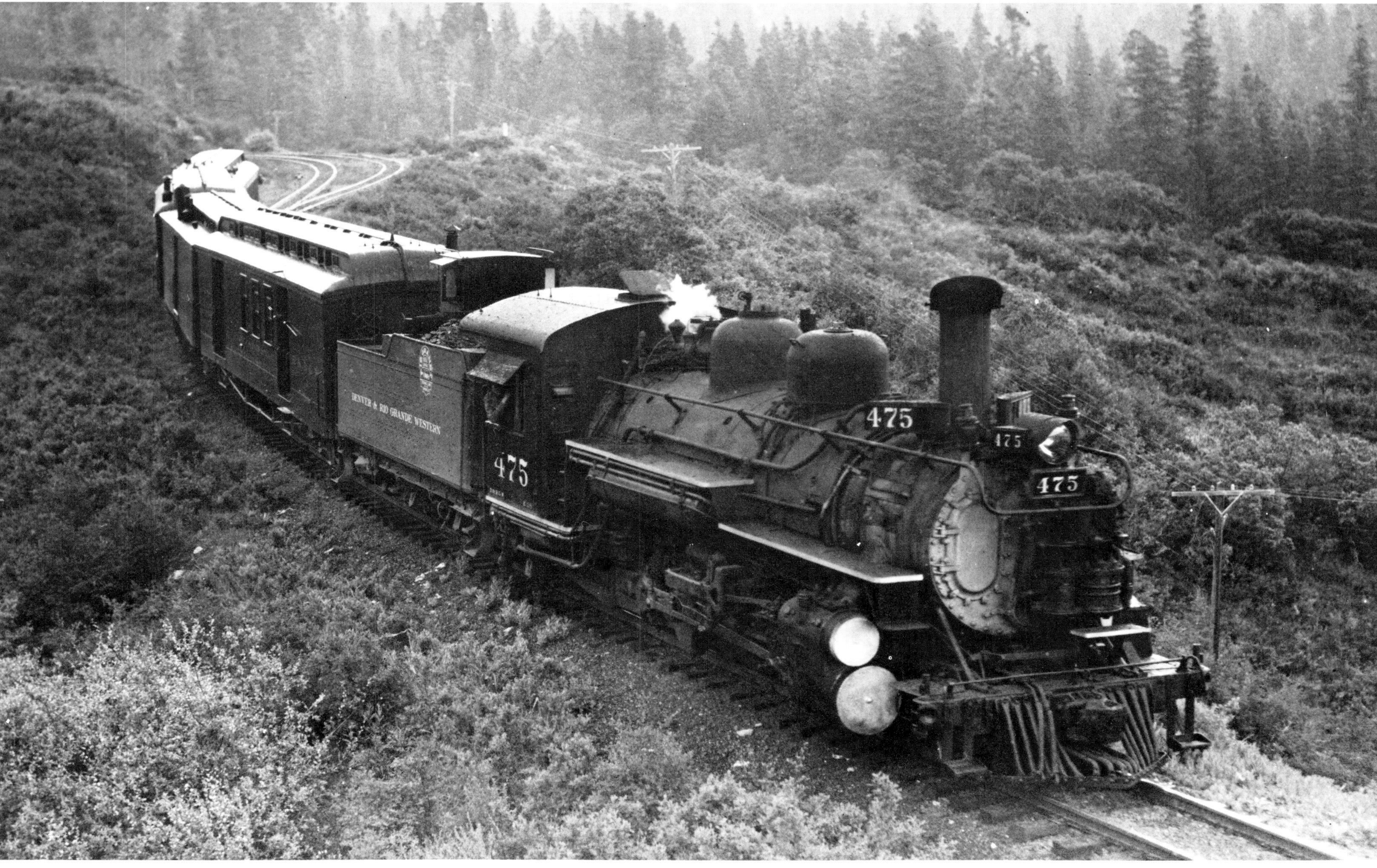

We're below Cresco with the *San Juan* as she makes her way on a damp, rainy day in June of 1940. *Otto Perry/Denver Public Library, Western History Dept.*

word they might have to go to work early next morning. On the way back to their boarding houses, still traveling as a group, they stopped for a last drink alongside an adobe wall built around a private home. Someone leaned against it and it wobbled a bit; then others, and finally they were chanting the tracklayers "yo - heaveho" and pushing on the wall. It toppled over as the owner came out of the house. Making up a pot to pay for a new wall, they soon quieted the owner. He went back in his house and the wild men, arm in arm, paraded up the street with a sweet-voiced Welshman singing "And the Walls of Jericho Came Tumbling Down."

Before another decade had passed the Rio Grande railroaders were no longer the darlings of Santa Fe, business had fallen off and the high jenks ceased.

...Some warm day in summer, if you are at Garfield Monument at the west end of the Toltec Tunnel and feel strong and adventuresome, climb down into the Gorge. Just below the wall at the portal you will find six trucks of narrow gauge cars buried intermittently, depending on water conditions, in river bottom. They are all that remain of three cars of lumber that derailed and tumbled to the bottom of the Gorge.

Crummies on the narrow gauge were not equipped with electric lights and the tin can kerosene lanterns gave a very inferior illumination. Some agent's handwriting were not candidates for penmanship prizes, and waybills were often written with indelible pencils and the indelible blurred if it got wet. Anyway, one fall when I came to work, I was informed that two cars of sheep were setting on a track at a place called Darlington. The waybills were in Alamosa and called for two cars of sheep for Burlington, a station on the CB&Q. They has violated their 36-hour release by this time. The first problem was to get a train to pick them up; the second to find out what had happened. The culprit was the conductor handling the sheep out of Durango. For one reason or another, he had misread the waybills and did not question his own literacy; to him the destination read "Darlington," so he set the two cars out.

...I never find myself nostalgic for the narrow gauge as I knew it, but I do suffer from nostalgia when I think of my experiences with the Mexican people who lived and worked along the narrow gauge. And they were *Mexicans*. That is what we called them, and what they called themselves. They were neither "chicanos," "Spanish-Americans," "New Mexicans," nor the "minority," nor, later, "La Raza"—Por Dios!! They were "Mexicans" and proud of it. They could trace their lineage back further than the Americanos—to conquistadores, missionary padres and the most royal of Indian maidens. They were old in the land before the Pilgrims and Jamestown and, except for frauds and strong military forces, their land would still be Mexico. But, since this was not true, then they would be good citizens of the country but, por Dios, they were Mexicans.

Over the years a number of people have accused me of being a "Mexican lover." For the generation of Mexicans, my own, I lived with and among on the narrow gauge, I cannot deny it. For the present generation, La Raza, chicanos—not having lived with them to develop the same rapport and empathy, I cannot say.

DISTINCT RACE

...The people I knew along the Rio Grande, Navajo and San Juan Rivers were of a distinct race. They were proud, clean, loyal, trustworthy, intelligent and industrious. Neither myself or any of my family ever was lied to or stolen from. Within certain limits beyond which we could not intrude, we were received and accepted by the Mexican people. The secret was to learn where the borderline lay and what it consisted of. It was an intuitive knowledge, rather than being laid out in defined words.

Early age impressions stay with you through life. In my younger years I came to believe the epitomy of womanhood was represented by the Mexican women. To me their beauty affected me the same way a blooded Tennessee Walker horse, a highly-bred coon dog or a new Winchester rifle did. (At that stage of my life I related more to the latter three, women were only an abstraction, but my early impressions were so deeply ingrained I married an Irish colleen, a brunet, who resembled, and could have held her own, with any latina beauty. Of course, being Irish, she was not as compliant or submissive.)

A mixed freight with three passenger cars tacked on the rear crosses a trestle near Leonard, Colorado, on the Rio Grande Southern in 1940. ***Otto Perry/Denver Public Library, Western History Dept.***

What I miss most are the story tellings by los ancianos, the old ones, the bitter black coffee and munchies of goat cheese, the chicharones (cracklings), dulces, sweets, and brown paper cigarettes.

...Near the west end of Monero Canyon where it debouches into Amargo Flats, there is a knife-like sandstone structure left as a relic of some age-old channel change of Monero Creek. On top of its flat surface are three balanced rocks—one large, one small and one between these in size. The old Mexicans tell a story of how these came to be there.

Many, many years ago when the people of the Rio Grande valley were moving to the new lands on the San Juan River, they came by way of the Chama River, over Horse Lake Pass and down the Monero Canyon to strike the Navajo River. A man, muy rico, with his wife and two daughters, left the settlement at San Juan with his property and gold to make this move. They camped one night at the rock of the Three Women. While the father was away putting the animals to graze, some mal hombres, bandidos, attacked the camp, killed the three women and stole the gold.

The husband and father grieved for his dead, then buried them on top of the mesita and piled stones over each body. In the years to come, these mounds of stone took the shape of his three women and became the three balanced rocks. Without gold, or a will to live away from his wife and daughters, he found a cueva, a grotto, from which he could watch his graves. At the mouth of the grotto he built a wall, and behind it made his home. There he lived.

Other travelers gave him food, a few goats and sheep and seeds. He planted crops each year and tended his animals within sight of his dead. He became renowned as a curandero (a healer), a wise and sympathetic man, respected and loved and visited by many. They named him "El Tecolote," The Owl. (There are other words for owl but tecolote was used for the old man.)

El Tecolote lived to be a very old man and some travelers were there when he died. They told the story that when they went to bury him at sunrise, they saw a great gray owl fly from his body to a niche in the cliff above his grotto. The people say that from that day on, a gray owl has always used that niche as a roosting place.

SPIRIT IS AN OWL

It may be that El Tecolote's spirit became an owl and is there yet watching his dead. At least, when the *San Juans* were still running, if you knew where to look, you could see the tumbled rocks that walled in his grotto and above it, if you look carefully and closely, you could see a large gray owl perched in the niche and looking toward the Three Women.

...Reminiscent of the legend of the Winged Serpent in old Mexico and depicted on the Mexican seal and money, are the stories told along sections of the narrow gauge where

#268 makes black smoke into the clear blue Western skies as part of the abandonment/clean-up operations on the Narrow Gauge. ***John Krause/Dr. Richard Severance collection***

standstone or lava cliffs harbored many rattlesnakes. The stories tell of a very large rattlesnake living in a den in a cliff (each location is different for each community). It has been there since the first settlers came and is mucho grande. Once each moon in the dark of the night it comes out and takes one goat or one sheep for food, but it never harms any human. Nobody every claimed to have seen the serpent, but they *know* it is there.

He is spoken of variously: as El Anciano, the Old One; as El Serpiente, The Serpent; as Tio Culebra, Uncle Snake; and as Abuelo Vibora, Grandfather Rattlesnake.

An area of Mexican life we whites did not intrude upon was the religion within a religion, Los Hermanos, the Penitentes. This Mexican secret ritual (religion) was a carry-over from the Mexican colonial days when the Indians and newborn of Spanish gentleman and Indian maiden were taken into the Church and thereafter interpreted its rituals as best they could. They were especially taken with ceremonies of the Lenten season and the story of Christ going to his Crucifixion up Calvary.

They began to simulate this pageant, and their re-enactment was extremely realistic. The Catholic padres

Same train as on previous page, pulling the same converted box car. *John Krause/Dr. Richard Severance collection*

Rio Grande locomotive #318 sits quietly as a Rio Grande Southern train of varnish stops for passengers to view Lizard Head in background. *Ruth Gregory collection*

frowned upon their actions and strove mightily to stop them, but without success. Los Hermanos, The Penitentes, became deeply entrenched in the Mexican villagers' lives and each community somewhere had a secret "morado," literally a dwelling but, related to the Penitentes, a church.

Lent was celebrated in all its rituals in the morado by Los Hermanos. The climax came with the choosing of a Cristo, Christ, who carried the Cross up Calvary, falling and being whipped along the way by brother Penitentes swinging "flagelos," whips, made of woven strands of yucca or Spanish Bayonet with the spiny tips left protruding. Reaching Calvary, Cristo was symbolically crucified by being tied to the Cross which was then erected in a previously dug hole.

The Crucifixion over, the "dead" Cristo was borne to the Morado to be resurrected on Easter morning. As a mark of veneration in the future, Cristo had a small blue cross tattooed on his forehead just above the eyebrow line. No few members of our section laborers carried this tattoo.

(I can speak first-hand about the march up Calvary and the Crucifixion. I hid once when I was about 14 years old and watched it from a hillside. Los Hermanos probably would not have hurt me if they found me, but I spent several hours worrying about what they would do if they did discover me.)

Then there was the story of "El Monstruo" told by the people in the Monero-Lumberton district. When the first coal mine was being opened in Monero, and the miners had their entry some hundreds of feet into the vein of coal, it was drilled and charged with black powder to break up coal for the day's work. When the shot was fired, it opened up a large cavity that was in the vein. From the cavity a "monster" ran out on its hind legs. It looked just like one of the small lizards but it was as large as a man. Still running on its hind legs and with its long tail dragging, it raced from the mine and fled up the canyon.

It was never seen again and no more were ever found in the coal veins of Monero or Lumberton, but ever after mothers made their misbehaving children be good by threatening that "El Monstruo" would get them.

The Mexicans often made realistic and practicable adjustments in their life style as dictated by factors such as geography, isolation and lack of public officers. One of these adjustments was in their marriage customs.

Very few of the small communities had permanently located Catholic priests (or other clergy) or justices of the peace or other officers. Thus, there were no church authorities readily available to perform marriage ceremonies or to issue license to wed. But these people accepted the fact that a time came in the lives of maturing boys and girls they were so physically attracted to each other it was impossible to deny the urge to unite. They were a moral people and frowned on clandestine couplings in the montes (bushes) that could result in unwedded mothers. Realistically, they accepted, if

#268 and clean-up train. *John Krause/Dr. Richard Severance collection*

268
268
285

Form E. B. No. 2

D. & R. G. R. R.

Local Excess Check.
AGENT'S STUB.

Date 4-18 1907
From [illegible]
To [illegible]
Gross Wt. 400 Ex. Wt. 250
Rate 60 No. of Fares 1
Cash Collected
Coupons Collected 1.50
Coupon Book No. 7840
Issued by [illegible] R. R.
Prepaid Permit No.
IF CHECKED ON P. P. P.
Issued by R. R.
Nos. of other Checks, if any.
37495-96

C 53934

Form E. B. No. 2

D. & R. G. R. R.

Local Excess Check.
AGENT'S STUB.

Date 6/14 1910
From Farmington N M
To Durango Colo
Gross Wt. 600 Ex. Wt. 450
Rate No. of Fares 1
Cash Collected 1.35
Coupons Collected
Coupon Book No.
Issued by D&RG R. R.
Prepaid Permit No.
IF CHECKED ON P. P. P.
Issued by R. R.
Nos. of other Checks, if any.

D 83245

Collection of Doug Harley

the two must be together let them be so under the approved auspices of all.

A young man worked on the railroad, in the mines or with sheep until he had saved some money. With it he returned home with the view in mind of setting up housekeeping with a girl he had been long attracted to. He informed his mother of his choice and she in turn told her esposo (husband). The elder uncles then decided if the girl was suitable and not related by blood to their family. If the word was "go" the eldest uncle then approached an uncle of the girl and the process flowed in reverse until at last the girl approved (there was seldom a question of this, for the boy and girl had already reached a meeting of minds).

UNCLES MEET

A meeting of the two groups of uncles, attended by the village matchmaker, was then held and the match either approved or disapproved. If approved, the girl's uncles carried the word back to her. If for some reason the boy's uncles did not approve, they did not openly so state, but during the night following the negotiations a calabazo (a knotty, gray squash) was placed at the door of the girl's home. The young people might be heartbroken, but they seldom rebelled against their elders' decision.

If the match was approved, the boy purchased a large, substantial trunk which was delivered to the girl. In it was placed all her personal possessions plus bedclothes, linens and such. Another container was filled with other housekeeping items given by her family. The trunk and container were then carried to the boy's home accompanied by the girl. There in a room set aside for the young people they became, in the eyes of the village, legally and actually man and wife. Then, a plot of ground being selected, both families and others of the community built a house for the young couple.

Later, sometimes much later, when a priest was available, if the young couple had enough money for a gratuity to the priest, a marriage, almost always sans marriage license, was confirmed in the church. As was often the case, a priest was a long time coming to the village or money was not available or, for many other reasons, the couple's confirmation of their marriage was delayed so long, the first-born son might have reached an age old enough to be out herding the family goats. Or the couple might appear before the priest with two or three of their children and another on the way.

To its credit, and to the credit of a practical people, this custom worked, not for better or worse, but until death do us part. If some strait-laced person tried to imply to these people that the custom was not kosher, or according to the laws of the land, all that person would get was a smile, a shrug of the shoulders and, "De nada, no es importe." (So what? It is not worth mentioning, of no importance.)

Season followed season, children were born and old folks died, crops were either good or bad as God willed; there was little excitement or intensity in their life, that is, until the word, *tesoro* (treasure) entered a conversation. These people believed fervently that there were numerous minas perdidas (lost mines) and tesoros perdidas (lost treasures) to be found and all of them were muy rico (very rich). Every family had in its keepsakes an old soiled, tattered derrotero or plata (a map or chart) showing where one of these could be found. Many sheepherders, as they tended their flocks, walked the terrain using a vara de virtud (a witching rod that it was thought would detect buried minerals or metals.).

But, after much excited speculation about what they would do if they found such a mina or tesoro, some old man or

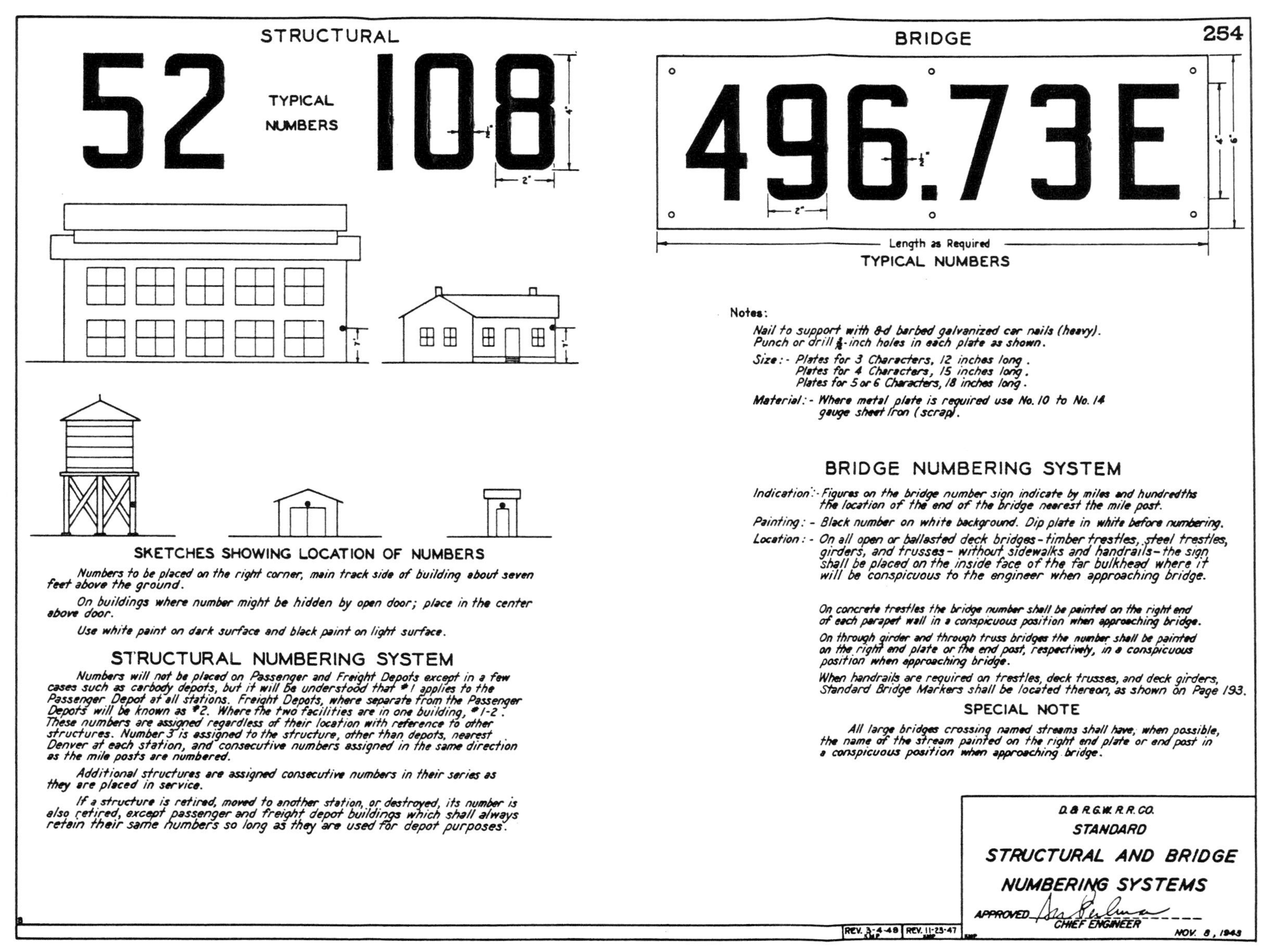

STRUCTURAL

52 TYPICAL NUMBERS 108

BRIDGE

254

496.73E

Length as Required

TYPICAL NUMBERS

Notes:

Nail to support with 8-d barbed galvanized car nails (heavy). Punch or drill ⅛-inch holes in each plate as shown.

Size: - Plates for 3 Characters, 12 inches long.
Plates for 4 Characters, 15 inches long.
Plates for 5 or 6 Characters, 18 inches long.

Material: - Where metal plate is required use No. 10 to No. 14 gauge sheet iron (scrap).

SKETCHES SHOWING LOCATION OF NUMBERS

Numbers to be placed on the right corner, main track side of building about seven feet above the ground.

On buildings where number might be hidden by open door; place in the center above door.

Use white paint on dark surface and black paint on light surface.

STRUCTURAL NUMBERING SYSTEM

Numbers will not be placed on Passenger and Freight Depots except in a few cases such as carbody depots, but it will be understood that #1 applies to the Passenger Depot at all stations. Freight Depots, where separate from the Passenger Depots will be known as #2. Where the two facilities are in one building, #1-2. These numbers are assigned regardless of their location with reference to other structures. Number 3 is assigned to the structure, other than depots, nearest Denver at each station, and consecutive numbers assigned in the same direction as the mile posts are numbered.

Additional structures are assigned consecutive numbers in their series as they are placed in service.

If a structure is retired, moved to another station, or destroyed, its number is also retired, except passenger and freight depot buildings which shall always retain their same numbers so long as they are used for depot purposes.

BRIDGE NUMBERING SYSTEM

Indication: - Figures on the bridge number sign indicate by miles and hundredths the location of the end of the bridge nearest the mile post.

Painting: - Black number on white background. Dip plate in white before numbering.

Location: - On all open or ballasted deck bridges - timber trestles, steel trestles, girders, and trusses - without sidewalks and handrails - the sign shall be placed on the inside face of the far bulkhead where it will be conspicuous to the engineer when approaching bridge.

On concrete trestles the bridge number shall be painted on the right end of each parapet wall in a conspicuous position when approaching bridge.

On through girder and through truss bridges the number shall be painted on the right end plate or the end post, respectively, in a conspicuous position when approaching bridge.

When handrails are required on trestles, deck trusses, and deck girders, Standard Bridge Markers shall be located thereon, as shown on Page 193.

SPECIAL NOTE

All large bridges crossing named streams shall have, when possible, the name of the stream painted on the right end plate or end post in a conspicuous position when approaching bridge.

D.&R.G.W. R.R. CO.
STANDARD
STRUCTURAL AND BRIDGE NUMBERING SYSTEMS
APPROVED [signature] CHIEF ENGINEER
NOV. 8, 1943

REV. 3-4-48 | REV. 11-25-47

woman would quench the young people's fire with this wisdom. "Ay," he would mourn, "it is well to think of these things, but do not forget los chisos and Patrones (the spirits and the ghostly guardians). If you are the one not chosen to find that tesoro by the Patrones, you will lose it or you may suffer." There would be dejected sighs from the group, "Si, es una cosa de verdad, estar necesitado de cuidado." (Yes, it is a thing of truth, it is necessary to be careful.)

To prove this, the old man tells the story of the tesoro of the Resaca del Castor Ciego, the Marsh of the Blind Beaver, that, when the land was less arid, was situated between Amargo and Lumberton, a couple of miles north of the narrow gauge tracks.

A sheepherder tending his flock on the slopes of Archuleta Mountain southwest of Lumberton found a large cache of gold coins. He placed it in a bag, packed his camp burro, saddled his horse, and headed for home at Monero. His route took him across the marsh which seemed firm enough to carry him and his animals. He and his horse negotiated the wet ground safely, but the burro followed behind, browsing as it came, reached the middle of the marsh then, before the eyes of its owner, disappeared quickly out of sight in the muck of the

Engine #318 travels southbound on the Ouray branch in June of 1952. ***John Krause/Dr. Richard Severance collection***

Train #461, a mixed, north of Durango, with 13 cars in September of 1941. *Otto Perry/Denver Public Library, Western History Dept.*

Train #426, a mixed, on its last run north of No Agua, New Mexico. *Otto Perry/Denver Public Library, Western History Dept.*

swamp. The sheepherder obtained a long pole, cautiously crept out to where the burro had left his sight and probed. It was a long pole, but he could not feel the burro in the muck.

The old man ended his story with, "That man was not the one the Patron wanted to have the gold."

About halfway between Pagosa Junction and Arboles there is a prominent, gently sloping hill that extends from the cliffs to the railroad. Father Escalante on his journey from Santa Fe, trying to find a route to the missions in California, was carrying a chest of golden church vessels and reliquaries for the missions on the Pacific. Soon after reaching the San Juan River, for some reason, he reached a decision to bury this treasure to be reclaimed later. A hole was dug on top of the slope a short distance from the river, and the treasures placed in it.

Mexicans in the district claimed that on dark nights they saw blue lights as tall as men dancing on this hill. (The few Americanos could never see them.) These blue lights, the natives believed, were los chisos appearing to remind anyone coveting the treasure they were on guard. Then, one dark and stormy night, it is said there was one great blue flame on the hill and a burst of sound. Next day, rosaries in hand to protect them, some men went to see what had happened. They found a mound of dirt with a shovel and pick on it beside a hole three or four feet deep. In the hole was a pair of shoes burned and charred as if from great heat, but there was no body in the shoes. Carefully the men filled the dirt back into the hole and placed a cross in its center.

A few miles farther west, across the San Juan from Arboles, a second treasure was concealed (maybe it was recovered). A canyon led off the hills toward the river. Between its mouth and the river there was a small cultivated plot, an adobe house and a brush goat corral. A Mexican farmer, his wife and two teenage sons lived here. The sons took turns tending the goats up the canyon.

TRICKLE OF WATER

Near the head of the canyon, in the sandstone walls, was a grotto and in the grotto a never-failing trickle of water filled a depression in the floor of the grotto. The boys watered their goats here each day and took a siesta in the cool cave. Several feet above the entrance to the grotto a large slab of sandstone was wedged on a ledge. On the rock was chiseled a Maltese cross. The members of the family often speculated about this cross, as did others, but never gave any serious thought as to why it was there.

One day when the family, except for the youngest son, was absent, two Americanos with packs on their backs came to the ranch. They engaged the young boy in conversation and asked him if he knew of any caves in the area. He told them of the one where he watered his goats. Then one asked if there was a cross near it. When told there was, they offered him a whole silver dollar to lead them there. He took the money with pleasure, although he probably would have done it for nothing.

At the cave the men told him they were tired, the cave was a good resting place and there was water, so they would spend the night there.

The following day when the older boy, whose turn it was to herd the goats, arrived at the grotto, he discovered the large slab with the cross laying at the entrance on the ledge. Where the slab had been was a large hole and in it were the remains of two rotted rawhide aparejos (containers designed to be used with packsaddles of horses, mules or burros.)

The father, when told there may have been a treasure, only

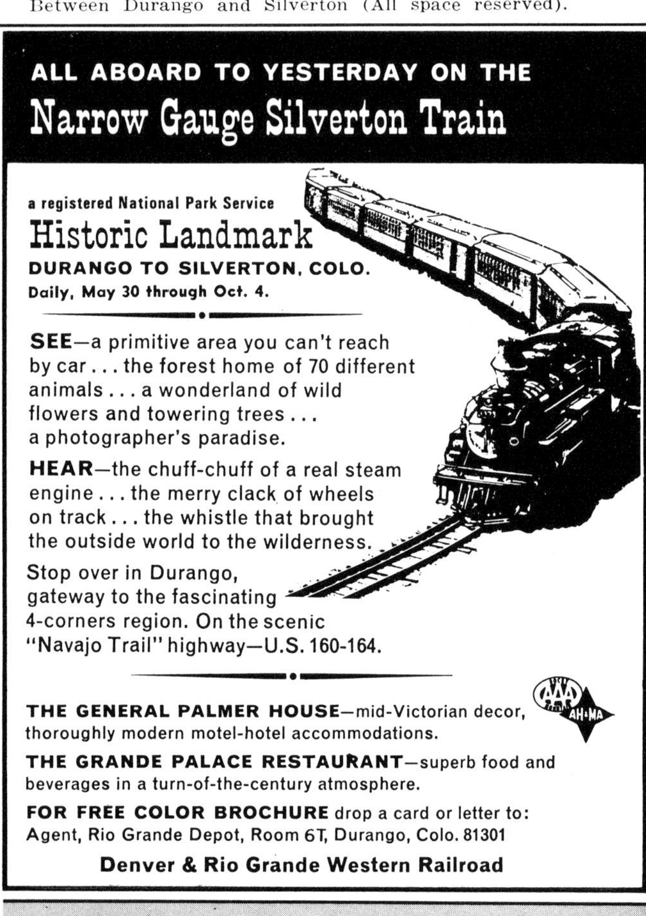

commented it was not intended for them. If the Americanos took it and destroyed the cross, the Patron would punish them. Maybe the Patron did just that. They were never seen again.

...A story told was of a large city in a canyon from which the inhabitants had fled. Before leaving, they buried a huge treasure of turquoise in line with and near the base of a great towering rock. And the priests of these people declared this rock to be the Patron of their treasure, and enjoined him to fall on and kill any who came to take the treasure. (Chaco Canyon, maybe? There are the ruins of a large community of the Anasazi there; a great slab of rock *did* fall and destroy some of the ruins, and its rubble has never been dug into, and archeologists have found hundreds of pieces of crafted and unworked turquoise in the ruins. Maybe some searcher did dig into the treasure and El Patron fell on him.) Quien sabe?

Most of the stories from the Durango area tell more of lost mines than of treasures. Nearly every canyon tributary to the main Animas River canyon has its tale of a lost mine. You cannot stay in Durango or Silverton long, or ride the Silverton train, without hearing some of these stories.

The old Pagosa Springs Branch also had its stories. One is of a great lost placer discovery, the Stewart Placers, some miles west of Pagosa Springs. Then, there is the story of four horse loads of gold dust being carried by Americanos riding east and crossing the Piedra River where they accidentally set a Ute Indian camp on fire. The Utes ambushed them, killed three of the riders and the fourth escaped. The Indians took all the horses and paraphernalia, but the eight sacks of gold dust they threw into an arroya and caved its walls in on top the treasure. This was somewhere in the vicinity of a station named Dyke, on Stolsteimer Creek. It may be there, yet buried under the now-abandoned roadbed. Again, quien sabe? The Utes aren't talking, and the Mexicans want no part of this treasure's Patron and chisos.

CHROMO MOUNTAIN

West of Chama and near the narrow gauge tracks, due north of the old Azotea sectionhouse, is Chromo Mountain. It also has its stories of hidden and lost treasures. If you continued on north over the mountain a few miles, you come to the Navajo River at a point about where a branch of the

Train #315, the *Shavano*, pulls five cars of varnish west of Mears Junction, Colorado, in September of 1939. *Otto Perry/Denver Public Library, Western History Dept.*

Near Otowi, New Mexico, Train #426 plys the rails with a cut of five cars. ***Otto Perry/Denver Public Library, Western History Dept.***

old Rio Grande and Pagosa Springs Railroad ended. A mile or so beyond this point on a low bluff is a large flat surface of rock in place. On this surface is chiseled a petroglyph of a snake, and its curved body has the same number and changes of direction of curves of the Navajo River above this point. There are also petroglyphs of objects and signs usually associated with derroteros for treasures drawn on paper or hides.

Some believe if you could decipher it, you could find the "Lost Frenchmen's Gold," a horde of gold (400 horses supposedly were needed to carry it all) that was buried somewhere in the vicinity of Cumbres Pass when the French expedition of about A.D. 1800 (rumored, not authenticated) either died of illnesses or were massacred by Indians and survivors buried the treasure. A lot of Americanos have spent a lot of time trying to find this cache, or even part of it. The Mexicans say, "No way, senores. That much treasure will be guarded by hundreds of chisos and almost as many Patrones."

There is a dearth of lost treasure or lost mines in the communities served by the old Chili Line through the upper Rio Grande Valley. This is understandable, because here the Padres of the Catholic missions were strongly entrenched and in control. Any wealth in any form, or mines discovered, quickly came to the knowledge of the Padres. They adhered to the principle that all such should accrue to the glorification of God and the church. So no one kept possession of enough treasure long enough to bury it and put it under protection of a Patron.

The Fathers figured it was best for them to take it over and keep it safe by packing it off immediately to Mother Church either in Spain or Mexico. On the way from the Rio Grande Valley to Mexico, the Fathers furnished their own chisos and Patrones in the form of well-armed troops.

On the remainder of the narrow gauge, Mexicans constituted a small minority of the populace and consequently their legends did not extend to these areas.

...Our family came to the Chama area in 1929 and moved to Monero shortly after. The country between these two points, once designated as the "Chama Pinery" was, except for grass and scrub oak, almost bare. As far as the eye could see in any direction were thousands of rotting tree stumps

all at the height that two men using a crosscut saw would most easily reach. Erosion was advanced and continuing. What denudation that was not attributable to the early day logging could be charged to overgrazing by numerous flocks of sheep. By the end of June each year the watercourses were dry except for puddles, and these are alkaline. A stream flowed to a degree the year around from Biggs Spur west, but the stream bed was bare rock and slimy mud, heavy with alkali. Any small rock on the banks, or in the course, was of slatey sandstone and bits of shale.

Yet, H.A. "Auz" Rogers, who had part in teaching me Morse telegraphy, often described to me what the land starting at the line of pine trees on the west side of Cumbres Pass to Durango was like for a few years after the railroad came and the timbering was in full swing. Auz worked as a mail messenger on passenger trains first before being employed as an agent-telegrapher on the Rio Grande narrow gauge.

SCARCELY SEE

He recounted that the pines were growing so densely west of Chama you could scarcely see through them. Dead needles blanketed the ground and hampered the growth of grass or underbrush. Many streams, flowing sweet and clear over graveled bottoms, were there and in them there were many native trout. Along these water courses there were berries, grass and wild game, big and small. Wild turkeys were especially plentiful, also blue grouse. Some of the streams flowed into numerous small lakes and waterfowl was plentiful on them. Down vistas through the trees many deer could be seen and occasionally, elk.

On the shores of a few of the lakes there were hunting camps of Ute and Jicarilla Apache Indians, harvesting and preserving the flesh and hides of the game killed. In season their children were active in gathering berries, to be eaten fresh or dried for winter. Auz and his wife, Helen, lived at Pagosa Junction until the Pagosa Springs Branch was abandoned. Both had many occasions during these years to travel by train

The *San Juan* crosses a small trestle near Falfa, Colorado, with four cars. This is Train #116 on October 17, 1941. *Otto Perry/Denver Public Library, Western History Dept.*

over the route. They watched the land and environment change rapidly as the thoughtless lumbermen clear-cut all the pines, leaving not even an occasional seed tree.

They saw the Indians go and the game, the trees and the birds. They saw the clean gravel bottoms of streams being scoured away by waters, not retained by the thick mat of needles, rushing and flooding, and the polished gravel bottoms give way to bare rock and mud. They saw the trout disappear as streams dried and waters turned brackish and alkaline. Finally, only a small chub tolerant of alkali swum in the stinking pools in the arroyas. The loggers, having slaughtered the country, left and a cover of grass slowly appeared, then the sheep came.

The land had been murdered and no one took responsibility.

End sill of old Rio Grande narrow gauge car shows attached metal hardware. ***Don Winter***

It took two steamers, Nos. #485 and #483, to tackle these 11 Gramps tank cars. They're near Lobato. Date is 1942. ***Otto Perry/Denver Public Library, Western History Dept.***

Engine #461, a Rio Grande locomotive sold to the Rio Grande Southern and dismantled in 1953, is southbound near Durango with 14 cars. Date is September 21, 1943. Note log truck at right of locomotive. *Otto Perry/Denver Public Library, Western History Dept.*

This was one of the last trains to arrive at Antonito from the Chili Line. Date is June 30, 1941. ***Colorado RR Museum/R.W. Richardson***

Chapter 28

Mergers, Acquisitions, and Abandonments

One sunny spring day, several months after I had been appointed Chief Dispatcher at Alamosa, there was not much doing after I had issued the next day's operating program, and I had a bad case of wanting to be outside. So I left my secretary to run the railroad (she was capable of doing it) and rambled off down to the car shops and roundhouse.

That little bit of playing hooky was to prove to be a crucial day in my railroad career.

I had need of a visit to the relief station at the car shops, and as I entered, I heard the sound of rushing water. Walking up to the trough (there were no shining vitreous urinals or stools) I watched a torrent of water flowing down the ancient wooden channel. Above and at one end of this disposal unit was a 50-gallon metal barrel with a pipe leading into its tops and a second pipe coming out of the bottom and ending at the head of the trough. I could hear water running into the barrel.

By the time I had relieved myself and zippered up, another

torrent of water came rushing down the channel. Out of idle curiosity I timed the rate of filling and emptying the tank, and found it was, give or take a few seconds, 10 minutes. So I found a ladder and inspected the contrivance to see how the automatic dumping worked. It was done by a float that came up as the barrel filled, and when the water level reached a point of about 40 gallons capacity, it tripped a valve and the water flowed out, just like a modern flush toilet.

Still curious, I went over to the roundhouse and found a similar arrangement and relief facility. The timing was practically the same as at the car shop. After some questioning it became apparent this operation was continuous every day of the year and the water just kept dumping every day and every hour. It was never shut off during the night when crews were not on duty.

Back at the office I got out my slide rule and came up with a figure of approximately 2 million gallons of water per year going down each drain, or a total of 4 million gallons for the two facilities. The Superintendent's Chief Clerk was able to give me the rate we were paying for water, and as I recall we were paying between $4,000 and $5,000 annually to flush the sanitary facility that probably was installed when the relief areas were first built.

AS A JOKE

Next day as a joke I wrote up a proposal that we replace the existing sanitary facilities at the car shop and roundhouse with modern equipment, and stated the net saving I had estimated. When I gave it to the Superintendent I expected him to laugh, but instead he says, "Well, I'll be damned", called the Division Engineer to his office and told him to prepare an "A.F.E.", Authority for Expenditure, and get cracking on remodeling the mechanical sanitary facilities.

That single incident cooked my goose. From then on I was handed more and more items to research, evaluate and recommend changes.

And that little bit of playing hooky and indulgence in some quasi-humor 20 years later led to me being pulled out of the line and assigned to work on mergers, acquisitions, and abandonments—all of them at the time the hottest issues on American railroads.

Mergers were in many respects the most challenging, yet most interesting, of the three issues to work. Without question the UP-CRI&P was the longest, the roughest and most challenging of any I was assigned to. Months were spent working with our Traffic Department correlating data and practical usage of Rock Island trackage the Rio Grande hoped

A nine-car mixed freight clanks along the tracks south of Antonito in May of 1939, loaded partially with pipe destined for the Farmington, New Mexico, oil fields. *Otto Perry/Denver Public Library, Western History Dept.*

TOP. Santa Fe, New Mexico, paints itself a picture of Spanish style churches (middle of the train) and quiet abode style homes. Here #478 is in charge of Train #426, a mixed, on December 4, 1937. *Otto Perry/Denver Public Library, Western History Dept.*

This was the last scheduled revenue train on the Chili Line. The ICC authorized abandonment effective Sept. 1, 1941. *Museum of New Mexico*

to gain from the case. Then there were many weeks and many miles of travel given to the physical survey of the line and hundreds of hours spent with Rock Island personnel accumulating data. Much of the latter had to be done sub rosa, for the U.P. at an early date exerted influence on the Rock Island to make the Rio Grande's and other protestant's task difficult, if not impossible.

However, the personnel including the officials were not sympathetic with the U.P.'s goals and I, for one, built up a wonderful rapport with all on the Rock Island from section men up to but not including their president. After the merger hearing was over, I later spent more months on the Rock Island on the entire system making an evaluation to determine whether or not the Rio Grande wanted to acquire the line under bankruptcy which by then was apparent would be the outcome. It was just as apparent also, by them, that the road had deteriorated to a point it would cost between $35 and $50 million to rehabilitate the property to a competitive level. It *did* go into bankruptcy and at the end no other railroad wanted it. The cost was too high.

During the hearing, in addition to presenting testimony, I was assigned to be with our lawyers constantly available for consultation. Our group spent three months or so in residence at the Union League Club in Chicago, conferring, planning, plotting and eating and drinking too much.

At times it was very boring and at all times there was a tension in the air. The latter was due to a facet of working with lawyers, I soon became aware of. In the hearing room there were no allies or friends, while at night the hostilities of the day were locked away and everybody was bosom buddies. (Of course, this did not apply to U.P. adherents.)

What I listened to and observed while in these lawyers' company soon convinced me there is no justice, only law as it is interpreted in the exigency of the moment. Too, that there are so many laws it is no problem to find those that are apropos and, if well-founded in the legal profession, to find ways of applying them. I soon realized that there was a well understood code of ethics among them: testimony must be valid; it must be true; it must be pertinent and defensible; and above all, it must appear reasonable. How shrewdly and effectively it was presented was the key. The desired result was not to prove what was right or wrong but to win, under the law.

I ate (and drank) many a luncheon or dinner with the lawyers. At lunch a group of usually four to eight would gather at a table and, while eating, decide whose throat they would cut during the afternoon. At other tables there were other coteries engaged in the same pastime. At dinner, on a larger scale, attacks were planned for the next day. What amazed me was that there were no cliques, only coteries, and the makeup of these varied day by day. An ally at lunch could in all probability be in another circle for dinner. Just as probable, after dinner members of both luncheon or dinner groups or complete outsiders would get together in some lawyer's suite for a general discussion of the case. It was never forgotten the enemy of all of us was the U.P., but there was no conniving at the evening parties.

OUTSIDE HELP

The Rio Grande had hired an outside legal firm to represent it at the hearing. The lawyer assigned was brilliant and well-versed in the law, but after about two months at Chicago, a personal weakness and problem of his kept getting worse. At last I contacted his partners and told them what the situation was. They said they would send his wife to stay with him awhile as she could usually control him. However, she was as powerless as I had been, and after five or six days, we put him under a doctor's care, and I asked permission from our president to ship him home. This was done and the Rio Grande attorney, E.P. (Ernest) Porter was sent to Chicago to take over. He was to prove more than competent and was a pleasure to work with. In the following years we were teamed in a number of cases.

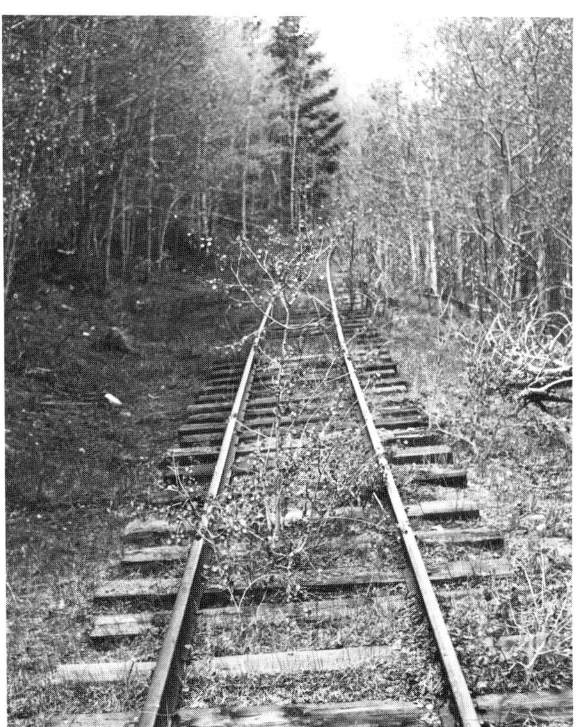

The days of glory and romance are gone. The rail just waits for the salvage crews to start pulling spikes. Scene is a location on Marshall Pass.

The hearing moved from Chicago to Denver then to San Francisco. I testified at San Francisco and during this testimony reveled in the pleasure of leading the Examiner to publicly chastising one of the more obnoxious lawyers. I had learned long ago it was possible to drive a non-railroader up the wall by using railroad language which he did not understand. This lawyer asked me a question that actually had no bearing on the case and I told him so. He became indignant and insisted I answer. So I did, using as many railroad words as I could. I could see his confusion building up and he asked the question again, and I answered him again in the same language.

He reworded the question and asked it again. I made answer almost word for word as previously. Twice more the question was put and I answered. By now the Examiner was sitting very upright, playing with some papers and his face was getting very red. The lawyer started to ask the same question but did not get to finish it.

The Examiner exploded, "Sir, you have asked the same question over and over again and it is irrelevant. The witness has answered you again and again clearly and understandably. At least I understand what he is saying and the answer will be in the transcript. Now, spare us anymore of this kind of behavior and get on with your interrogation."

The lawyer slammed his pencil on the table, sat down and said, "I have no more questions."

To illustrate the premise that lawyers are a breed apart, that

Rocky Mountain Railroad Club members fill the *Silver Vista* on an excursion special east of Iola, Colorado, in May of 1949. ***Otto Perry/Denver Public Library, Western History Dept.***

evening while our Rio Grande party was at the table, and I was enjoying some good California wine, this lawyer came over to me and laid a hand on my shoulder. "Norwood", he says, "that was just plain masterful the way you handled me today." Live and learn; first I was cynical about lawyers' actions, but before the hearing was over I had come to give them the respect any good craftsman deserves.

The hearing at San Francisco was held about the time the bars there went topless. I disgraced all rough railroaders and sophisticated lawyers the first time I went to one of these as part of a group. As my drink I ordered a double John Bushmills Irish whiskey. The waitress was behind me serving the table, and the first knowledge I had of her condition was when she leaned over my drink to pass another across the table. An oversize nipple plopped into my drink. I got up and left.

FIRST HEARING

For some reason the Rio Grande did not get into the first hearing of the Burlington Northern merger, but did appear as a protestant at the second, a rehearing. R.L. Jacobsen, from Engineering, and I were assigned to develop testimony to counter Burlington claims. We did not have a transcript of the first hearing and none were available except at the I.C.C. library in Washington. We went there to review it and take excerpts, but found we would be allowed to take all the notes we wanted to but could not photocopy any portion. As a result, we spent a couple of weeks reading and writing.

Back in Denver we reviewed our notes with our lawyers

to decide what to concentrate on. The Traffic Department went to work on a traffic impact study, and Jacobsen and I took off to check on engineering features. In a bit less than a month we hit all major terminals and many intermediate engineering locations on the three railroads involved, Burlington, Great Northern and Northern Pacific, from the Pacific to the Twin Cities and north to Duluth.

We made a good case disruptive of many of the BN claims at the hearing in Washington. It became apparent early we had a lot of information backed by detailed photos of items the BN had not updated for the rehearing. We did not win our case, but the merger was held up a bit more than a year while new evidence, ours included, was studied.

About halfway through the hearing one of the top BN representatives caught me alone in the hall and he was somewhat irate. First he wanted to know how we had picked out their weak points. I told him they stuck out like sore thumbs. Then he demanded to know who we had suborned on the BN. Of course, we had not found it necessary or practical to do that.

I informed him, pleasantly, that what we were presenting was easily obtained if you were willing to go without sleep, were willing to fly at night between locations, and spent a small fortune on helicopters and small planes to get pictures. He was especially concerned about the many items we were disclosing where the work had already been done and were no longer valid to be used as required expenditures after merging of the three lines. There were a number of them, and there were others that good engineering practices accompanied by clear photos to explain them proved some of their plans were impractical.

One item BN was pushing hard was the iron ore movement at Duluth, claiming only by merger and the expenditure of a couple of millions could it remain efficient. Their figures called for upgrading of equipment, lines and loading docks. Jacobsen and I had flown into Duluth late in the evening and registered at one of the better hotels. In its lobby was a large display of new developments in the iron ore industry, basically a change over from pit-mining of ore sent to smelters in the crude condition. The new method, in full swing and

The excursion car *Silver Vista* was destroyed in a shop fire in Alamosa. Date of photo was October 1, 1953. *Otto Perry/Denver Public Library, Western History Dept.*

This is the next to last narrow gauge train to cross Highway #285 at Mears Junction at the bottom of Poncha Pass. The train is picking up track materials along the right-of-way. ***Museum of New Mexico***

developed in the past year or so, explained how a better method, the taconite one, was changing the entire picture.

We spent a day of research on this, then the following morning chartered a four seat plane and pilot to take pictures. No helicopter was available so the pilot took a door off on my side. Approaching a location we wanted to photograph, he would take a long run, then wing over so I could get photos. At Duluth, in the middle of March, that is a mighty cold way to get pictures, but we got them. Pictures that showed the loading docks unused, hundreds of hopper cars stored on auxiliary tracks out in the boonies and small trees growing up around and between them. This testimony when presented caused a stir among the I.C.C. bench and the BN could not answer questions about it satisfactorily.

The BN merger out of the way, Rio Grande considered the possibility of acquiring the Colorado Southern-Ft. Worth & Denver between Wendover, Wyoming, and Galveston, Texas. A team of four was assigned to make an evaluation of the lines, and there was no doubt it would be a solid acquisition. It never came to pass because in the end the BN would not deal with us. I remember best of this study sitting on a shady patio of a hotel in Galveston with the cool Gulf breezes blowing while an attentive waiter or two rushed all kinds of seafood to us, especially the grilled prawns. Fortunately one of the SP men we had come in contact with supplied us with a couple of bottles of good Scotch, so we did not have to eat our food dry. Since then, Texas has become a bit more lenient with their beverage laws.

When time permitted I was still involved on the Rock Island case. Then a rumor began to fly that the Milwaukee was up for grabs. I started at Louisville with the Monon and worked up to the Milwaukee, gathering data and evaluating the property. It was midsummer and the heat and humidity was almost unbearable, but after three months, I turned in a negative report. The Milwaukee property as far west as Mobridge was in almost as bad shape relatively as the Rock Island Lines.

I had two unpleasant recollections of this assignment, not including the heat and being away from home so long. One was eating a meal of contaminated catfish somewhere in Indiana, or maybe the ice in the drinks was the culprit. Anyway, I was so sick I thought I was going to die, and was wishing I would. There was no doctor in the small town but a fine old druggist finally mixed up a bitter concoction for me. Its effect was horrendous, but it purged me completely. For the next few days I was on a warm milk and toast diet, but by the time I got to Chicago I was almost well. Luckily, for trying to find O'Hare field coming in from the south during a driving rainstorm and night, I got lost, and I mean, *really* lost. An accommodating police officer somewhere in Cicero got me straightened out.

ACQUIRE GM&O

The Milwaukee stint out of the way, I had a few weeks at home, and then we took a flyer at trying to acquire the GM&O before the IC could tie it up with their merger. A court decision knocked out this possibility when it ruled we could only take it as an outright purchase. It could not be tied into any Rock Island possibilities because we had no actual Rio Grande connection at any point with the GM&O.

I had spent about a month on the GM&O before we had to get out. Too bad, for the GM&O was in topnotch shape in every way. Track maintenance and condition was excellent; bridge program was the same way and there was an overall aspect of good management by a competent bunch of officers. It was comparable in every fashion to what I was used to on the Rio Grande.

The KCS could enter as a protestant, which it did, and there was good rapport with that line and ours. I was loaned to the KCS for the preparation of their case and its presentation to make use of the information I had already accumulated. However, the IC came out the winner, and the Illinois Central Gulf is the result.

Back home the preliminaries were taking place for putting a petition before the I.C.C. to abandon the narrow gauge.

September 17, 1917, E. L. Bronley, Missouri Pacific, published from St. Louis an in depth study of what was necessary to be done on the Denver and Rio Grande Western and the Western Pacific in order to make these two lines combined with Missouri Pacific standards to make the combination of the three railroads profitable in the future.

The study recommended spending about $31 million dollars on the Rio Grande and $6 million on the Western Pacific. It also recommended standard gauging segments of the existing narrow gauge lines. A total of $6.5 million was projected for a new line via South Fork thence to Pagosa Springs and down the San Juan River to join the existing line at Juanita and on to Durango. An alternate plan was Antonito to Chama and west. Another $3.45 million for the Antonito to Chama segment and $2.25 million on to Durango. (Eventual standard gauging of the balance of the narrow gauge to come later at a projected cost of $2.65 million.)

30-POUND RAILS

Narrow gauge main line was listed as 820 miles. There was still some 30-pound rail in the tracks. A total of 27.41% was listed as 45-pound or under. Tie replacement would be heavy as the ties were described as native yellow pine (at that time untreated) with an estimated life of only four to eight years. The roadbed was described as being native, with only a small percentage in cinder or gravel ballast. All the narrow gauge, if converted, would require ballasting.

It was an excellent study, but it had two faults: it did not contemplate any connections with the AT&SF or SP west of Durango and hence revenue would have to come from local production. At the time, 1917, only 176,000 acres were under irrigation with 916,000 more possible to irrigate if *private* money could be induced to build a huge irrigation sytem.

Control of the Rio Grande was shortly returned to it by court

Sometimes the #268's job took it to beautiful—but lonely—territory. ***John Krause/Dr. Richard Severance collection***

action. The MP was out, and the standard gauging hopes died aborning. So did any hopes of finding enough private money to build an irrigation system, and WWI came and with it great changes in the areas served by the narrow gauge.

There were some comments in the study that took almost 50 years to the month to come to pass.

"Present narrow gauge operations are a source of serious loss to the Company;

"Operation of Company's narrow gauge line is unduly expensive—deficit in 1916 was $60,303;

"(Conclusion) It is necessary that the D&RGW reach an early decision as to whether operation of the narrow gauge lines shall be perpetuated or whether such of these lines as have further traffic development possibilities shall be relocated and reconstructed to provide economical standard gauge operations."

The Rio Grande finally made that decision in September, 1967, a half-century later, and filed for abandonment with the I.C.C., Colorado Public Utilities Commission, and the New Mexico State Corporation Commission. The I.C.C. assigned a docket number, FD No. 24745. (A second file number was combined with this: I.C.C. No. 34843, covering a complaint by the Colorado, New Mexico Better Transportation Assocation versus the Denver and Rio Grande Western Railroad Company for failure to provide service and for the deliberate downgrading of all activities in connection with this branch of the railroad.)

PROLONGED BATTLE

We anticipated a prolonged battle, a bloody one similar to the one we went through when the Santa Fe Branch was up for abandonment. Consequently, a great deal of care was put into the preparation of our testimony, with me being assigned to appear as the "expert witness" (the one the opposition does its best to shoot down).

Considering how much effort had been expended to prepare our case and the trepidation we felt approaching the hearing, the actual confrontation was an enervating let down, almost a disappointment. The opposition was almost non-existent. On local levels, community witnesses and representation, there had been no homework or preparation. Colorado Public Utilities attorneys were better prepared, but surprisingly were not in the least aggressive. The Colorado, New Mexico Better Transportation Association had been reorganized and appeared as the Four Corners Regional Commission. The witness put on the stand for this organization got off to a bad start. First, he had not been in the area long enough to be geographically or historically oriented. Under cross-examination he stated that the Commission he represented was essentially interested in having developed an improved network of highways and airline capabilities.

The hearing began at Farmington, New Mexico, April 29, 1968, and ended there early the following day. The hearing room had been set up for a couple of hundred people. Less than 40 seats were used by spectators. It required 19 more for the examiner, his secretary and attorneys with their witnesses.

Ernest Porter, assisted by John Walker, our attorneys, had advised me to expect at least a full day under the gun on the stand. Actually, I went to the stand about 2:00 p.m. the first day and was excused by the Examiner about 4:00 p.m.

The coterie from the New Mexico State Corporation Commission included a bombastic attorney who was proud of his voice and presence. His performance was apparently patterned after Perry Mason. The first hearing being in New Mexico he led the charge, holding back his main attack until I was on the stand. He asked questions, sometimes ambigiously worded, in a tone of voice louder than was necessary, considering how few were in the room. I answered each one that was clear in its meaning as clearly and concisely as possible. Each time he put a question obviously intended as a trap, I asked him to repeat it, and explain what he meant by some of the terms. My written testimony had contained some references to geologic conditions on the line that gave us problems and he requested me to expand on this testimony.

I was happy to do so. In describing a trouble spot just east of Cresco, I testified we often had earth subsidence here due to the presence of a great deal of rotten schist. The court reporter, a lady in her mid-twenties, interrupted me to ask the Examiner if she should put that in the transcript. The Examiner, Robert N. Burchmore, grinned and said, "The word

Eastbound clean-up train makes smoke in September of 1954 on the Sapinero Branch. *John Krause/Dr. Richard Severance collection*

View near end of standard gauge rail, west of Antonito, June, 1943. ***Otto Perry/Denver Public Library, Western History Dept.***

All I need...

"Elena, the gracious old Mexican lady needed her rosary to recall the past—all I need is the sight of a picture, a few words from an old-timer, or a railfan, and the beads of my rosary start racing through my mind."
John Norwood

is schist, not what you evidently thought it was." The response from the hearing room was an unanimous burst of laughter. I felt sorry for the poor girl and the heat of her embarassment.

Well, that attorney just let me talk, and when I finished, he arose from his chair like a coyote ready to pounce on a juicy rabbit and quietly thanked me for the education in geology. He stood silent a long minute and turned to go back to his seat. Before reaching it he swiftly turned and almost yelled, "Tell me about your background in geology. What degrees do you have and where did you receive them?"

I answered, "Sir, I regret you asked that question. You see, sir, I'm just a third grade dropout from a little red schoolhouse down in the hills of Arkansas."

He got redder in the face than the lady court reporter had been and started to say something. Then he looked at the Examiner who was trying to hide his laughter behind his handkerchief; others in the audience, including lawyers, were either laughing or smiling. He drew in a few deep breaths and said, "No more questions."

A couple more opposition attorneys asked a few questions that were easily answered and the Examiner excused me, and called a short recess.

Our attorney, Ernest Porter, took me to one side and congratulated me on cutting down the New Mexico group, then told me to beat it to our motel to check out and get lost so well I could not be found in case anyone wanted to recall me to the stand. We agreed I would do it, and keep in touch to meet him at the next hearing at Durango. I got lost down in the Chaco National Monument looking at pueblo ruins and taking pictures, a real enjoyable "getting lost."

I rejoined our group in Durango where we stayed at the Strater Hotel. Ernest Porter announced the Legal Department would pick up the tab for the evening meal and furnish a few drinks. I had the drinks and at dinner, since I was not paying for it, I ordered lobster and drawn butter. That lobster (or the ice in the drinks) was contaminated with the same bug as the catfish in Indiana. But Durango had doctors and one of them mixed up an elixir that, if anything, was more bitter and more potent than the one the Indiana druggist gave me. And, more effective. By morning I was again in good shape.

WITNESSES UNPREPARED

For all practical purposes the hearing at Durango might as well not have been held. Protestant witnesses were unprepared, confused and did their case more harm than good. The entire hearing lasted less than one day, was closed and we drove on to Alamosa for the last of three hearings.

The Alamosa hearing lasted only about three hours due to the lack of witnesses. It was, if possible, more farcical than the one at Durango.

On July 30, 1968, Examiner Burchmore's recommendations to permit abandonment of the last of the narrow gauge, excluding the Silverton Branch, was published by the Secretary of the I.C.C. The document was officially served to all interested parties on August 16.

With the final decision granting permission to abandon came to an end the 3-foot gauge railroad that extended from Alamosa to Santa Fe, Durango, Silverton and Farmington, the first rail of which was laid at Alamosa on February 20, 1880.

And with it, with the exception of a few short assignments on the Silverton Branch, came to an end my active involvement on the narrow gauge that began in the fall of 1929. Regardless of my loyalty to the Rio Grande management I was sorrier, maybe more so, than any of the protestants that the decision to abandon had been given.

Appendix

ABOVE. No. 157 refrigerator car was a 40-footer. Note how it is sway backed. Car could carry 25 tons of goods. BELOW. 3000-series 30-ft. box car. *Both photos, Don Winter*

No. 3446 was one of 712 3000-series box cars. These cars had 50,000-pound capacities. Height of cars was 12 feet. Photo taken in Gunnison, Colorado, in November of 1945. *Otto Perry/Denver Public Library, Western History Dept.*

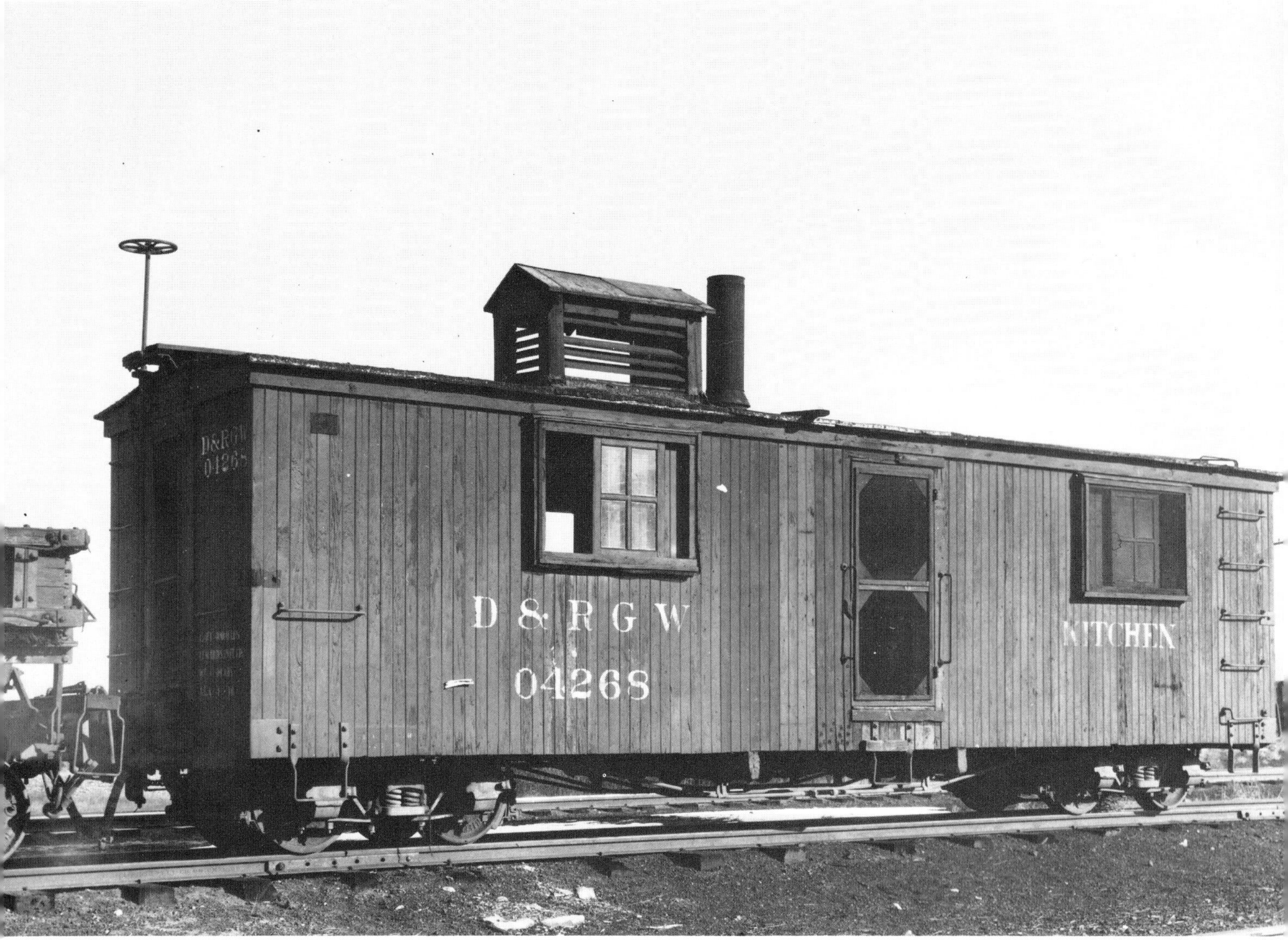

Rio Grande
D & R G W
5627

Safety
MAIN LINE
Rio Grande
THRU THE ROCKIES
Service

LEFT. **#04268 was a kitchen car with a vent at top. Photo taken in 1945 at Gunnison.** ***Otto Perry/Denver Public Library, Western History Dept.***

LEFT, BELOW. Stock car #5627 is a 30-footer with a capacity of 50,000 pounds. ***Don Winter***

BELOW. A maintenance-of-way car sits on the house track at Gato, Colorado, on June 21, 1945. ***Otto Perry/Denver Public Library, Western History Dept.***

ABOVE. Gondola with open ends, probably of the 9000-series. BELOW. Flat car turned gondola? Photo taken at Chama.
Both photos, Don Winter

ABOVE. D&RGW dump bottom coal car #859 at Chama. BELOW. High-side gondola with some of the boards missing portions. *Both photos Don Winter*

D&RGW 1000 high-side flat-bottomed gondola was part of series 1000 to 1499, built in 1902 by the American Car & Foundry Co. They were 32-foot-long cars with a marked capacity of 50,000 pounds. ***Don Winter***

This is a leased "Gramps" UTLX tank car, at Alamosa in the 1950's. ***Otto Perry/Denver Public Library, Western History Dept.***

Leased UTLX tank cars at Chama in 1939. *Otto Perry/Denver Public Library, Western History Dept.*

A D&RGW flat car with two pieces of light rail secured to the top. *Don Winter*

D&RGW flatcar #6613. *Don Winter*

D&RGW #6512, a 41-foot flat car, sports a wood ramp on top. *Don Winter*

D&RGW #6706 was at Alamosa in October of 1955 and appears to be newly outshopped.

D&RGW OS air dump car at Gunnison in 1945. ***Both photos this page, Otto Perry/Denver Public Library, Western History Dept.***

D&RGW spreader OV was at Gunnison in September of 1951 when this photo was taken. ***Otto Perry/Denver Public Library, Western History Dept.***

D&RGW baggage outfit car #053 was formerly a Railway Post Office car. Photo was taken at Durango on October 17, 1951. ***Otto Perry/Denver Public Library, Western History Dept.***

Parlor-buffet car *Durango* was built by Jackson & Sharp in 1880 and rebuilt by the D&RGW in 1937. It's a 41′11″-long car, with a wood roof covered with tin. Interior finish was walnut with electric lighting and steam-vapor heating. There were four chairs for dining and 10 revolving parlor seats. This photo was taken in 1938. *Otto Perry/Denver Public Library, Western History Dept.*

The coach *Alamosa* was built in 1880 by Jackson & Sharp, rebuilt by the D&RGW in 1937 and remodeled in 1957. The car carried 50 persons. It had formerly been numbered 25 and 403. This photo was taken in 1942. *Otto Perry/Denver Public Library, Western History Dept.*

D&RGW #0524 short caboose just recently outshopped. *Don Winter*

D&RGW caboose #0500 is at Durango in the fall of 1941. *Otto Perry/Denver Public Library, Western History Dept.*

Caboose #0503 isn't completely re-lettered for the Toltec Scenic RR yet. *Don Winter*

ACKNOWLEDGEMENTS

It is becoming more of a chore to gather data and suitable illustrations to do a railroad book than it is to write it. Thankfully, there is still a vast reservoir to draw on, and possessors of rail memorabilia are the world's best people and the most cooperative.

This book owes much of its appeal to those folks below to whom I give my heartfelt thanks. Any I have not included have not been omitted intentionally. If I have, please let me know so I may give you my most abject apologies.

Chris Burritt
Cameo Restaurant
Colorado RR Museum
Mary Ann Davis
Denver Public Library - Western History Department
D&RGW Railroad
Ruth and Marvin Gregory
Doug Harley
Doug Jones
Steve Kirby
John Krause
Mason M. Light, M.D.
Terry McGowan
Museum of New Mexico
Avery Norlin
Mike Pearsall
Robert Richardson
San Juan Historical Society
Dr. Richard Severance
Thomas Shirk
Bob Sloan
Jackson C. Thode
Bill Wilson
Don Winter
Charles Zeiler

INDEX

AT&SF, 15, 249
Abandonments, 6
Alamosa, 266
Alamosa Courier, 67
Alamosa, NM, 18, 37, 39, 40, 45, 47, 57-60, 62, 64, 67, 69, 71, 79, 82, 91, 94, 95, 99-101, 103, 107, 108, 111, 112, 114, 116, 118, 123, 124, 126, 131, 159, 160, 166, 169, 172, 174, 200-202, 222, 223, 226, 242, 247, 253, 260, 263
Amargo Canyon, 10, 172
Amargo Flats, 227
Amox, Dean, 29
Anderson, Andy, 175
Anderson, Dr. Sidney, 66, 67, 71
Animas Canyon, 46, 49, 52, 54, 63, 76, 117
Animas River, 73, 74, 77, 80, 120, 148
Annie's Cafe, Chama, NM, 166
Antonito, CO, 6, 31, 33, 37, 40, 41, 57, 62, 67, 94, 95, 107, 167, 174, 181, 208, 209, 222, 242, 249
Arboles, CO, 6, 19, 23, 25, 223, 236, 243, 252
Archuleta County, 25
Archuleta Mountain, 234
Ashbrook, Walter, 16, 160, 162
Aydelott, Gus, 74, 80
Azotea, NM, 16, 18, 94, 175
Aztec, NM, 31, 97
Bakers Park, 51, 80
Baldwin Branch, 6, 94, 107, 157, 174
Ball, Johnny, 58-60
Barranca Hill, 14, 66
Baughman, Norma, 45
Bendure, Dick, 14
Berkey, Arthur, 79
Big George, 151-153
Big Horn, NM, 39, 57, 67, 114, 201
Biggs Spur, 16, 239
Black Canyon of the Gunnison, 144
Blanca, CO, 201, 202
Boucher, 175
Boyer, "Old Dad", 31
Brankamp, Laura, 145
Bridal Veil Falls, CO, 184
Bronley, E.L., 248
Brown, Lynn, 49
Buchanan, "Buck", 53
Burchmore, Robert N., 251, 253
Bureau of Reclamation, 10, 27
Burlington Northern RR, 246
Burlington, CO, 160, 226
Carantas Family, 18
Carantas' Store, 11
Carbon Junction, CO, 148
Carpenter, C.B., 222
Carracas, CO, 25
Cascade Park, 73, 74
Cascade Water Tank, 77
Cebolla Creek, 87
Cerro-Summit, 83, 107
Chama "Reading Room", 161, 162, 164
Chama Mercantile, 27, 29, 116
Chama River, 227
Chama, NM, 8, 10, 14-16, 19, 25-37, 39, 42, 45, 56-60, 62, 67, 69, 71, 94-97, 107, 108, 111, 116, 150, 157, 160, 161, 164, 166, 172, 174, 175, 188, 200, 205, 215, 222, 238, 239, 249, 258, 259, 261
Chicago, IL, 245, 248
Chilkoot Pass, 111
Chili Line, 15, 66, 80, 83, 107, 166, 167, 222, 223, 238, 242, 244
Chromo Mountain, 237
Chromo Pass, 28
Cimarron, CO, 105, 107
Cimmaron-Cerro Summit District, 6
Civliian Conservation Corps., 173
Cleveland Slide, 49, 51
Coleman, L.B., 99
Colorado Coal & Iron Corp., 96
Colorado Division of Wildlife, 53
Colorado Fuel & Iron, 175, 215, 219
Colorado Public Utilities Commission, 48, 62, 112, 250
Conductor's Manifest, 25
Conejos Canyon, 62, 63
Confinement Law, 83
Connor, Steve, 49, 51
Continental Divide, 16, 94, 172
Coxo, CO, 34, 45, 56-59, 65
Creed, CO, 107
Cresco, NM, 58-60, 69, 157, 174, 225, 251
Crested Butte Branch, 94, 97, 107
Crested Butte, CO, 6, 174, 175, 215, 219, 222
Crowley Family, 83
Cumbres & Toltec Scenic RR, 36, 57, 89
Cumbres Loop, 63
Cumbres Pass, 6, 16, 31, 36, 37, 39, 40, 42, 45, 47, 53, 56-58, 62-67, 69, 83, 91, 94, 107, 111, 113, 121, 123, 157, 160, 164, 169, 172, 174, 175, 185, 200, 210, 238
Cummins, Tom J., 40, 42, 44, 45
D&RGW map, 12, 13
Dalla, Joe, 37, 39, 69
Dallas Divide, 222
Darlington Siding, 160, 226
Davis, R.E., 62
Dean, Ernie, 175
Del Norte, CO, 28
Delores, CO, 174
Denver Post, 67
Denver, CO, 18, 19, 29, 56, 60, 67, 74, 99, 201
Dieckman, John, 49, 51
Donaldson, Ed, 40, 44, 45
Dulce, NM, 8, 25, 26, 44, 124, 175, 181
Duluth, MN, 247
Dunham, J.I., 27, 31, 33, 35, 36, 116, 222
Durango, 265
Durango, CO, 6, 14, 15, 20, 25, 30, 47-49, 51, 52, 54, 56, 57, 74, 80, 83, 95, 97, 100, 107, 108, 112, 116-118, 124, 144, 152, 160, 169, 172, 174, 175, 178, 179, 186, 187, 192, 193, 200, 206, 207, 235, 237, 239, 241, 249, 253, 264, 267
Durango-Silverton Branch, 73, 120, 122, 212, 213
Duxstad, Granny, 15
Edmisten, Hugh, 22, 23

Edmiston, Stame, 25, 26
El Vado, NM, 108
Elena, 174, 176
Elk Creek, 51
Elk Park, 49-54, 80
Embudo Canyon, MN, 14, 80
Embudo, NM, 166, 175, 181, 188
Ensenada, NM 35, 36
Escalante, Father, 236
Espanola Mercantile, 167
Espanola, NM, 59, 83, 115, 122, 167
Evans, W.O., 29
Falfa Hill, 83
Falfa, CO, 239
Farmington, NM, 84, 86-88, 97, 101, 108, 111, 206, 207, 243, 251, 253
Farmington-Aztec District, 83
Farmington Branch, 94, 97, 148, 174, 175
Fin, 59, 60
Fir, CO, 201, 202, 210
Fitzhugh Family, 83
Fitzpatrick Family, 83
Florence & Cripple Creek RR, 20
Fort Carson, 57, 59
Foster's Hotel, 164, 166
Fruit Specials, 83
Ft. Garland, CO, 201
GM&O RR, 248
Gallinas, NM, 108, 151
Garfield Monument, 15, 226
Gato, CO, 15, 16, 19, 28, 175, 223, 256, 257
Gavin, Mike, 219
Gertrude, 164, 165
Gilbert, Bill, 219
Gomez Family, 83
Gomez, Felix, 19, 23-25, 169
Gonzales Family, 83
Graebing, 175
Graham Family, 83
Grand Junction, CO, 99, 108, 145
Groshart, Charlie, 40
Gunnison River, 71, 171
Gunnison, CO, 6, 7, 82, 83, 88, 91, 94-96, 100, 107, 108, 111, 144, 157, 174, 175, 188, 215, 217, 255-257, 263, 264
Haase, Ed, 52
Hale, Leonard, 222
Hammond, Special Agent, 15
Hermosa, CO, 52, 54, 73, 74, 117
High Line, 74, 120
Hindelang, Ben, 40
Hines, D.H. (Henry), 91
Holly, Dan, 67, 69, 70
Hooper, Col. Shadrach K., 144, 145
Hooper, CO, 19, 28, 85
Horse Lake, 9, 30
Horse Lake Pass, 227
Hotter, Henry, 48, 49
Huntington, Dr. Harry, 116
Ignacio, CO, 152
Illinois Central RR, 248
Iola, CO, 83, 88, 246
Jacobsen, R.L., 246
Jacona Siding, 130
Jarrett, K.M., 99
Jicarilla Apache Indians, 9, 11, 44, 239
Johnson, H.C., 202
Jones, Sargent, 59, 60
Juanita, CO, 249
Jumping Jenny Slide, 49
Kettle Mountain, 114
Kirkland, Wallace, 112-117
Klondike Rush in 1898, 111
Kramer, Norman, 39, 42
Krenz, Nora, 33
Krille-Nichols Wood & Hide Co., 192
La Manga Pass, 62-65
La Madera NM, 24, 94
La Veta Pass, 59, 126, 157, 160, 201, 202, 214
Lake City Branch, 94, 107, 153, 174
Lake Fork, 87
Lake Shalano, 74, 120
Lava Water Tank, 40, 201
Leonard, CO, 182, 183, 227
Life Magazine, 67, 112-117
Lime Creek, 73, 77
Linderholm, Gus, 101
Lira, Johnny, 37, 39, 69
Lively, C.R., 174
Lizard Head, 144, 176, 230
Lobato Trestle, 36, 58, 194, 208, 209
Lobato, NM, 42, 57, 93, 96, 121, 174, 240
Looney, Tim, 175
Los Pinos Creek, 116
Los Pinos, CO, 39, 42, 44, 58, 63, 64, 69, 162, 200, 214
Luchetti Commissary Bldg., 15
Luebke, W.G. (Gus), 114-117
Lumberton, NM, 16, 94, 108, 111, 151, 160, 166, 175, 234
Lyons, Alva, 15, 120
Ma Foster's Restaurant, 35
Manzanarez, Antonio & Eulalia, 167
Marshall Pass, 6, 7, 55, 59, 60, 64, 83, 89, 91, 94, 107, 108, 111, 124, 144, 159, 174, 211, 245
Max Read's General Store, 166
Maysville Loop, 68
McCarthy, Wilson, 145
McEnany, C.E., 52
McIvor, Jim, 169, 172
Mears Junction, 85, 94, 159, 248
Mears, Otto, 144, 177
Meek, Hubert, 58, 59
Mesa Verde, CO, 118
Mining Camps, 32
Minnequa, CO, 96, 215
Missionary Ridge, 117
Missouri Pacific RR, 248, 249
Moffat Tunnel, 145
Monarch Branch, 68, 142, 147, 168, 174
Monarch Quarry, 215
Monero Canyon, 172, 227
Monero Coal Mines, 151
Monero Creek, 10, 14, 227
Monero, NM, 8-12, 15, 16, 18, 19, 30, 31, 152, 166, 176, 230, 234, 238
Montrose, CO, 6, 82, 94, 95, 107, 108, 111, 174, 175, 218
Morgan, Ed, 67, 69-71
Moriarty, K.L., 67, 99
Mountain & Cold Weather Command, 57, 58, 60
Murphy, Roadmaster, 175
Murray, R.S., 49
Navajo River, 172, 227, 237
Navajo Sheep Movement, 84, 86
Navajo, CO, 23
Needleton Creek, 80
Needleton, CO, 77, 79, 80
New Mexico State Corporation Commission, 251
No Agua, NM, 235
Nolan, Bill, 11
North Star Sultan, 79
Oliver, Eddy, 28
Osier, CO, 28, 39, 40, 44, 45, 58, 216
Otowi, NM, 25, 130
Ouray Branch, 81, 85, 97, 100, 234
Ouray, CO, 11, 85, 94, 99, 108, 111, 144, 174
Pagosa Junction, CO, 19, 20, 22-26, 94, 111, 169, 175, 223, 236, 239
Pagosa Springs Branch, 94, 107, 237, 239
Pagosa Springs, CO, 19, 107, 169, 174, 223, 237, 249
Palmer, Wm. Jackson, 6, 10
Pandora, CO, 184
Peacock Coal Co., 14, 15
Peak, CO, 222
Pearson, A.P. (Primus), 67
Peg Leg Steve, 152, 153
Perlman, A.E., 99
Phantom Curve, 57, 69

Piedra River, 237
Pig Specials, 15, 83
Pitkin Branch, 174
Placerville, CO, 15, 173, 175, 177
Pollard, Henry, 14
Poncha Junction, CO, 70, 215
Poncha Pass, 248
Porter, Earnest P., 245, 251, 253
Posta, CO, 148
Pound Brothers Lumber Co., 27
Powderhorn Pool, 82-84, 87, 88, 217
Prohibition, 30, 31
Pueblo, CO, 29, 59, 96, 100, 201
Purcell, Bill, 175, 219
Railway Express, 20, 22, 28
Rainbow Route, 144
Ray, Myrtle, 29
Red Mountain Pass, 144
Red Young Slide, 52
Reddington, Pat, 30, 31
Reddy, 40, 42
Ridgway, CO, 78, 83, 85, 94, 99, 100, 107, 108, 111, 126, 144
Rio Arriba County, 35
Rio Arriba State Bank, 28, 29
Rio Grande & Pagosa Springs, 108
Rio Grande & Southwestern, 108
Rio Grande Southern RR, 78, 83, 100, 107, 126, 144, 174, 176, 177, 182-184, 222, 227, 230, 241
Rock Island RR, 245
Rockwood, CO, 48, 49, 74, 120, 172
Rocky Mountain RR Club, 246
Rogers, H.A., "Auz", 19, 239
Romeo, CO, 19, 28
"Rose of Azotea", 18, 175
Royal Gorge, 144
Ruby Anthracite, 107
Ruby Canyon, 145
Rust, L.K., 175
Salida, CO, 82, 94, 95, 99, 100, 107, 108, 124, 157, 162, 174, 190, 191, 215, 222, 223
Salt Lake City, UT, 99
San Francisco, CA, 245
San Juan, 10, 18, 66, 67, 71, 112, 116, 117, 144, 164, 166, 175, 185-187, 194, 210, 220, 221, 225, 239
San Juan Basin, 111
San Juan Mountains, 37, 59
San Juan River, 25, 116, 175, 227, 236, 249
San Juan Route, 6
San Luis Valley, 19, 114, 126, 160
Sanchez Family, 83
Sangre de Cristo Range, 58, 114
Sante Fe Branch, 6, 91, 94, 107, 166, 181, 222
Santa Fe, NM, 15, 29, 83, 94, 130, 151, 167, 174, 196, 197, 224, 226, 244, 253
Sapinero Branch, 71, 90, 91, 251
Sapinero, CO, 83, 105, 171
Sargent, CO, 6, 55, 59, 88, 94, 106-108
Sargent, Ed, 83
Selby, Joe, 48
Shamrock Hotel, Chama, 116
Shavano, 70
Sheepherders' Gap, 63, 69
Shehan Family, 83
Shell, Leroy, 40
Shenandoah, Dives Zinc Operation, 48, 49, 54
Sierra, CO, 201, 202
Sills, Carleton, 145
Silver Vista, 117, 190, 191, 246, 247
Silverton Branch, 40, 47-49, 51, 53, 55, 72-74, 94, 108, 118, 175, 253
Silverton, CO, 6, 46-54, 79, 80, 117, 118, 144, 172, 174, 237
Skarda, NM, 224
Skirvin, Sid, 67, 70, 71
Slate Creek, 175
South Fork, CO, 249
Spearman, Newt, 51, 58
Springett, Ralph, 25
Stackhouse, W.B., 28
Stephens, Jim, 40
Steve, Peg Leg, 152, 153
Stewart Placers, 237
Strater Hotel, Durango, 116, 117, 253
Sublette, NM, 31, 39, 40, 57, 114-116, 201
Sultan Mountain, 79
Summit, CO, 94
Sunny, Parlor car attendant, 67, 69, 71
Swan, Henry, 145
Tacoma, CO, 49, 74, 80
Tanglefoot Curve, 39, 41, 45, 63, 69
Taos Junction, NM, 24
Taylor, Herb, 40, 44
Tefft, CO, 52
Tennessee Pass, 144
Tequ, Norman, 11
Tierra Amarilla, NM, 35
Toltec Gorge, 66, 226
Toltec Scenic RR, 267
Toltec Tunnel, 60, 226
Toltec, CO, 40
Trinidad, CO, 100
Trotter, Milton E., 28, 35
Twin Shed Slide, 49, 51, 52
US Army Transportation Corps., 154
Uncompahgre River, 111
Union League Club, Chicago, 245
Ute Indians, 120, 239
Ute Mountain, 114
Vallecitos, CO, 117
Ventura, Joe, 219
Walker, John, 251
Wallace, Agent, 175
Walsenburg, CO, 100
Walsh Hotel, 64
Waring, Ed, 56, 58
Warman, Cy, 111
Western Pacific RR, 24, 88, 249
Western Union, 20, 22, 23, 28, 126
White Rock, NM, 224
Whitehorse Water Chute, 51, 52, 54, 86
Willow Creek, 18, 150, 160
Windy Point, 34, 39, 45, 58, 64, 69, 113, 157, 174
Winkel, Mechanical Foreman, 58
Wirt, Emmet, 44, 175
Wolf Creek, 174
Wolf Creek Bridge, 45, 56, 174
Wolf Creek Pass, 59
Zabriskie, Walter, 19, 22-24

Here's a charcoal sketch by the late rail artist Barton Kyle Davis, showing the Denver & Rio Grande Western No. 461 lumbering across trestles high in the mountains of Colorado. In later years, Barton's feelings for the romance of the railroads and a painstaking attention to detail made his custom-drawn charcoal originals the envy of those who commissioned them...or even one of the high-quality lithographs he produced. Trained as an aeronautical engineer, his love for planes was sidetracked years ago by one even greater—steamers on crack passenger trains—and the electric interurbans of his native Ohio, where he met his wife and life-long, train-riding companion, Mary Ann. *Ted Lemen*